Everyman, I will go with thee,
and be thy guide

D0493405

H. G. Wells

ANN VERONICA

Edited by
SYLVIA HARDY

EVERYMAN
J. M. DENT · LONDON
CHARLES E. TUTTLE
VERMONT

Introduction and other critical endmatter
© J. M. Dent 1993

Text copyright by the Literary Executors
of the Estate of H. G. Wells

First published by J. M. Dent in Everyman's Library 1943
Last reprinted 1962
First Everyman paperback edition 1993

Typeset in Great Britain by ROM-Data Corporation Ltd,
Falmouth, Cornwall

Printed in Great Britain by
The Guernsey Press Co. Ltd,
Guernsey, Channel Islands

J. M. Dent
Orion Publishing Group
Orion House
5 Upper St Martin's Lane, London WC2H 9EA
and
Charles E. Tuttle Co. Inc.
28 South Main Street, Rutland, Vermont
05071, USA

British Library Cataloguing-in-Publication Data
is available upon request

ISBN 0-460-87306-7

CONTENTS

NOTE ON THE AUTHOR AND EDITOR

H. G. WELLS was born in Bromley, Kent, in 1866. His parents ran a china and sporting goods shop in Bromley High Street, and although their financial situation was precarious, Mrs Wells ensured that the family clung on to the lower-middle-class status accorded to tradespeople. After working as a draper's apprentice and pupil-teacher, young Wells won a scholarship to the Normal School of Science, South Kensington, in 1884, which enabled him to study under T. H. Huxley. He left without a degree in 1887, and went back to teaching, and worked hard enough at his studies to achieve a first-class honours degree in biology from London University in 1890. During these years, Wells was experimenting with writing of all kinds – his first published work was a textbook in biology which appeared in 1893. Ill health forced him to give up teaching and *The Time Machine* (1895) launched his literary career. He married his cousin Isabel in 1891, but the marriage ended in divorce after he eloped with one of his students, Amy Catherine Robbins. They were married in 1895, but this was the first step in a pattern of philandering which continued throughout Wells's life. In these early years he published a wide range of writings – short stories, science fiction and fantasy such as *The Wonderful Visit* (1895) and *The War of the Worlds* (1898), novels such as *Love and Mr Lewisham* (1900), *Kipps* (1905) and *Tono-Bungay* (1909), and books on sociology and politics such as *Anticipations* (1901) and *New Worlds for Old* (1908). Although changes in literary fashion after the First World War led to Wells's decline as a literary figure, he continued to publish at least one novel a year until a few years before his death. During the latter part of his career he was, however, better known as the author of non-fiction books such as *The Outline of History* (1920) and *The Science of Life* (1933), and as a journalist and public figure – he remained an active and vigorous political campaigner until his final illness in 1946. Much has been made of what some critics have described as Wells's underlying pessimism which, it is claimed, came to dominate his thinking in later life. Admittedly his hopes for the future of human-kind could not fail to have been affected by the Second World War and the bombing of Hiroshima, but it could equally well be argued that all his work shows evidence of both optimism and pessimism, and that his prolific and varied output during the last decade of his life displays extraordinary vigour and energy. Significantly, the titles of his two last pieces of writing – *The Happy Turning* (1945) and *Mind at the End of its Tether* (1945) – reflect both these tendencies.

SYLVIA HARDY was born in Weymouth, Dorset and educated at the University of Wales and later at London. She is a senior lecturer in English at Nene College, Northampton, as well as Honorary General Secretary of the H. G. Wells Society and editor of *The Wellsian*. Current research projects include Modernism and Edwardian literature, with a particular interest in language and stylistics, and the work of Elizabeth Von Arnim.

NOTE ON THE TEXT

The first edition of *Ann Veronica* appeared in 1909, published by T. Fisher Unwin. The novel is dedicated 'To A. J.', and Wells's subsequent comments would suggest that 'A' stands for Amber [Reeves] whilst 'J' probably indicates his wife, Jane. When Wells reread and revised his writings for *The Atlantic Edition of the Works of H. G. Wells* in 1924, he made very few changes to the text of the novel, but its original subtitle, 'A Modern Love Story', was deleted. The first Everyman edition, which used the text of the first edition, appeared in 1943, and this is the text that is reprinted here.

Year	Age	Life
1866		Born 21 September, Bromley, Kent, to a lower-middle class family: father a gardener, shopkeeper and cricketer; mother a maid and housekeeper
1873	7	Entered Thomas Morley's Bromley Academy

CHRONOLOGY OF HIS TIMES

Year	Arts & Science	History & Politics
1865	Mendel's *Law of Heredity*	End of American Civil War; Lincoln assassinated
1866	Dostoevsky's *Crime and Punishment*	Russia defeated Austria at Sadowa
1867	Ibsen's *Peer Gynt*; Lister experiments with sterile surgery	Dominion of Canada founded
1868	Browning's *The Ring and the Book*; typewriter first patented	Gladstone Prime Minister
1869	Jules Verne's *Twenty-Thousand Leagues Under the Sea*; Flaubert's *Education Sentimentale*; John Stuart Mill's *On the Subjection of Women*	Suez Canal opened
1870	Charles Dickens dies; T. H. Huxley's *Theory of Biogenesis*	Franco-Prussian War; Prussia defeats France at Sedan; fall of Napoleon III; Education Act, introducing elementary education for 5–13 year olds
1871	Lewis Carroll's *Alice Through the Looking Glass*; George Eliot's *Middlemarch*; Charles Darwin's *The Descent of Man*	Paris Commune suppressed; the Chicago Fire; unification of Germany
1872	Edison's duplex telegraph	The Secret Ballot Act
1873	Tolstoy's *Anna Karenina*; James Clarke Maxwell's *Electricity and Magnetism*	Napoleon III dies in exile in Kent; David Livingstone dies in what is now Zambia
1874	Thomas Hardy's *Far from the Madding Crowd*; First Impressionist exhibition in Paris	Disraeli Prime Minister; Factory Act introduces fifty-six and a half hour week
1875	Bizet's *Carmen*	London Medical School for Women founded
1876	Alexander Graham Bell's telephone; Twain's *Tom Sawyer*	Battle of Little Bighorn; death of General Custer; Queen Victoria becomes Empress of India

Year	Age	Life
1880	14	Apprenticed to Rodgers and Benyer, Drapers, at Windsor
1881	15	Pupil-teacher at Alfred Williams' school at Wookey, Somerset; pupil at Midhurst Grammar School; apprenticed to Southsea Drapery Emporium
1883–4		Under-master at Midhurst Grammar School; wins scholarship and bursary at Normal School of Science, South Kensington
1884–7		Studies under T. H. Huxley at the Normal School of Science; begins to write; first published work appears in May 1887 in the Science Schools Journal – *A Tale of the Twentieth Century*
1887	20	Teacher at Holt Academy, Wrexham
1888	22	Returns to London after illness, working as a teacher; *The Chronic Argonauts* published in Science Schools Journal
1890	24	B.Sci degree
1891	25	Tutor for University Correspondence College; marries his cousin, Isabel Wells; *The Rediscovery of the Unique* published in the Fortnightly Review

Year	Arts & Science	History & Politics
1877	Thomas Edison's phonograph	Britain annexes the Transvaal
1879	Dostoevsky's *The Brothers Karamazov*	Zulu Wars, South Africa
1880	Electric light devised by T. A. Edison (USA) and by J. W. Swan (Scotland)	Boer uprising in the Transvaal
1881	Henry James's *Portrait of a Lady*	President Garfield murdered, USA
1882	R. L. Stevenson's *Treasure Island*	Married Woman's Property Act
1883	Death of Karl Marx; William Thomson (later, Lord Kelvin) publishes *On the Size of Atoms*; first skyscraper in Chicago	Fabian Society founded
1884	Twain's *Huckleberry Finn*; invention of Maxim machine gun	Berlin Conference on division of Africa; Gladstone's Reform Act extends vote to country householders
1885	Zola's *Germinal*; Pasteur's vaccine to cure hydrophobia; Karl Benz's automobile	Battle of Khartoum; Death of General Gordon
1886	R. L. Stevenson's *Dr Jekyll and Mr Hyde*; Rimbaud's *Les Illuminations*	Lord Salisbury Prime Minister
1887	H. W. Goodwin's celluloid film invented; speed of light measured	Queen Victoria's Golden Jubilee
1888	Kipling's *Plain Tales from the Hills*; Eastman's box camera; Dunlop's pneumatic tyre; Hertz discovers electromagnetic waves	Kaiser Frederick III dies after only three months as Emperor of Germany; accession of Wilhelm II
1889	Death of Robert Browning; T. H. Huxley's *Agnosticism*; Eiffel Tower built	Archduke Rudolf, heir to the Emperor, commits suicide at Mayerling, Austria
1890	Emily Dickinson's *Poems*; discovery of tetanus and diptheria viruses	Bismarck dismissed by the Kaiser; the 'O'Shea' scandal; Charles Parnell resigns as leader of Irish party
1891	Wilde's *The Picture of Dorian Grey*; Hardy's *Tess of the D'Urbervilles*	

Year	Age	Life
1892	26	Meets Amy Catherine Robbins – 'Jane'
1893	27	Elopes with Jane; in poor health; first published book, *A Text Book of Biology*; lives by writing for the rest of his life
1895	29	Marries Jane; they settle in Woking; meets George Bernard Shaw; *The Time Machine*; *Select Conversations with an Uncle*; *The Wonderful Visit*; *The Stolen Bacillus*
1896	30	*The Island of Doctor Moreau*; *The Wheels of Chance*; meets George Gissing
1897	31	*The Invisible Man*; *The Plattner Story and Others*; *Thirty Strange Stories*; *The Star*
1898	32	In poor health again; travels to Italy; meets Edmund Gosse, Henry James, Joseph Conrad, J. M. Barrie; *The War of the Worlds*
1899	33	*When the Sleeper Awakes*; *Tales of Space and Time*
1900	34	Now rich enough to have house built at Sandgate, Kent; *Love and Mr Lewisham*
1901	35	*Anticipations*; *The First Men in the Moon*; birth of first son 'Gip', G. P. Wells

Year	Arts & Science	History & Politics
1892	Kipling's *Barrack Room Ballads*; Diesel's internal combustion engine	Keir Hardie wins first seat in Parliament for Labour (ILP)
1893	Henry Ford's first automobile	Gladstone's Irish Home Rule Bill defeated
1894	Shaw's *Arms and the Man*; Edison's Kinetoscope Parlour, New York; Emile Berliner's gramophone disc	Death of Alexander III, Tsar of Russia; accession of Nicholas II
1895	Conrad's *Almayer's Folly*; Freud's *Studies in Hysteria*; Wilhelm Rontgen introduces X-rays; Gillette's safety razor.	Hispano-Cuban war; London School of Economics founded; Jameson Raid, South Africa
1896	Chekhov's *The Sea Gull*; Nobel Prizes instituted; William Ramsay discovers helium. Rutherford publishes researches into magnetic detection of electrical waves; Becquerel determines radioactivity of Uranium	Cecil Rhodes resigns as PM of Cape Colony
1897	Shaw's *Candida*; The Webbs's *Industrial Democracy*; Havelock Ellis's *Studies in the Psychology of Sex*; Robert Ross discovers the cause of malaria; Marconi's first radio transmission	Queen Victoria's Diamond Jubilee; Indian revolt on North West Frontier
1898	Zola's *J'Accuse*; Wilde's *The Ballad of Reading Gaol*; Henry James's *The Turn of the Screw*; the Curies discover radium	Cuban-American War; death of Bismarck; Battle of Omdurman, Sudan; General Kitchener retakes Khartoum
1899	Wilde's *The Importance of Being Earnest*	Dreyfus pardoned; Boer War begins
1900	Conrad's *Lord Jim*; Chekhov's *Uncle Vanya*; Freud's *The Interpretation of Dreams*; Planck's Quantum Theory; deaths of Ruskin and Wilde	Boxer Rebellion in China
1901	Kipling's *Kim*; Thomas Mann's *Buddenbrooks*; Marconi transmits radio communication across the Atlantic	Assassination of President McKinley, USA; Theodore Roosevelt succeeds; Queen Victoria dies; accession of Edward VII

Year	Age	Life
1902	36	*The Sea Lady; The Discovery of the Future*
1903	37	Joins Fabian Society, the Coefficients, and the Reform Club; birth of second son, Frank; *Twelve Stories and a Dream; Mankind in the Making*
1904	38	*The Food of the Gods*
1905	39	*Kipps; A Modern Utopia*
1906	40	Affairs with Amber Reeves and Rosamund Bland; meets Gorky in New York; *In the Days of the Comet; Socialism and the Family; The Future in America; This Misery of Boots; The So-called Science of Sociology*
1908	42	Resigns from the Fabians; *First and Last Things; The War in the Air; New Worlds for Old*
1909	43	Birth of Wells's daughter, Anna, to Amber Reeves; Wells and Jane move to Hampstead; *Tono-Bungay; Ann Veronica*
1910	44	*The History of Mr Polly*

Year	Arts & Science	History & Politics
1902	Conrad's *Heart of Darkness*; Bennett's *Anna of the Five Towns*; William James's *The Varieties of Religious Experience*; Caruso's first record	End of the Boer War
1903	The Wright Brothers succeed in powered flight; Henry Ford starts Ford Motors; Samuel Butler's *The Way of All Flesh*; Shaw's *Man & Superman*	Bolshevik-Menshevik split in Russian socialists; Lenin becomes Bolshevik leader
1904	Picasso's *The Two Sisters*; Freud's *The Psychopathology of Everyday Life*; Chekhov's *The Cherry Orchard*	Russo-Japanese War begins; Theodore Roosevelt re-elected
1905	Einstein's Special Theory of Relativity; Debussy's *La Mer*; Cézanne's *Les Grandes Baigneuses*; Edith Wharton's *House of Mirth*; Shaw's *Major Barbara* forbidden by New York police	Russia defeated by Japan; riots in St Petersburg, 'the Potemkin' mutinies
1906	J. J. Thompson wins Nobel Prize for Physics	American occupation of Cuba; Liberal victory in General Election – maj. 218; Labour win 54 seats
1907	First Cubist exhibition in Paris; Kipling's Nobel Prize for Literature; Conrad's *The Secret Agent*	Defeat of Labour bill to give votes to women; arrest of fifty-seven suffragettes in London
1908	Arnold Bennett's *The Old Wives' Tale*; E. M. Forster's *A Room with a View*; Rutherford wins Nobel Prize for Physics; Wright Brothers tour Europe	Asquith Prime Minister; Mrs Pankhurst imprisoned
1909	Diaghilev's Russian Ballet in Paris; Peary Expedition at North Pole; Bleriot flies the Channel	Murderer Dr Crippen arrested
1910	Marie Curie's *Treatise on Radiography*; Stravinsky's *Firebird*; Roger Fry's Post-Impressionist Exhibition in London; E. M. Forster's *Howards End*; Tolstoy dies	Death of Edward VII; accession of George V

Year	Age	Life
1911	45	*The New Machiavelli*; *The Country of the Blind and Other Stories*; *Floor Games* (for children); moves to Easton Glebe, Essex
1912	46	Meets Rebecca West; *Marriage*
1913	47	*The Passionate Friends*; *Little Wars*
1914	48	Birth of Wells's son, Anthony, to Rebecca West; visits Russia with Maurice Baring; *The Wife of Sir Isaac Harman*; *The World Set Free*; *An Englishman Looks at the World*; *The War That Will End War*
1915	49	*Boon* (originally published under the pseudonym Reginald Bliss); break with Henry James; *The Research Magnificent*; *Bealby*
1916	50	Visits Western Front in France and Italy; *Mr Britling Sees it Through*; *The Elements of Reconstruction*; *What is Coming?*
1917	51	*The Soul of a Bishop*; *War and the Future*; *God, the Invisible King*
1918	52	*Joan and Peter*; joins Ministry of Information under Lord Northcliffe
1919	53	*The Undying Fire*; *History is One*; contributor to *The Idea of a League of Nations*

Year	Arts & Science	History & Politics
1911	Amundsen at South Pole; Rutherford's *Theory of Atomic Structure*; D. H. Lawrence's *The White Peacock*; Ezra Pound's *Cantos*; Rupert Brooke's *Poems*	Lords Reform Bill passed in Lords after intervention of the King; Liberals announce first measures for National Insurance
1912	Schoenberg's *Pierrot Lunaire*; Jung's *The Theory of Psychoanalysis*	The *Titanic* disaster; Woodrow Wilson elected US President
1913	Vitamin A isolated at Yale, by Elmer McCollum; Lawrence's *Sons and Lovers*	Panama Canal opened; hunger strikes by suffragettes in prison
1914	J. H. Jean's *Radiation and the Quantum Theory*; James Joyce's *Dubliners*	Assassination of Archduke Franz Ferdinand of Austria in Sarajevo; the Great War starts
1915	D. W. Griffith's film *Birth of a Nation*; Somerset Maugham's *Of Human Bondage*; Lawrence's *The Rainbow* banned; Joseph Conrad's *Victory*	The Allied failure at Gallipoli; Zeppelins attack London; The *Lusitania* sinking; Coalition Government formed in Britain
1916	Death of Henry James; James Joyce's *Portrait of the Artist as a Young Man*; Dadaism in Zurich	The battle of Verdun; the Easter Rising, Dublin; Battle of Jutland; President Wilson's plea for peace; Lloyd George Prime Minister
1917	Freud's *Introduction to Psychoanalysis*; T. S. Eliot's *Prufrock*	America enters the war; Russian Revolution; Lenin in power; Woodrow Wilson re-elected
1918	Matisse's *Odalisques*; Joyce's *Ulysses*	Collapse of the Central Powers ends the Great War; Versailles Peace Conference; vote given to women over thirty and men over twenty-one; first woman elected to Parliament – Countess Markiewicz (Sinn Fein)
1919	Thomas H. Morgan's *The Physical Basis of Heredity*; Thomas Hardy's *Collected Poems*; Maugham's *The Moon and Sixpence*; J. M. Keynes's *The Economic Consequences of the Peace*; Bauhaus founded; Alcock and Brown fly the Atlantic	Herbert Hoover takes control of European Relief; Prohibition in America; Versailles Treaty signed; President Wilson awarded Nobel Peace Prize; socialist uprising in Berlin crushed by troops; murder of Rosa Luxembourg

Year	Age	Life
1920	54	Visits Russia; meets Lenin and Moura Budberg; *The Outline of History*; *Russia in the Shadows*
1921	55	Visits USA; *The Salvaging of Civilization*
1922	56	*A Short History of the World*; *The Secret Places of the Heart*; unsuccessful as a Labour Parliamentary candidate for London University
1923	57	*Men Like Gods*; *The Story of a Great Schoolmaster*; *The Dream*; stands for Parliament again but defeated
1924	58	Begins affair with Odette Keun
1925	59	*Christina Alberta's Father*
1926	60	*The World of William Clissold*
1927	61	Death of Jane Wells; *Meanwhile*; *Collected Short Stories*; *Democracy Under Revision*; *Collected H. G. Wells* (Atlantic edition) completed in USA
1928	62	*The Open Conspiracy: Blue Prints for a World Revolution*; *Mr Blettsworthy on Rampole Island*; introduction to *The Book of Catherine Wells*

Year	Arts & Science	History & Politics
1920	Eddington's *Space, Time and Gravitation*; F. Scott Fitzgerald's *This Side of Paradise*; Sinclair Lewis's *Main Street*; Edith Wharton's *The Age of Innocence*	America rejects the League of Nations; National Socialist Workers party (NAZI) publishes manifesto, Germany
1921	Einstein wins Nobel Prize for Physics	Victory of Red Army in Russian Civil War
1922	T. S. Eliot's *The Waste Land*; first transmissions by BBC	Mussolini establishes dictatorship in Italy; Irish Free State established
1923	Gershwin's *Rhapsody in Blue*; E. N. da C. Andrade's *The Structure of the Atom*; Freud's *The Ego and the Id*; W. B. Yeats awarded Nobel Prize for Literature	Hitler's NAZI coup fails in Munich; Stanley Baldwin Prime Minister; Matrimonial Bill passed, allowing wives to divorce husbands; British Mandate in Palestine
1924	E. M. Forster's *A Passage to India*; Thomas Mann's *Magic Mountain*	Lenin dies; Minority Labour government; Ramsay MacDonald Prime Minister
1925	John Logie Baird's successful television experiments; Eisenstein's film *Battleship Potemkin*; Chaplin's *The Gold Rush*; Fitzgerald's *The Great Gatsby*	Hitler publishes *Mein Kampf*
1926	Fritz Lang's film *Metropolis*; William Faulkner's *Soldier's Pay*; Kafka's *The Castle*; Hemingway's *The Sun also Rises*; R. H. Tawney's *Religion and the Rise of Capitalism*	British troops withdraw from the Rhineland; British Commonwealth instituted; General Strike
1927	Lindbergh's flight from New York to Paris; Abel Gance's film *Napoleon*; Virginia Woolf's *To the Lighthouse*; *The Jazz Singer* (first talkie); completion of Proust's *A la Recherche du Temps Perdu*	Trotsky expelled from Russian Communist Party
1928	J. L. Baird demonstrates colour TV; Eisenstein's film *October*	Vote given to women over twenty-one – equal rights; Chiang Kai-shek President of China

Year	Arts & Science	History & Politics
1929	Robert Graves's *Goodbye to All That*; Hemingway's *A Farewell to Arms*; Thomas Mann wins Nobel Prize for Literature	Crash of New York Stock Exchange, Wall Street; Second Minority Labour Government; thirteen women elected to Parliament; NAZI victory in Bavarian elections
1930	Freud's *Civilization and its Discontents*; W. H. Auden's *Poems*; Robert Frost's *Collected Poems*; Sinclair Lewis wins Nobel Prize for Literature; Amy Johnson's flight from London to Australia; death of D. H. Lawrence	Haile Selassie (Ras Tafari) becomes Emperor of Ethiopia; Gandhi's Salt March, India; NAZI party becomes second largest in Germany
1931	Death of Edison; Empire State Building completed; Chaplin's *City Lights*; Schweitzer's *My Life and Thoughts*; Faulkner's *Sanctuary*	World slump begins with the collapse of the Credit Anstadt bank, Vienna; first woman elected to the American Senate; National Government, Britain; Franklin D. Roosevelt wins US Presidential election; New Deal initiated; Stalin purges begin, Russia
1932	James Chadwick discovers the neutron; Fritz Lang's film of Huxley's *Brave New World*; Galsworthy's Nobel Prize for Literature	
1933	A. N. Whitehead's *Adventures of Ideas*; Jung's *Psychology and Religion*; Orwell's *Down and Out in Paris and London*	Hitler becomes Chancellor; start of anti-Jewish measures in Germany; first concentration camps; Germany leaves League of Nations
1934	Gershwin's *Porgy and Bess*; Graves's *I Claudius*	'Night of the Long Knives' massacre in Germany; Hitler assumes title of 'Führer', after plebiscite
1935	The Curies awarded Nobel Prize for Chemistry, having synthesized radioactive elements; The Webbs's *Soviet Communism: A New Civilization*; Graham Greene's *England Made Me*; T. S. Eliot's *Murder in the Cathedral*	Hitler denounces Versailles Treaty, forms Air Force and imposes conscription; Russian Show Trials; Italy invades Abyssinia

Year	Age	Life
1936	70	Awarded Hon.D.Litt by London University; *The Anatomy of Frustration*; *The Croquet Player*; *The Man Who Could Work Miracles*; *The Idea of a World Encyclopaedia*
1937	71	*Brynhild*; *Star Begotten*; *The Camford Visitation*
1938	72	*Apropos of Dolores*; *World Brain*; *The Brothers*
1939	73	Visits Sweden; *The Fate of Homo Sapiens*; *Travels of a Republican Radical In Search of Hot Water*; *The Holy Terror*
1940	74	In London during Blitz; speaking tour of USA; *The Commonsense of War and Peace* ; *Babes in the Darkling Wood*; *A Aboard for Ararat*
1941	75	*Guide to the New World*; *You Can't be Too Careful*
1942	76	*Phoenix*; *Science and the World Mind*; *The Conquest of Time* (final revision of *First and Last Things*)
1943	77	*Crux Ansata*

Year	Arts & Science	History & Politics
1936	Chaplin's *Modern Times*; Alexander Korda's film *Things to Come*; Dylan Thomas's *Twenty Five Poems*; Kipling, Houseman and Chesterton die; A. J. Ayer's *Language, Truth and Logic*	Hitler reoccupies the Rhineland; Spanish Civil War begins; Rome–Berlin Axis announced; death of George V; Edward VIII accedes in January, abdicates in December; 'Battle of Cable St' in London's East End
1937	Picasso's *Guernica*; Steinbeck's *Of Mice and Men*; Orwell's *The Road to Wigan Pier*; Sartre's *La Nausée*; Wallace Carothers invents Nylon	Stalin purges high Party and military officials; Japanese Imperialism in China, Peking and Shanghai captured
1938	Orson Welles's radio feature of H. G. Wells's *The War of the Worlds* terrifies America	Austria falls to Hitler; Munich Conference over Czecho-Slovakia; Appeasement Policy confirmed; Franco's victories in Spain; Roosevelt appeals to the dictators for peace
1939	Death of Freud; Jolie-Curie shows the potential of nuclear fission. Henry Moore's *Reclining Figure*; Joyce's *Finnegan's Wake*; Steinbeck's *The Grapes of Wrath*; death of Yeats, and of Ford Madox Ford	Germany invades Poland; Second World War begins; Hitler–Stalin Pact; Russia invades Finland and Poland; fall of Madrid to Franco
1940	Koestler's *Darkness at Noon*	Churchill Prime Minister; Battle of Britain; start of Blitz on London; murder of Trotsky
1941	Welles's *Citizen Kane*; Carrol Reed's film *Kipps*	Hitler invades Russia; Japan bombs Pearl Harbor; America enters the War
1942	Evelyn Waugh's *Put Out More Flags*	Japan invades Burma, Malaya, Dutch East Indies; Singapore surrenders; Americans bomb Tokyo; Stalingrad siege begins; Montgomery wins El Alamein; start of Hitler's 'Final Solution'
1943	Henry Moore's sculpture *Madonna and Child*	Russian victory at Stalingrad; Warsaw Ghetto killings; Allies finally conquer North Africa; fall of Mussolini, Italy surrenders

Year	Age	Life
1944	78	'42 to '44: A Contemporary Memoir; thesis for Doctorate of Science (On the Quality of Illusion in Continuity of the Individual Life in the Higher Metazoa with Particular Reference to the Species of Homo Sapiens); in London during rocket attacks
1945	79	Mind at the End of Its Tether; The Happy Turning
1946		Dies in London, 13 August

Year	Arts & Science	History & Politics
1944	T. S. Eliot's *Four Quartets*	Leningrad relieved; Allies capture Rome and land in Normandy; de Gaulle enters Paris; V1 and V2 rocket raids on London
1945	Orwell's *Animal Farm*; Nobel Prize for medicine to Alexander Fleming, E. B. Chain and Howard Florey, for discovery of penicillin	Yalta Conference; Russians capture Warsaw and Berlin; Mussolini executed, Hitler's suicide; United Nations Charter; end of the Second World War in Europe; death of President Roosevelt; atomic bombs dropped on Hiroshima and Nagasaki; Japan surrenders; Labour win General Election; Attlee Prime Minister
1946	Electronic Brain constructed at Pennsylvania University; Cocteau's film *La Belle et La Bête*; Eugene O'Neill's *The Iceman Cometh*	First General Assembly of the United Nations; nationalization of Civil Aviation, coal and the Bank of England; Churchill's 'Iron Curtain' speech
1947	Transistor invented	GATT established
1948	Norman Mailer's *The Naked and the Dead*	National Health Service; Israel founded; East German blockade of Berlin; Allied airlift into Berlin
1949	Orwell's *1984*	West Germany established, confirming division of Europe
1950	Death of Orwell	Start of Korean War

INTRODUCTION

When H. G. Wells began writing *Ann Veronica* in 1908, he was already a well-established author who had written in a variety of forms, from popular journalism and science fiction to sociology, politics and philosophy. By the time of his death in 1946, Wells had become one of the best known, the most prolific, and certainly one of the most versatile writers of his generation, an achievement which is all the more remarkable when one considers the circumstances of his birth and upbringing.

Herbert George Wells was born in Bromley, Kent, on 21 September 1866, the youngest of three brothers. His mother, Sarah, had been a lady's maid at Up Park, Sussex, and it was there that she met his father, Joseph Wells, then a gardener on the estate. After their marriage they set up a shop in what is now the centre of Bromley, selling china and sporting goods – Joseph was also a professional cricketer. The shop was never successful, but the family eked out a living and Wells's mother ensured that all her sons received a private education. Although Wells's later accounts indicate just how limited and constricting an education this proved to be, it did maintain the lower-middle class status of the family.

When, in 1880, the family fortunes declined, Sarah Wells returned to Up Park as housekeeper, and thirteen-year-old Bertie was sent to Windsor as an apprentice to a draper.[1] He hated the dull and uninspiring jobs found for him over the next few years – pupil-teacher, assistant in a chemist's shop, then another drapery. The only relief was provided by visits to Up Park, where he had access to the library, and first acquired his passion for politics and philosophy. During his brief period with the Midhurst chemist, Wells had come to know the headmaster of the local grammar school, and had so impressed him by his intelligence and ability that, in 1882, he was offered a student assistantship, which provided an opportunity to study as well as teach. His parents, who had paid for the drapery apprenticeship, were reluctant to let him go, but Wells embarked on one of his many struggles to fight his way out of constraints, and eventually his rational arguments and irrational appeals – at one point he threatened suicide – overcame their resistance.

Within a year, Wells had passed examinations so efficiently that he won a state scholarship to the Normal School of Science, South Kensington (now Imperial College). In his first year he was inspired by the lectures of T. H. Huxley – portrayed as Russell in *Ann Veronica* – but in subsequent years the teaching was less interesting, and he became so absorbed in politics and debates that he failed his exams, leaving college in 1887 without a degree. He was distracted, too, by falling in love for the first time, with his cousin Isabel.

He found work where he could, and it was while he was teaching at a private school that he received an injury to one of his kidneys. For the next ten years or so, Wells suffered a series of lung haemorrhages, plus recurrent kidney problems, and in these periods as an invalid he began writing seriously. He also returned to his zoological studies and, in 1890, obtained his BSc from London University. When he became biology tutor for a correspondence college in 1891, he felt sufficiently secure to marry Isabel, but from the beginning the marriage was a failure; it seems clear, from Wells's subsequent comments, that Isabel was sexually unresponsive, and he began what proved to be a lifetime pattern of seeking consolation from other women. One of these women was a bright, pretty biology student, Amy Catherine Robbins (whom Wells soon began calling 'Jane'). They ran away together and, in his autobiography, Wells records that they were both 'in reality in flight from conditions of intolerably narrow living'.

Just before this flight, Wells had suffered a particularly severe lung haemorrhage, which convinced him that he must give up tutoring. He would become a professional writer. He threw himself into writing book and play reviews, newspaper and magazine articles and short stories. He also wrote a number of speculative articles on science, which led to the production of one of his most popular books, *The Time Machine*, published in 1895 – the year in which his divorce from Isabel was finalized and he and Jane were married.

The Time Machine was an immediate success, and Wells followed it with a number of scientific romances and fantasies:

The Wonderful Visit, The Island of Doctor Moreau, The Invisible Man and *The War of the Worlds*. This was a period when the publishing trade was booming. There was a huge demand for undemanding reading matter which, in turn, produced an explosion of light fiction and journalism. Given the rigid class distinctions of the period, it is hard to think of any other career which could have enabled Wells to break out of his under-privileged background so thoroughly and so effectively. As he records in his autobiography, 'The last decade of the nineteenth century was an extraordinarily favourable time for new writers and my individual good luck was set in the luck of a whole generation of aspirants. Quite a lot of us from nowhere were "getting on" ' (p. 506).

Feminist critics have pointed to the way in which the opening up of literary circles to men from underprivileged backgrounds in the early years of the century coincided with the struggles of vast numbers of young women to break away from the constraints of home and parental authority.[2] In this respect, H. G. Wells was certainly well placed to identify with Ann Veronica's need to break out. He, too, was a rebel and knew what it was to struggle for advancement and opportunity. He knew, too, from bitter personal experience – as his heroine soon discovers – that freedom cannot be achieved without economic independence.[3]

H. G. Wells made his name as a writer of scientific romances but at the turn of the century he wanted to write novels dealing with contemporary social issues, since he believed that the novel could change attitudes and affect conduct as effectively – often more effectively – than non-fictional writing. Thus Wells regarded *Love and Mr Lewisham*, published in 1901, as his first real novel, since it explores the problems which ensue when educational aspiration conflicts with sexual desire. In 1905 came *Kipps* which, although a comedy, also examines serious issues of class prejudice and exploitation. When he began writing *Ann Veronica*, in 1908, Wells must have been aware that he was tackling head-on one of the most hotly debated social issues of the day – the so-called 'woman question'. In the period leading up to the First World War, the apparent stabilities and certainties of the Victorian era were giving way to deeply disturbing uncertainties and anxieties[4] – fears of national decline, which embodied questions about the physical deterioration of the British race itself were interwoven with concern about the decay of parental authority and 'the degradation of the marriage tie'.[5] Debates about the role of woman in society and, indeed, about the nature of woman herself, were central to all of these issues, and the outraged reaction to Wells's fictional representation of rebellious young womanhood in *Ann Veronica* is in part a reflection of these uncertainties. In this introduction I want first to examine the ways in which the novel relates to the women's cause in its own period, then to explore the extent to which *Ann Veronica* can be considered a feminist text.

H. G. Wells was no stranger to controversy. By 1908 he had already shocked conservative opinion by his advocacy of free love and the emancipation of women, which he saw as interdependent. These ideas had been developed in a number of Wells's non-fictional writings[6] and had been explored in fictional form in *In the Days of the Comet*, published two years earlier.[7] These earlier publications had certainly provoked comment, but the furore caused by *Ann Veronica* was both more intense and more acrimonious. This was partly because *In the Days of the Comet* took the form of fantasy, whilst *Ann Veronica* purported to represent contemporary reality; but it was prompted, too, by the personal scandal threatening to break about its author's ears in the summer of 1909. H. G. Wells, then a forty-four-year-old married man with two young children, was deeply involved in a passionate love affair with Amber Reeves, the beautiful and brilliant daughter of fellow Fabian Society members, who was twenty-five years his junior.[8] When Amber became pregnant, the lovers fled to France. It seemed more than likely that Wells would leave his wife, but in the event a marriage with an old admirer was arranged for Amber in July 1909, and she gave birth to a daughter on New Year's Eve. Many who knew of the affair saw *Ann Veronica* as wish fulfilment, and in his autobiography, written over twenty years later, Wells appears to endorse the links between the novel and the Amber Reeves affair when he writes that 'Ann Veronica came as near to being a living character as anyone in [his] earlier love stories. This was so because in some particulars she was drawn from life.'[9] (p. 470)

Since the first appearance of the novel, then, many commentators have seen *Ann Veronica* and its message of free love and sexual liberation as a product of Wells's own sexual proclivities rather than as an expression of principle.[10] By his own admission,

Wells suffered from what he called 'Domestic claustrophobia'; he needed a stable home-life, but soon became restless when obliged to spend much time at home. By 1908 he had embarked on what was to be a lifelong pattern of unfaithfulness to his wife Jane – apparently with her collusion, although it is clear that the impetus came from him – which included affairs with Rebecca West, Elizabeth von Arnim, Dorothy Richardson and many other independent and able women. In the third volume of his autobiography, *H. G. Wells in Love*, Wells claims that throughout his life he has been searching – unsuccessfully – for what he calls his 'lover shadow' – a woman who would be the perfect sexual and intellectual complement of himself, his female counterpart.[11]

In a consideration of Wells's claims to be a feminist, it is interesting to note that although he makes out a good theoretical case for freer sexual relations, two of his young mistresses[12] – Amber Reeves and Rebecca West – bore him children, and it is clear that it was their lives, and not his, which were subsequently determined by these events: Rebecca West certainly felt that her literary career had been hampered because she was obliged to live in the country with her young son,[13] whilst Amber Reeves, who seemed likely to have a brilliant future – she had attained a double first in the Cambridge Moral Science Tripos at the height of the affair with Wells – retired into domesticity. As Ruth Brandon puts it in *The Young Women and the Old Men*, 'Whatever Amber's intellectual potential may have been, she was never given a chance to realize it. By the time the obsession with H. G. Wells had abated she had a husband and, more to the point, a baby.'[14]

Given such a background is it possible to see H. G. Wells as a feminist novelist, and *Ann Veronica* as a novel which can still interest readers in women's issues in the 1990s? His contemporaries certainly considered him to be a supporter of the woman's cause, and many women readers in the years leading up to the First World War seem to have taken it for granted that Wells was speaking to and for them;[15] novels like *Ann Veronica* seemed, in fact, to open up hitherto undreamt of possibilities for women. And this did not apply only to the middle-class intelligentsia. In 1911 a young working woman, Ruth Slate, urged her friend Eva Slawson to read Wells's latest novel, *The New Machiavelli*: 'I wanted to read you wild, splendid passages from Wells,' she writes

' – how he stirs the rebel in one!'[16] Eva clearly responded with enthusiasm. In September 1913, she describes in her diary how she and a friend had talked about the Woman's Movement, and comments: 'I had the horrible sensation that she was absolutely hanging upon my words; as Gertie said to me afterwards, "Anyone would have thought you were H. G. Wells!"'[17]

David Smith, in his critical biography of Wells, suggests that Wells continued to be popular with feminists of later generations, but this is arguable.[18] There were, in fact, many successful women in the 1920s and 1930s who felt that they had been very much influenced by Wells during their formative years but later outgrew his ideas. The American, Freda Kirchwey, for instance, who became editor of the New York Nation in the 1930s, wrote 'A Private Letter to H. G. Wells', published in Nation in November 1928, which hails him as 'the ideal father'. But, she adds, he is ideal because he presents ideas which she has discarded: 'You stayed just exactly the same age; but we grew up.' Other writers had influenced her, she acknowledges:

> But you were the most energetic and intimate of our fathers. You covered so much ground. You opened so many doors. You delighted and excited and angered us. You offered us all the world in tempting cans with lively labels: Socialism, Free Love, Marriage, Education, World Organisation and H. G. Wells's Patented Feminism – Very Perishable. Down they went. And gradually, on this varied if not always very digestible diet, the children grew older.[19]

But just how perishable is Wells's feminism? This can only be assessed in relation to Ann Veronica by looking at the text of the novel itself.

One obvious problem is Wells's depiction of the suffrage movement in Ann Veronica. Wells believed that the WSPU was far too narrow in its aims because he maintained all along that far more than the vote was required if women were going to achieve the freedom and independence they wanted. 'We have indeed', he argues, 'to work out an entire new system of relations between men and women, that will be free from servitude, aggression, provocation, or parasitism.'[20] In the novel it is the 'aggressive and disagreeable' suffragette Kitty Brett who exemplifies this narrowness. The goal of the women's movement, she declares is 'Freedom! Citizenship! And the way to that – the way to everything – is the Vote' (p. 165). Ann Veronica's arguments about the need for a general change of ideas are brushed aside dismissively: '"The vote is the symbol of everything," said Miss Brett' (p. 166).

But although Wells makes out a good case for considering the WSPU as too narrow, and he was by no means alone in this view,[21] it would be difficult for any reader nowadays to see his one-sided depiction of its followers as other than anti-feminist. The suffragettes who appear in *Ann Veronica* are ridiculous figures. It is significant, for instance, that Miss Miniver, the most prominent representative of the movement in the novel, is not only physically unattractive[22] – 'Miss Miniver looked out on the world through large emotional blue eyes that were further magnified by the glasses she wore, and her nose was pinched and pink' (p. 25) – her appearance also denotes an absurd fanaticism. On her visit to Ann Veronica in London, 'There was a wild light in her eye, and her straight hair was out demonstrating and suffragetting upon some independent notions of its own' (p. 96). What is worse, she possesses 'a weakly rhetorical mind' incapable of logical reasoning or sustaining an argument, and, to Ann Veronica's dismay, Miss Miniver's 'long, confused and emphatic discourse on the position of women, full of wonderful statements' degenerates into a 'fluent muddle' (p. 28). But Wells reserves his deepest scorn for the repressed feelings of excitement underlying Miss Miniver's disgust for male sexuality. On such occasions, we learn, 'A flush of excitement crept into her cheeks' (p. 27), her face acquires 'an unaccustomed pink' (p. 127). Kitty Brett, too, sees sex antagonism as a necessary part of the women's movement at least as long as women are unable to obtain justice.[23] Patricia Stubbs queries whether Wells's own responses to sexuality, the fact that he saw women 'in an exclusively sexual light' made him particularly resistant to anything he saw as anti-sex.[24]

Whatever one thinks of the justice of Wells's descriptions of Miss Miniver and Kitty Brett, however, it is clear that showing suffragettes as neurotic manhaters in *Ann Veronica* is an effective literary device. These women provide a striking contrast to what the novel presents as the common-sense normality of its heroine. Ann Veronica has rebelled against the patriarchal view of women, but finds herself unable to adopt the suffragette attitudes. In prison after the WSPU raid, she concludes: 'The real reason why I am out of place here ... is because I like men. I can talk to them. I've never found them hostile. I've got no feminine class feelings' (p. 180).

Whether or not we accept Ann Veronica as the standard by which womanhood should be judged is, of course, disputable, but the novel requires us to do so.

The narrative form of *Ann Veronica* does, in fact, reflect a feminist bias in a number of ways. Although Wells has been accused by feminist critics of always taking the male point of view in his fiction – 'The woman is secondary,' writes Patricia Stubbs, 'something for the man to cope with, never something of interest in herself'[25] – this is clearly not true of the narration in *Ann Veronica*, which is the only one of Wells's novels to be written primarily from the perspective of a woman. There is, of course, a neutral, third person narrator but Ann Veronica is, in Henry James's phrase, the 'centre of consciousness'. Either she is the centre of focus or, more often, she herself is the focalizer – that is, it is through her eyes and through her responses that events are presented. We never know, for instance, what Canongate Prison is like in objective terms, but we receive a vivid impression of Ann Veronica's reactions to it.

The narrative structure of the novel as a whole also foregrounds women's experience against the constraints society imposes on them. From our first view of Ann Veronica on the train to Morningside Park, we enter the psyche of a young woman who is intelligent, direct, hungry for knowledge and experience – but is only too well aware that:

> All the world about her seemed to be – how can one put it? – in wrappers, like a house when people leave it in the summer. The blinds were all drawn, the sunlight kept out, one could not tell what colours these grey swathings hid. She wanted to know. And there was no intimation whatever that the blinds would ever go up or the windows or doors ever be opened, or the chandeliers which seemed to promise such a blaze of fire, unveiled and furnished and lit. Dim souls flitted about her, not only speaking but it would seem even thinking in undertones. . . . (p. 5)

This recurrent metaphor of the 'wrappered world' in *Ann Veronica* encapsulates the power structures – personal, social and institutional – which determine not only how young women should behave but also how they should see themselves, and each of these power structures is embodied in a different character, whose behaviour is based on a different patriarchal assumption. The most important figure in Ann Veronica's life at the beginning of the novel is her father, and his attitude to women is unequivocally Victorian. All women, he believes, belong to one of two classes: 'they were creatures, he thought, either too bad for a modern vocabulary, and then frequently most undesirably desirable, or too pure and good for life' (p. 10). His task, therefore, is to protect Ann Veronica from the 'prowling pitfalls' (p. 12) of modern life – from anything, in fact, which might change her from the latter kind of woman to the former.[26] He has no problems with authority, because he considers his daughters to be 'his absolute property, bound to obey him, his to give away or his to keep to be a comfort in his declining years, just as he thought fit' (p. 11). The eligible suitor, Mr Manning, on the other hand, eschews power. He describes himself as 'a woman worshipper' (p. 36) and disconcerts Ann Veronica by maintaining fervently that women 'should never come into contact with politics or economics – or any of those things. And we men would work for them and serve them in loyal fealty' (p. 37). It is women, he claims, who possess power, not directly, but 'as influences, as inspirations' (p. 37). But Ann Veronica comes to realize that Mr Manning is not interested in women as individuals, nor in herself as a person: 'she was in fact just a mannequin for her lover's imagination' (p. 204). The middle-aged philanderer, Mr Ramage, on the other hand, pretends an enthusiasm about modern ideas as a way of obtaining power over Ann Veronica. He does, in fact, despise women – 'You're all dependents – all of you. By instinct' (p. 149–50) is his response to rejection, 'Only you good ones – shirk. You shirk a straightforward and decent return for what you get from us.' For all his pretence of liberalism, his philosophy of sexual difference is, in fact, a cruder version of Mr Stanley's.

After Ramage shows himself in his true colours, Ann Veronica realizes that the problem is larger than she had supposed: 'I thought I was just up against Morningside Park and father, but it's the whole order of things – the whole blessed order of things', and the structure of the remainder of *Ann Veronica* reveals the ideological premise on which the novel as a whole is based. In terms of a conventional feminist reading it is obvious that Ann Veronica never does achieve independence and autonomy in the way she had hoped. Her lack of education and experience mean that she cannot provide for herself by getting a job. Admittedly, she does enter on a possible route to independence – the scientific education she wanted so badly – but it could not have been obtained without Ramage's money and is abandoned, apparently without a backward glance, when she falls in love with her instructor and runs away with him. Worst of all, the novel ends with a conventional marriage, and Ann Veronica happily pregnant and reconciled with her family. At first glance, this is scarcely an acceptable feminist solution to the problems faced by the heroine.[27] In defence of Wells's feminist credentials, it should be stressed that to allow Ann Veronica a happy future after she has defied her father, run away with a married man and 'lived in sin' was in itself provocative, a slap in the face of Edwardian conventional opinion.[28] What is more, although the ending of the novel may seem tame to the modern reader, it is less conventionally bourgeois than has often been suggested. There is, after all, an uneasy awareness in Ann Veronica's final comments that something has been lost, that she and Capes are already 'hedged about with discretions – and all this furniture' (p. 257). For Wells, as for E. M. Forster, the significant problems in human relationships occur after the marriage vows, and this is hinted at even in this ostensibly fairytale ending.[29]

Wells is in advance of his period, too, in his approach to female sexuality – although he had considerable doubts about the institution of monogamous marriage, he had none about the importance of sex. A striking feature of *Ann Veronica*, in fact, is that even though, as its most condemnatory critic concedes, the novel 'has not a coarse word in it, nor are the most "suggestive" passages open to very severe criticism,'[30] sexuality is present as an undercurrent throughout the text[31] and Ann Veronica's developing love for Capes is described in sensual not romantic terms.[32] Wells, I would suggest, is undeniably a feminist novelist in one very important respect – he believes not only that women are sexual beings, but also that there should be free and guiltless sexual choice between men and women. Therefore, although it may come as a shock to the modern reader to hear so enlightened a heroine declare, as Ann Veronica does in prison:

> A woman wants a proper alliance with a man, a man who is better stuff than herself. She wants that and needs it more than anything else in the world. It may not be just, it may not be fair, but things are so. It isn't law, nor custom, nor masculine violence settled that. It is just how things happen to be. She wants to be free – she wants to be legally and economically free, so as not to be subject to the wrong man; but only God, who made the world, can alter things to prevent her being slave to the right one (p. 180).

– it is important to remember that the crucial factor is *choice*. For Ann Veronica, for instance, her sister's frequent pregnancies cannot be compared with her own – 'Quite different. She didn't choose her man' (p. 256).

This is a choice, moreover, which does not have to be initiated by the man. Writing about *Ann Veronica* in his autobiography many years later, Wells suggests that this was the 'particular offence' which aroused so much outrage when the novel first appeared:

> Ann Veronica was a virgin who fell in love and showed it, instead of waiting as all popular heroines had hitherto done, for someone to make love to her. It was held to be an unspeakable offence that an adolescent female should be sex-conscious before the thing was forced upon her attention. But Ann Veronica wanted a particular man who excited her and she pursued him and got him. With gusto (p. 470).

Even today, Ann Veronica's unabashed directness comes as something of a shock. It is she who insists that Capes walk with her to Waterloo, and when he asks 'What do you want?' she replies with a single word: 'You!' After he has told her about his marriage and pleaded with her to be cautious, to think carefully before rushing into anything, Ann Veronica still insists: '"I want you. I want you to be my lover. I want to give myself to you. I want to be whatever I can to you." She paused for a moment. "Is that plain?" she asked' (p. 220).

The ideological premise on which *Ann Veronica* is based, however, derives from the fact that for Wells, the biologist and Darwinist, there are some areas of human life where choice is not available; 'things are so', as Ann Veronica puts it, because the good of the species requires it. So far as Wells is concerned, men and women have evolved to perform different functions, and woman's role is motherhood.[33] Thus, he advocates the social and political equality and personal freedom of women, but at the same time seeks ways of reconciling this emancipation with the evolutionary process.[34] Wells's solution is 'Endowed Motherhood', a system by which the state is required to pay a wage to a woman who is, or is about to become, a mother.[35] The patriarchal family structure, where the male head of the family virtually owned and controlled the lives of the women in his family, would be replaced by the power of the socialist state. Feminist critics have reacted in various ways to this idea. Cliona Murphy, for instance, claims that Wells gave insufficient attention to women's education because he considered it unimportant, he 'saw women playing a major role as breeders in his new race',[36] but Patricia Stubbs argues that although the plan does nothing to free women from domesticity, 'at least Wells was moving in the right direction and understood something of the economic aspects of women's oppression'.[37] Not surprisingly, after she has met Capes, the idea appears to Ann Veronica herself as the ideal solution to a problem which she is beginning to see as insurmountable – ideal because it would enable her to choose of her own free will:

> She let her mind run into dreams of that cloud paradise of an altered world in which the Goopes and Minivers, the Fabians and reforming people believed. Across that world was written in letters of light: 'Endowment of Motherhood.' Suppose in some complex yet conceivable way women were endowed, were no longer economically and socially dependent on men. 'If one was free,' she said, 'one could go to him. . . . This vile hovering to catch a man's eye! . . . One could go to him and tell him one loved him. I want to love him . . .' (p. 161)

– but there's no doubt in *Ann Veronica* about who is going to stay home and look after the children!

It would appear, then, that there are no easy answers to the question I raised at the beginning of this Introduction. In some ways *Ann Veronica* can be seen as very much a feminist novel, but there are a number of problems. For those who reject the essentialist theory of sexual difference, and deny that there are any temperamental and psychological differences between women and men which are not culturally produced, *Ann Veronica* will always be an unsatisfactory novel, full of contradictions and ambivalences. This is because it is structured round a heroine who has not only broken away from home in an unconscious search for a mate – 'You came out like an ant for your nuptial flight' (p. 238), says Capes – but also has disclaimed modernity: 'Modern indeed! She was going to be as primordial as chipped flint' (p. 228). One thing can be said for sure, however: the novel raises questions about relationships between men and women and about social attitudes towards women which are still of considerable interest and relevance to today's readers. Wells may not always have provided satisfactory answers, but in *Ann Veronica* he does oblige us to look at the problems.

Notes

[1]Sarah Wells apprenticed all three of her sons to drapery establishments. 'Almost as unquestioning as her belief in Our Father and Saviour,' writes Wells, 'was her belief in drapers.' (H. G. Wells, *Experiment in Autobiography*, London, Cape, 1934, p.434.)

[2]Rosalind Miles does, in fact, refers to this social and intellectual mobility as the 'H. G. Wells Syndrome' (*The Fiction of Sex*, New York, Barnes & Noble, 1974, p.89) and points out that this mobility coincided with the emergence of many young women writers.

[3]Wells was at this period very excited about his own good fortune. In a 1911 article he describes his early 'grim rebellion against the world' and the sudden illness which had decided his future: 'as I could do nothing else, I wrote, and in a year found myself free to live anywhere and write as I liked, twice as prosperous as I had ever been in my life before.' ('My Lucky Moment', *The View*, 29 April 1911, p.212.) V. S. Pritchett writes: 'Above all, in these early books, you catch Wells in his characteristic act, of breaking down mean barriers and setting you free. He has burst out himself and he wants everyone else to do the same.' (*The Living Novel*, London; Arrow Books, 1960, p.123.)

[4]These issues are discussed in detail in Samuel Hynes's *The Edwardian Turn of Mind* (New Jersey, Princeton UP, 1971).

[5]This phrase comes from the Manifesto of the National Council for Public Morals (founded in 1901 as the National Crusade for Social Purity) published in *The Times*, 31 May 1911.

[6]See *Anticipations* (1901), *Mankind in the Making* (1903), *A Modern Utopia* (1905), as well as Wells's 1906 address to the Fabian Society, 'Socialism and the Middle Classes' (published as 'Socialism and the Family') in which he argued that socialism should repudiate the private ownership of women accorded to the head of the family by ensuring that mothers were 'endowed' with sufficient money to be independent of their husbands.

[7]*In the Days of the Comet* is a fantasy in which a mysterious extraterrestrial gas from a passing comet transforms the whole of Britain into a land of peace and harmony, where there is no such thing as jealousy or proprietorial love, where 'unstinted love' is both possible and socially acceptable. In its review, the *Times Literary Supplement* commented: 'Socialistic men's wives, we gather, are, no less than their goods, to be held in common. Free love, according to Mr Wells, is to be of the essence of the new social contract.' (*TLS*, 14 September 1906.)

[8]Wells, who was at that time on the Fabian Society executive, had also had a brief sexual relationship with Rosamund Bland, the twenty-year-old daughter of Hubert Bland and E. Nesbit, an affair which had been nipped in the bud by her father. It is hard, in fact, to detach Wells's protracted quarrel with the Fabian Society on matters of policy from the

scandal caused by his love affairs – as Samuel Hynes reports, Beatrice Webb 'was especially shocked that the union [with Amber Reeves] had been consummated within the very walls of Newnham College'. (*Edwardian Turn of Mind*, pp.118–19.)

[9] In the later volume of autobiography, *H. G. Wells in Love: Postscript to an Experiment in Autobiography*, ed. G. P. Wells (London, Faber, 1984) p.84, Wells writes: 'A pallid reflection of some aspects of our situation – or rather of the sentiments of our situation – appeared in *Ann Veronica* and *The New Machiavelli*.'

[10] Contemporary feminist critics have tended to look at Wells's 'feminist' writings in relation to what is known of his life and his numerous sexual relationships. See: Ruth Brandon, *The New Women and the Old Men*; Bonnie Kime-Scott, 'Uncle Wells and Women: A Revisionary Reading of the Social Romances'; *H. G. Wells Under Revision*, eds. Patrick Parrinder & Christopher Rolfe, London; Associated UP, 1990; Nancy Steffen-Fluhr, 'Paper Tiger: Women and H. G. Wells', *Science Fiction Studies* Vol. 37, 1985; Patricia Stubbs, *Women and Fiction: Feminism and the Novel 1880–1920*, London, Methuen, 1979.

[11] *H. G. Wells in Love*, pp.51–7. This book was written in 1935–6, immediately after the publication of the first two volumes of autobiography, which dealt in detail with his early life, but concentrates on his public life during his mature years. In the third volume, Wells describes what had to be omitted from the earlier books – his diverse and complicated love life. He left a note to say that he did not know whether this Postscript to his autobiography would ever be published, but he clearly hopes that it will be possible to do so 'When ***** and Moura and Dusa are either dead or consenting – for Odette does not matter a rap; Rebecca, bless her, is fully able to take care of herself; ***** won't mind, and nobody else has any justification for complaint ... ' His son Gyp, who edited the text for publication, replaced names with asterisks, and adds a footnote to the last announcing 'She did'! In fact, the text was published in 1984, the year following Rebecca West's death.

[12] Dorothy Richardson, who had a sexual relationship with Wells a few years before the Amber Reeves affair, discovered she was pregnant by him in 1906. Showalter claims that 'she was determined to follow the Fabian gospel by raising the child completely on her own. Unhappily – for she had an intense maternal drive – she had a miscarriage in 1907, around Easter.' (Elaine Showalter, *A Literature of Their Own: British Women Novelists from Brontë to Lessing*, London, Virago, 1982, p.252.)

[13] See Gordon N. Ray, *H. G. Wells and Rebecca West* (London, Macmillan, 1974).

[14] Ruth Brandon, *The New Women and the Old Men: Love, Sex and the Woman Question* (London, Flamingo, 1991) p.187.

[15] Admittedly, Rebecca West denounced Wells as anti-women and anti-sex, as 'the old maid among novelists' in her review of his 1912 novel,

Marriage in *The New Freewoman*. But in the light of subsequent events – the review led to a meeting and a sexual relationship which lasted for ten years – the attack could be seen as deliberately provocative. See *The Young Rebecca: Writings of Rebecca West 1911–7*. (London, Macmillan, 1982) pp.64–70.

[16] Tierl Thompson, ed., *Dear Girl: The Diaries and Letters of Two Working Women (1897–1917)* (London, Women's Press, 1987) p.158–9.

[17] Tierl Thompson, p.185.

[18] David Smith, *H. G. Wells: Desperately Mortal* (New Haven, Yale UP, 1986) ch.15.

[19] Freda Kirchwey, 'A Private Letter to H. G. Wells', *H. G. Wells: The Critical Heritage*, ed. Patrick Parrinder (London, Routledge, 1972) p.308.

[20] 'The Great State', *An Englishman Looks at the World*, p.129.

[21] No one disputes the fervency of Rebecca West's feminism, and yet she was advancing exactly these ideas between 1912 and 1914, in *The New Freewoman* and *The Clarion*. She, like Wells, had reservations about militancy, and she too complained that the suffragettes seemed not to realize that the emancipation of women required huge changes in attitudes *and* in social structures. 'It is strange,' she writes, 'that the middle-class woman, who forms the backbone of the suffrage societies, should believe that one can superimpose the emancipation of women on the social system as one sticks a halfpenny stamp on a postcard' and, she concludes, 'That is why women should not concentrate their intelligences too fixedly on the vote without preparing for the tremendous issues that follow.' ('Women Who are Parasites', *Clarion*, 1 November 1912. *The Young Rebecca West*, pp.111–15.)

[22] Anti-feminist slogans castigated the suffragettes as women who had embraced the cause because no one would embrace them.

[23] Wells managed to incur the wrath of both wings of the suffrage movement. Moderate opinion was alarmed by his emphasis on doing away with private property within marriage, and he lost the support of militant feminists who saw women as the victims of male oppression. He notes in his autobiography, 'It became increasingly obvious to me that a large part of the women's movement was animated less by the desire for freedom and fullness of life, than by a passionate jealousy and hatred of the relative liberties of men.' (*Experiment in Autobiography*, p.483.)

[24] Stubbs, p.187. Although it is undeniable that Wells presents a highly partial view of the suffrage movement in his novels, there undoubtedly was a strong element of puritanism within the WSPU. Rebecca West, for instance, in a 1913 article, deplores the generalized 'rancour against men' shown by Christabel Pankhurst in a recent issue of the *Suffragette*. 'It would be as well,' writes West, 'if Miss Pankhurst would put a note at the head of her article: "For man read immoral man."' (*The Young Rebecca West*, p.207.)

[25] Stubbs, p.193.

[26] One of the dangers, so far as Mr Stanley is concerned, is advanced education. It is interesting that when Ann Veronica makes 'a valiant fight' for higher education either at Girton (which at that period was acquiring a reputation for academic rigour) or Newnham (which pursued less strenuous courses and made more concessions to its women students), Mr Stanley makes no distinction between them. His opposition to genuine education for women is anti-feminist and therefore global: 'that sort of thing unsexed a woman'.

[27] Ann Veronica bemoans the fact that 'A woman's life is all chance. It's artificially chance', but for Wells this is as much a matter of class as it is of gender. In *Kipps* he explores this idea in relation to a man, an underprivileged draper's assistant, who on two occasions has his fortunes determined, arbitrarily and by chance, through no effort or merit of his own.

[28] Victorian and Edwardian novels abound in heroines who offend against the sexual moral code, but they all come to a bad end. In Dickens' *David Copperfield*, Little Em'ly is forgiven but banished to Australia, Hardy's Sue Bridehead in *Jude the Obscure* returns to a husband she loathes; Tess in *Tess of the d'Urbervilles* is hanged. Even Grant Allen's heroine in *The Woman Who Did* commits suicide.

[29] Admittedly the sudden conversion of Capes from disgraced lecturer to successful playwright does strain credibility. This could be a consequence of Wells's decision to make the novel shorter than he had originally intended or it could reflect his belief that writing plays was a quick way to make money. In 1904, Wells had, according to Arnold Bennett, 'talked seriously of gambling with six months of his time in order to try to do a couple or so of plays that would possibly bring in a fortune. He said he wanted £20,000 as a capital basis.' (*The Journals*, Harmondsworth, Penguin, 1971 p.108.)

[30] This comment is taken from the unsigned review in the *Spectator*, quoted at length in 'H. G. Wells and his critics' (p. 267–8).

[31] When it comes to conveying a range of sexual responses, Wells overcomes the problem of explicit statement faced by the Edwardian writer by employing a variety of textual strategies. One of the most striking is the way links are established between protuberant eyes and male sexuality. The man Ann Veronica believes is following her in London is described as having 'bluish eyes that were rather protuberant', whilst from his first appearance, the philandering Mr Ramsay is characterized by his 'rather protuberant black eyes' – a description which is repeated five times in the course of his meetings with Ann Veronica. By the time we reach the seduction scene in the *cabinet particulier*, the link has been established, and when he seizes Ann Veronica and 'Her eye met his four inches away, and his was glaring, immense, and full of resolution, an enormous monster of an eye' the reader is in no doubt about its significance. Interestingly, in *The Interpretation of Dreams*, Freud makes

a link between eyes, Oedipal dreams and the male genitals. (*The Inter-pretation of Dreams*, Harmondsworth, Penguin Freud Library, 1986, p.522n.)

[32] This is subtly and delicately conveyed through Ann Veronica's growing awareness of Capes's body – as he sits next to her at the microscope 'She ... saw that the sunlight was gleaming on his cheeks, and that all over his cheeks was a fine golden down of delicate hairs' – and, in a parallel passage, of her own: 'as she sat on her bed that night, musing and half undressed, she began to run one hand down her arm and scrutinize the soft flow of muscle under the skin, and all the delightfulness of living texture. On the back of her arm she found the faintest down of hair in the world.'

[33] Wells's ideas derive ultimately from Darwin's *Descent of Man*, but at the time *Ann Veronica* was written there were many writers at the forefront of cultural and psychological studies who thought exactly as he did. In *A Modern Utopia* Wells cites Havelock Ellis's *Man and Woman* – the psychological text of its time – in support of the view that 'The trend of evolutionary forces through long centuries of time has been on the whole ... towards differentiation.' (*A Modern Utopia*, London, Chapman & Hall, 1905, p.202.) In 1908, Wells published a book which explained his personal philosophy, and in the section entitled 'Sex' he declares: 'If, for example, it is for the good of the species that a whole half of its individuals should be specialized and subordinated to the physical sexual life, as in certain phases of human development women have tended to be, then certainly we must do nothing to prevent that.' (*First and Last Things: A Confession of Faith and a Rule of Life*, New York, Putnams, 1908, pp.261–2.)

[34] There was a general anxiety about the birth rate in which had been dropping since the turn of the century.

[35] See *A Modern Utopia*, ch.6.3; *The New Machiavelli*, Bk. 3, ch.4.6; 'The Endowment of Motherhood', *An Englishman Looks at the World*, pp.229–34.

[36] Murphy, p.221.

[37] Stubbs, p.188.

ANN VERONICA

Chapter I

Ann Veronica Talks to Her Father

One Wednesday afternoon in late September Ann Veronica Stanley came down from London in a state of solemn excitement and quite resolved to have things out with her father that very evening. She had trembled on the verge of such a resolution before, but this time quite definitely she made it. A crisis had been reached, and she was almost glad it had been reached. She made up her mind in the train home that it should be a decisive crisis. It is for that reason that this novel begins with her there, and neither earlier nor later, for it is the history of this crisis and its consequences that this novel has to tell.

She had a compartment to herself in the train from London to Morningside Park, and she sat with both her feet on the seat in an attitude that would certainly have distressed her mother to see and horrified her grandmother beyond measure; she sat with her knees up to her chin and her hands clasped before them, and she was so lost in thought that she discovered with a start, from a lettered lamp, that she was at Morningside Park, and thought she was moving out of the station, whereas she was only moving in. 'Lord!' she said. She jumped up at once, caught up a leather clutch containing note-books, a fat text-book, and a chocolate-and-yellow-covered pamphlet, and leaped neatly from the carriage, only to discover that the train was slowing down and that she had to traverse the full length of the platform past it again as the result of her precipitation. 'Sold again,' she remarked. 'Idiot!' She raged inwardly, while she walked along with that air of self-contained serenity that is proper to a young lady of nearly two-and-twenty under the eye of the world.

She walked down the station approach, past the neat, unobtrusive offices of the coal merchant and the house agent, and so to the wicket-gate by the butcher's shop that led to the field path to her home. Outside the post office stood a no-hatted, blond young man in grey flannels, who was elaborately affixing a stamp to a letter. At the sight of her he became rigid and a singularly bright shade of pink. She made herself serenely unaware of his existence, though it may be it was his presence that sent her by the field detour instead of by the direct path up the avenue.

'Umph!' he said, and regarded his letter doubtfully before consigning it to the pillar-box. 'Here goes,' he said. Then he hovered undecidedly for some seconds with his hands in his pockets and his mouth puckered to a whistle before he turned to go home by the Avenue.

Ann Veronica forgot him as soon as she was through the gate, and her face resumed its expression of stern preoccupation. 'It's either now or never,' she said to herself. . . .

Morningside Park was a suburb that had not altogether, as people say, come off. It consisted, like pre-Roman Gaul, of three parts. There was first the Avenue, which ran in a consciously elegant curve from the railway station into an undeveloped wilderness of agriculture, with big yellow brick villas on either side, and then there was the Pavement, the little clump of shops about the post office, and under the railway arch was a congestion of workmen's dwellings. The road from Surbiton and Epsom ran under the arch, and, like a bright fungoid growth in the ditch, there was now appearing a sort of fourth estate of little red-and-white rough-cast villas, with meretricious gables and very brassy window blinds. Behind the Avenue was a little hill, and an iron-fenced path went over the crest of this to a stile under an elm-tree, and forked there, with one branch going back into the Avenue again.

'It's either now or never,' said Ann Veronica again, ascending this stile. 'Much as I hate rows. I've either got to make a stand or give in altogether.'

She seated herself in a loose and easy attitude and surveyed the backs of the Avenue houses; then her eyes wandered to where the new red-and-white villas peeped among the trees. She seemed to be making some sort of inventory. 'Ye gods!' she said at last. '*What* a place!

'Stuffy isn't the word for it.

'I wonder what he takes me for?'

When presently she got down from the stile a certain note of internal conflict, a touch of doubt, had gone from her warm-tinted face. She had now the clear and tranquil expression of one whose mind is made up. Her back had stiffened, and her hazel eyes looked steadfastly ahead.

As she approached the corner of the Avenue the blond, no-hatted young man in grey flannels appeared. There was a certain air of forced fortuity in his manner. He saluted awkwardly. 'Hallo, Vee!' he said.

'Hallo, Teddy!' she answered.

He hung vaguely for a moment as she passed.

But it was clear she was in no mood for Teddys. He realized that he was committed to the path across the fields, an uninteresting walk at the best of times.

'Oh! dammit!' he remarked, 'dammit!' with great bitterness as he faced it.

2

Ann Veronica Stanley was twenty-one and a half years old. She had black hair, fine eyebrows, and a clear complexion; and the forces that had modelled her features had loved and lingered at their work and made them subtle and fine. She was slender, and sometimes she seemed tall, and walked and carried herself lightly and joyfully as one who commonly and habitually feels well, and sometimes she stooped a little and was preoccupied. Her lips came together with an expression between contentment and the faintest shadow of a smile, her manner was one of quiet reserve, and behind this mask she was wildly discontented and eager for freedom and life.

She wanted to live. She was vehemently impatient – she did not clearly know for what – to do, to be, to experience. And experience was slow in coming. All the world about her seemed to be – how can one put it? – in wrappers, like a house when people leave it in the summer. The blinds were all drawn, the sunlight kept out, one could not tell what colours these grey swathings hid. She wanted to know. And there was no intimation whatever that the blinds would ever go up or the windows or doors be opened, or the chandeliers, that seemed to promise such a blaze of fire, unveiled and furnished and lit. Dim souls flitted about her, not only speaking but it would seem even thinking in undertones. . . .

During her schooldays, especially her earlier schooldays, the world had been very explicit with her, telling her what to do, what not to do, giving her lessons to learn and games to play and interests of the most suitable and various kinds. Presently she woke up to the fact that there was a considerable group of interests called being in love and getting married, with certain attractive and amusing subsidiary developments, such as flirtation and 'being interested' in people of the opposite sex. She approached this field with her usual liveliness of apprehension. But here she met with a check. These interests her world promptly, through the agency of schoolmistresses, older schoolmates, her aunt, and a number of other responsible and authoritative people, assured her she must on no account think about. Miss Moffatt, the history and moral instruction mistress, was particularly explicit upon this score, and they all agreed in indicating contempt and pity for girls whose minds ran on such matters, and who betrayed it in their conversation or dress or bearing. It was, in fact, a group of interests quite unlike any other group, peculiar and special, and one to be thoroughly ashamed of. Nevertheless Ann Veronica found it a difficult matter not to think of these things. However, having a considerable amount of pride, she decided she would disavow these undesirable topics and keep her mind away from them just as far as she could; but it left her at the end of her schooldays with that wrapped feeling I have described, and rather at loose ends.

The world, she discovered, with these matters barred, had no particular place for her at all, nothing for her to do, except a functionless existence varied by calls, tennis, selected novels, walks, and dusting in her father's house. She thought study would be better. She was a clever girl, the best of her year in the high school, and she made a valiant fight for Somerville or Newnham, but her father had met and argued with a Somerville girl at a friend's dinner-table, and he thought that sort of thing unsexed a woman. He said simply that he wanted her to live at home. There was a certain amount of disputation, and meanwhile she went on at school. They compromised at length on the science course at the Tredgold Women's College – she had already matriculated into London University from school – she came of age, and she bickered with her aunt for latch-key privileges on the strength of that and her season ticket. Shamefaced curiosities began to come back into her mind, thinly disguised as literature and art. She read voraciously, and presently, because of her aunt's censorship, she took to smuggling any books she thought might be prohibited instead of bringing them home openly, and she went to the theatre whenever she could produce an acceptable friend to accompany her. She passed her general science examination with double honours and specialized in science. She happened to have an acute sense of form and unusual mental lucidity, and she found in biology, and particularly in comparative anatomy, a very considerable interest, albeit the illumination it cast upon her personal life was not altogether direct. She dissected well, and in a year she found herself chafing at the limitations of the lady B.Sc. who retailed a store of faded learning in the Tredgold laboratory. She had already realized that this instructress was hopelessly wrong and foggy – it is the test of the good comparative anatomist – upon the skull. She discovered a desire to enter as a student in the Imperial College at Westminster,* where Russell* taught, and go on with her work at the fountain head.

She had asked about that already, and her father had replied evasively: 'We'll have to see about that, little Vee; we'll have to see about that.' In that posture of being seen about the matter hung until she seemed committed to another session at the Tredgold College, and in the meantime a smaller conflict arose and brought the latch-key question, and in fact the question of Ann Veronica's position generally, to an acute issue.

In addition to the various business men, solicitors, civil servants, and widow ladies who lived in the Morningside Park Avenue, there was a certain family of alien sympathies and artistic quality, the Widgetts, with which Ann Veronica had become very friendly. Mr Widgett was a journalist and art critic, addicted to a greenish-grey tweed suit and 'art' brown ties; he smoked corn-cob pipes in the Avenue on Sunday morning, travelled third class to London by unusual trains, and openly despised golf. He occupied one of the smaller houses near the station. He had one son, who had been co-educated, and three daughters with peculiarly jolly red hair that Ann Veronica found adorable. Two of these had been her particular intimates at the high school, and had done much to send her mind exploring beyond the limits of the available literature at home. It was a cheerful, irresponsible, shamelessly hard-up family in the key of faded green and flattened purple, and the girls went on from the high school to the Fadden Art School and a bright, eventful life of art student dances, Socialist meetings, theatre galleries, talking about work, and even, at intervals, work; and ever and again they drew Ann Veronica from her sound persistent industry into the circle of these experiences. They had asked her to come to the first of the two great annual Fadden dances, the October one, and Ann Veronica had accepted with enthusiasm. And now her father said she must not go.

He had 'put his foot down,' and said she must not go.

Going involved two things that all Ann Veronica's tact had been ineffectual to conceal from her aunt and father. Her usual dignified reserve had availed her nothing. One point was that she was to wear fancy dress in the likeness of a corsair's bride, and the other was that she was to spend whatever vestiges of the night remained after the dance was over in London with the Widgett girls and a select party in 'quite a decent little hotel' near Fitzroy Square.

'But, my dear!' said Ann Veronica's aunt.

'You see,' said Ann Veronica, with the air of one who shares a difficulty. 'I've promised to go. I didn't realize—I don't see how I can get out of it now.'

Then it was her father issued his ultimatum. He had conveyed it to her, not verbally, but by means of a letter, which seemed to her a singularly ignoble method of prohibition. 'He couldn't look me in the face and say it,' said Ann Veronica. 'But of course it's aunt's doing really.'

And thus it was that as Ann Veronica neared the gates of home she said to herself: 'I'll have it out with him somehow. I'll have it out with him. And if he won't—'

But she did not give even unspoken words to the alternative at that time.

3

Ann Veronica's father was a solicitor with a good deal of company business: a lean, trustworthy, worried-looking, neuralgic, clean-shaven man of fifty-three, with a hard mouth, a sharp nose, iron-grey hair, grey eyes, gold-framed glasses, and a small circular baldness at the crown of his head. His name was Peter. He had had five children at irregular intervals, of whom Ann Veronica was the youngest, so that as a parent he came to her perhaps a little practised and jaded and inattentive; and he called her his 'little Vee,' and patted her unexpectedly and disconcertingly, and treated her promiscuously as of any age between eleven and eight-and-twenty. The City worried him a good deal, and what energy he had left over he spent partly in golf, a game he treated very seriously, and partly in the practices of microscopic petrography.

He 'went in' for microscopy in the unphilosophical Victorian manner as his 'hobby'. A birthday present of a microscope had turned his mind to technical microscopy when he was eighteen, and a chance friendship with a Holborn microscope dealer had confirmed that bent. He had remarkably skilful fingers and a love of detailed processes, and he had become one of the most dexterous amateur makers of rock sections in the world. He spent a good deal more money and time than he could afford upon the little room at the top of the house, in producing new lapidary apparatus and new microscopic accessories and in rubbing down slices of rock to a transparent thinness and mounting them in a beautiful and dignified manner. He did it, he said, 'to distract his mind'. His chief successes he exhibited to the Lowndean Microscopical Society, where their high technical merit never failed to excite admiration. Their scientific value was less considerable since he chose rocks entirely with a view to their difficulty of handling or their attractiveness at conversaziones when done. He had a great contempt for the sections the 'theorizers' produced. They proved all sorts of things perhaps, but they were thick, unequal, pitiful pieces of work. Yet an indiscriminating, wrong-headed world gave such fellows all sorts of distinctions. . . .

He read but little, and that chiefly healthy light fiction with chromatic titles, *The Red Sword, The Black Helmet, The Purple Robe*, also in order 'to distract his mind'. He read it in winter in the evening after dinner, and Ann Veronica associated it with a tendency to monopolize the lamp and to spread a very worn pair of dappled fawn-skin slippers across the fender. She wondered occasionally why his mind needed so much distraction. His favourite newspaper was *The Times*, which he began at breakfast in the morning, often with manifest irritation, and carried off to finish in the train, leaving no other paper at home.

It occurred to Ann Veronica once that she had known him when he was younger, but day had followed day, and each had largely obliterated the impression of its predecessor. But she certainly remembered that when she was a little girl he sometimes wore tennis flannels, and also rode a bicycle very dexterously in through the gates to the front door. And in those days, too, he used to help her mother with her gardening, and hover about her while she stood on the ladder and hammered creepers to the scullery wall.

It had been Ann Veronica's lot as the youngest child to live in a home that became less animated and various as she grew up. Her mother had died when she was thirteen, her two much elder sisters had married off – one submissively, one insubordinately; her two brothers had gone out into the world well ahead of her, and so she had made what she could of her father. But he was not a father one could make much of.

His ideas about girls and women were of a sentimental and modest quality; they were creatures, he thought, either too bad for a modern vocabulary, and then frequently most undesirably desirable, or too pure and good for life. He made this simple classification of a large and various sex to the exclusion of all intermediate kinds; he held that the two classes had to be kept apart even in thought and remote from one another. Women are made like the potter's vessels, either for worship or contumely, and are withal fragile vessels. He had never wanted daughters. Each time a daughter had been born to him he had concealed his chagrin with great tenderness and effusion from his wife, and had sworn unwontedly and with passionate sincerity in the bathroom. He was a manly man, free from any strong maternal strain, and he had loved his dark-eyed, dainty, bright-coloured, and active little wife with a real vein of passion in his sentiment. But he had always felt (he had never allowed himself to think of it) that the promptitude of their family was a little indelicate of her, and in a sense an intrusion. He had, however, planned brilliant careers for his two sons, and, with a certain human amount of warping and delay, they were pursuing these. One was in the Indian Civil Service and one in the rapidly developing motor business. The daughters, he had hoped, would be their mother's care.

He had no ideas about daughters. They happen to a man.

Of course a little daughter is a delightful thing enough. It runs about gaily, it romps, it is bright and pretty, it has enormous quantities of soft hair and more power of expressing affection than its brothers. It is a lovely little appendage to the mother who smiles over it, and it does things quaintly like her, gestures with her very gestures. It makes wonderful sentences that you can repeat in the City and are good enough for *Punch*. You call it a lot of nicknames: 'Babs' and 'Bibs' and 'Viddles' and 'Vee'; you whack at it playfully, and it whacks you back. It loves to sit on your knee. All that is jolly and as it should be.

But a little daughter is one thing and a daughter quite another. There one comes to a relationship that Mr Stanley had never thought out. When he found himself thinking about it, it upset him so that he at once resorted to distraction. The chromatic fiction with which he relieved his mind glanced but slightly at this aspect of life, and never with any quality of guidance. Its heroes never had daughters, they borrowed other people's. The one fault, indeed, of this school of fiction for him was that it had rather a light way with parental rights. His instinct was in the direction of considering his daughters his absolute property, bound to obey him, his to give away or his to keep to be a comfort in his declining years, just as he thought fit. About this conception of ownership he perceived and desired a certain sentimental glamour, he liked everything properly dressed, but it remained ownership. Owner-ship seemed only a reasonable return for the cares and expenses of a daughter's upbringing. Daughters were not like sons. He perceived, however, that both the novels he read and the world he lived in discountenanced these assumptions. Nothing else was put in their place, and they remained *sotto voce*, as it were, in his mind. The new and the old cancelled out; his daughters became quasi-independent dependants – which is absurd. One married as he wished and one against his wishes, and now here was Ann Veronica, his little Vee, discontented with her beautiful, safe, and sheltering home, going about with hatless friends to Socialist meetings and art-class dances, and displaying a disposition to carry her scientific ambitions to unwomanly lengths. She seemed to think he was merely the paymaster, handing over the means of her freedom. And now she insisted that she *must* leave the chastened security of the Tredgold Women's College for Russell's unbridled classes, and wanted to go to fancy dress dances in pirate costume and spend the residue of the night with Widgett's ram-shackle girls in some indescribable hotel in Soho!

He had done his best not to think about her at all, but the situation and his sister had become altogether too urgent. He had finally put aside *The Lilac Sunbonnet*, gone into his study, lit the gas fire, and written the letter that had brought these unsatisfac-tory relations to a head.

4

'MY DEAR VEE,' he wrote.

These daughters! He gnawed his pen and reflected, tore the sheet up, and began again.

'MY DEAR VERONICA, *Your aunt tells me you have involved yourself in some arrangement with the Widgett girls about a Fancy Dress Ball in London. I gather you wish to go up in some fantastic get-up, wrapped about in your opera cloak, and that after the festivities you propose to stay with these friends of yours, and without any older people in your party, at an hotel. Now I am sorry to cross you in anything you have set your heart upon, but I regret to say—*'

'H'm,' he reflected, and crossed out the last four words. '– but this cannot be.'

'No,' he said, and tried again: '*but I must tell you quite definitely that I feel it to be my duty to forbid any such exploit.*'

'Damn!' he remarked at the defaced letter; and, taking a fresh sheet, he recopied what he had written. A certain irritation crept into his manner as he did so.

'*I regret that you should ever have proposed it,*' he went on.

He meditated, and began a new paragraph.

'*The fact of it is, and this absurd project of yours only brings it to a head, you have begun to get hold of some very queer ideas about what a young lady in your position may or may not venture to do. I do not think you quite understand my ideals or what is becoming as between father and daughter. Your attitude to me—*'

He fell into a brown study. It was so difficult to put precisely. '*– and your aunt—*'

For a time he searched for the *mot juste*. Then he went on: '*– and, indeed, to most of the established things in life is, frankly, unsatisfactory. You are restless, aggressive, critical with all the crude unthinking criticism of youth. You have no grasp upon the essential facts of life (I pray God you never may), and in your rash ignorance you are prepared to dash into positions that may end in lifelong regret. The life of a young girl is set about with prowling pitfalls.*'

He was arrested for a moment by an indistinct picture of Veronica reading this last sentence. But he was now too deeply moved to trace a certain unsatisfactoriness to its source in a mixture of metaphors. 'Well,' he said argumentatively, '*it is.* That's all about it. It's time she knew.'

'*The life of a young girl is set about with prowling pitfalls, from which she must be shielded at all costs.*'

His lips tightened, and he frowned with solemn resolution.

'*So long as I am your father, so long as your life is entrusted to my care, I feel bound by every obligation to use my authority to check this odd disposition of yours towards extravagant enterprises. A day will come when you will thank me. It is not, my dear Veronica, that I think there is any harm in you; there is not. But a girl is soiled not only by evil but by the proximity of evil, and a reputation for rashness may do her as serious an injury as really reprehensible conduct. So do please believe that in this matter I am acting for the best.*'

He signed his name and reflected. Then he opened the study door and called 'Mollie!' and returned to assume an attitude of authority on the hearthrug, before the blue flames and orange glow of the gas fire.

His sister appeared.

She was dressed in one of those complicated dresses that are all lace and work and confused patternings of black and purple and cream about the body, and she was in many ways a younger feminine version of the same theme as himself. She had the same sharp nose – which, indeed, only Ann Veronica, of all the family, had escaped. She carried herself well, whereas her brother slouched, and there was a certain aristocratic dignity about her that she had acquired through her long engagement to a curate of family, a scion of the Wiltshire Edmondshaws. He had died before they married, and when her brother became a widower, she had come to his assistance, and taken over much of the care of his youngest daughter. But from the first her rather old-fashioned conception of life had jarred with the suburban atmosphere, the high school spirit and the memories of the light and little Mrs Stanley, whose family had been by any reckoning inconsiderable – to use the kindliest term. Miss Stanley had determined from the outset to have the warmest affection for her youngest niece and to be a second mother in her life – a second and a better one; but she had found much to battle with, and that there was much in herself that Ann Veronica failed to understand. She came in now with an air of reserved solicitude.

Mr Stanley pointed to the letter with a pipe he had drawn from his jacket pocket. 'What do you think of that?' he asked.

She took it up in her many-ringed hands and read it judicially. He filled his pipe slowly.

'Yes,' she said at last, 'it is firm and affectionate.'

'I could have said more.'

'You seem to have said just what had to be said. It seems to me exactly what is wanted. She really must not go to that affair.'

She paused, and he waited for her to speak.

'I don't think she quite sees the harm of those people or the sort of life to which they would draw her,' she said. 'They would spoil every chance.'

'She has chances?' he said, helping her out.

'She is an extremely attractive girl,' she said, and added, 'to some people. Of course, one doesn't like to talk about things until there are things to talk about.'

'All the more reason why she shouldn't get herself talked about.'

'That is exactly what I feel.'

Mr Stanley took the letter and stood with it in his hand thoughtfully for a time. 'I'd give anything,' he remarked, 'to see our little Vee happily and comfortably married.'

He gave the note to the parlourmaid next morning in an inadvertent, casual manner just as he was leaving the house to catch his London train. When Ann Veronica got it she had at first a wild, fantastic idea that it contained a tip.

5

Ann Veronica's resolve to have things out with her father was not accomplished without difficulty.

He was not due from the City until about six, and so she went and played badminton with the Widgett girls until dinner time. The atmosphere at dinner was not propitious. Her aunt was blandly amiable above a certain tremulous undertow, and talked as if to a caller about the alarming spread of marigolds that summer at the end of the garden, a sort of Yellow Peril to all the smaller hardy annuals, while her father brought some papers to table and presented himself as preoccupied with them. 'It really seems as if we shall have to put down marigolds altogether next year,' Aunt Molly repeated three times, 'and do away with marguerites. They seed beyond all reason.' Elizabeth, the parlourmaid, kept coming in to hand vegetables whenever there seemed a chance of Ann Veronica asking for an interview. Directly dinner was over Mr Stanley, having pretended to linger to smoke, fled suddenly upstairs to petrography, and when Veronica tapped he answered through the locked door: 'Go away, Vee! I'm busy,' and made a lapidary's wheel buzz loudly.

Breakfast, too, was an impossible occasion. He read *The Times* with an unusually passionate intentness, and then declared suddenly for the earlier of the two trains he used.

'I'll come to the station,' said Ann Veronica. 'I may as well come up by this train.'

'I may have to run,' said her father, with an appeal to his watch.

'I'll run too,' she volunteered.

Instead of which they walked sharply. . . .

'I say, daddy,' she began, and was suddenly short of breath.

'If it's about that dance project,' he said, 'it's no good, Veronica. I've made up my mind.'

'You'll make me look a fool before all my friends.'

'You shouldn't have made an engagement until you'd consulted your aunt.'

'I thought I was old enough,' she gasped between laughter and crying.

Her father's step quickened to a trot. 'I won't have you quarrelling and crying in the Avenue,' he said. 'Stop it! . . . If you've got anything to say, you must say it to your aunt—'

'But look here, daddy!'

He flapped *The Times* at her with an imperious gesture.

'It's settled. You're not to go. You're *not* to go.'

'But it's about other things.'

'I don't care. This isn't the place.'

'Then may I come to the study to-night – after dinner?'

'I'm – *busy*!'

'It's important. If I can't talk anywhere else – I *do* want an understanding.'

Ahead of them walked a gentleman whom it was evident they must at their present pace very speedily overtake. It was Ramage, the occupant of the big house at the end of the Avenue. He had recently made Mr Stanley's acquaintance in the train and shown him one or two trifling civilities. He was an outside broker, and the proprietor of a financial newspaper; he had come up very rapidly in the last few years, and Mr Stanley admired and detested him in almost equal measure. It was intolerable to think that he might overhear words and phrases. Mr Stanley's pace slackened.

'You've no right to badger me like this, Veronica,' he said. 'I can't see what possible benefit can come of discussing things that are settled. If you want advice your aunt is the person. However, if you must air your opinions—'

'To-night, then, daddy!'

He made an angry but conceivably an assenting noise, and then Ramage glanced back and stopped, saluted elaborately, and waited for them to come up. He was a square-faced man of nearly fifty, with iron-grey hair, a mobile clean-shaven mouth, and rather protuberant black eyes that now scrutinized Ann Veronica. He dressed rather after the fashion of the West End than the City, and affected a cultured urbanity that somehow disconcerted and always annoyed Ann Veronica's father extremely. He did not play golf, but took his exercise on horseback, which was also unsympathetic.

'Stuffy these trees make the avenue,' said Mr Stanley as they drew alongside, to account for his own ruffled and heated expression. 'They ought to have been lopped in the spring.'

'There's plenty of time,' said Ramage. 'Is Miss Stanley coming up with us?'

'I go second,' she said, 'and change at Wimbledon.'

'We'll all go second,' said Ramage, 'if we may?'

Mr Stanley wanted to object strongly, but as he could not immediately think how to put it he contented himself with a grunt, and the motion was carried. 'How's Mrs Ramage?' he asked.

'Very much as usual,' said Ramage. 'She finds lying up so much very irksome. But, you see, she *has* to lie up.'

The topic of his invalid wife bored him, and he turned at once to Ann Veronica. 'And where are *you* going?' he said. 'Are you going on again this winter with that scientific work of yours? It's an instance of heredity, I suppose.' For a moment Mr Stanley almost liked Ramage. 'You're a biologist, aren't you?'

He began to talk of his own impressions of biology as a commonplace magazine reader who had to get what he could

from the monthly reviews, and was glad to meet with any infor-
mation from nearer the fountain head. In a little while he and she
were talking quite easily and agreeably. They went on talking in
the train – it seemed to her father a slight want of deference to
him – and he listened and pretended to read *The Times*. He was
struck disagreeably by Ramage's air of gallant consideration and
Ann Veronica's self-possessed answers. These things did not
harmonize with his conception of the forthcoming (if unavoidable) interview. After all, it came to him suddenly as a harsh
discovery that she might be in a sense regarded as grown-up. He
was a man who in all things classified without nuance, and for
him there were in the matter of age just two feminine classes and
no more, girls and women. The distinction lay chiefly in the right
to pat their heads. But here was a girl – she must be a girl since
she was his daughter and pattable – imitating the woman quite
remarkably and cleverly. He resumed his listening. She was
discussing one of those modern advanced plays with a remarkable, with an extraordinary, confidence.

'His love-making,' she remarked, 'struck me as unconvincing.
He seemed too noisy.'

The full significance of her words did not instantly appear to
him. Then it dawned. Good heavens! She was discussing love-
making. For a time he heard no more, and stared with stony eyes
at a Book War proclamation in leaded type that filled half a
column of *The Times* that day. Could she understand what she
was talking about? Luckily it was a second-class carriage, and the
ordinary fellow travellers were not there. Everybody, he felt, must
be listening behind their papers.

Of course, girls repeat phrases and opinions of which they
cannot possibly understand the meaning. But a middle-aged man
like Ramage ought to know better than to draw out a girl, the
daughter of a friend and neighbour. . . .

Well, after all, he seemed to be turning the subject. 'Broddick
is a heavy man,' he was saying, 'and the main interest of the play
was the embezzlement.' Thank heaven! Mr Stanley allowed his
paper to drop a little, and scrutinized the hats and brows of their
three fellow travellers.

They reached Wimbledon, and Ramage whipped out to hand
Miss Stanley to the platform as though she had been a duchess,
and she descended as though such attentions from middle-aged,
but still gallant, merchants were a matter of course. Then, as

Ramage readjusted himself in a corner, he remarked: 'These young people shoot up, Stanley. It seems only yesterday that she was running down the Avenue all hair and legs.'

Mr Stanley regarded him through his glasses with something approaching animosity.

'Now she's all hat and ideas,' he said, with an air of humour.

'She seems an unusually clever girl,' said Ramage.

Mr Stanley regarded his neighbour's clean-shaven face almost warily. 'I'm not sure whether we don't rather overdo all this higher education,' he said, with an effect of conveying profound meanings.

6

He became quite sure, by a sort of accumulation of reflection, as the day wore on. He found his youngest daughter intrusive in his thoughts all through the morning, and still more so in the afternoon. He saw her young and graceful back as she descended from the carriage, severely ignoring him, and recalled a glimpse he had of her face, bright and serene, as his train ran out of Wimbledon. He recalled with exasperating perplexity her clear, matter-of-fact tone as she talked about love-making being unconvincing. He was really very proud of her, and extraordinarily angry and resentful at the innocent and audacious self-reliance that seemed to intimate her sense of absolute independence of him, her absolute security without him. After all, she only *looked* a woman. She was rash and ignorant, absolutely inexperienced. Absolutely. He began to think of speeches, very firm, explicit speeches, he would make.

He lunched in the Legal Club in Chancery Lane, and met Ogilvy. Daughters were in the air that day. Ogilvy was full of a client's trouble in that matter, a grave and even tragic trouble. He told some of the particulars.

'Curious case,' said Ogilvy, buttering his bread and cutting it up in a way he had. 'Curious case – and sets one thinking.'

He resumed after a mouthful. 'Here is a girl of sixteen or seventeen, seventeen and a half to be exact, running about, as one might say, in London. Schoolgirl. Her family are solid West End people. Kensington people. Father – dead. She goes out and comes home. Afterwards goes on to Oxford. Twenty-one, twenty-two.

Why doesn't she marry? Plenty of money under her father's will. Charming girl.'

He consumed Irish stew for some moments.

'Married already,' he said, with his mouth full. 'Shopman.'

'Good God!' said Mr Stanley.

'Good-looking rascal she met at Worthing. Very romantic and all that. He fixed it.'

'But—'

'He left her alone. Pure romantic nonsense on her part. Sheer calculation on his. Went up to Somerset House to examine the will before he did it. Yes. Nice position.'

'She doesn't care for him now?'

'Not a bit. What a girl of sixteen cares for is hair and a high colour and moonlight and a tenor voice. I suppose most of our daughters would marry organ grinders if they had a chance – at that age. My son wanted to marry a woman of thirty in a tobacconist's shop. Only a son's another story. We fixed that. Well, that's the situation. My people don't know what to do. Can't face a scandal. Can't ask the gent to go abroad and condone a bigamy. He misstated her age and address; but you can't get home on him for a thing like that. . . . There you are! Girl spoilt for life. Makes one want to go back to the oriental system!'

Mr Stanley poured wine. 'Damned Rascal!' he said; 'isn't there a brother to kick him?'

'Mere satisfaction,' reflected Ogilvy. 'Mere sensuality. I rather think they have kicked him, from the tone of some of the letters. Nice, of course. But it doesn't alter the situation.'

'It's these Rascals,' said Mr Stanley, and paused.

'Always has been,' said Ogilvy. 'Our interest lies in heading them off.'

'There was a time when girls didn't get these extravagant ideas.'

'Lydia Languish,* for example. Anyhow, they didn't run about so much.'

'Yes. That's about the beginning. It's these damned novels. All this torrent of misleading, spurious stuff that pours from the press. These sham ideals and advanced notions, Women who Dids,* and all that kind of thing. . . .'

Ogilvy reflected. 'This girl – she's really a very charming, frank person – had had her imagination fired, so she told me, by a school performance of *Romeo and Juliet*.'

Mr Stanley decided to treat that as irrelevant. 'There ought to be a censorship of books. We want it badly at the present time. Even *with* the censorship of plays there's hardly a decent thing to which a man can take his wife and daughters, a creeping taint of suggestion everywhere. What would it be without that safe-guard?'

Ogilvy pursued his own topic. 'I'm inclined to think, Stanley, myself that as a matter of fact it was the expurgated *Romeo and Juliet* did the mischief. If our young person hadn't had the nurse part cut out, eh? She might have known more and done less. I was curious about that. All they left it was the moon and stars. And the balcony and "My Romeo!" '

'Shakespeare is altogether different from the modern stuff. Altogether different. I'm not discussing Shakespeare. I don't want to bowdlerise Shakespeare. I'm not that sort. I quite agree. But this modern miasma—'

Mr Stanley took mustard savagely.

'Well, we won't go into Shakespeare,' said Ogilvy. 'What interests me is that our young women nowadays are running about as free as air practically, with registry offices and all sorts of accommodation round the corner. Nothing to check their proceedings but a declining habit of telling the truth and the limitations of their imaginations. And in that respect they stir up one another. Not my affair, of course, but I think we ought to teach them more or restrain them more. One or the other. They're too free for their innocence or too innocent for their freedom. That's my point. Are you going to have any apple tart, Stanley? The apple tart's been very good lately – very good!'

7

At the end of dinner that evening Ann Veronica began: 'Father!'

Her father looked at her over his glasses and spoke with grave deliberation. 'If there is anything you want to say to me,' he said, 'you must say it in the study. I am going to smoke a little here, and then I shall go to the study. I don't see what you can have to say. I should have thought my note – cleared up everything. There are some papers I have to look through to-night, important papers.'

'I won't keep you very long, daddy,' said Ann Veronica.

'I don't see, Mollie,' he remarked, taking a cigar from the box on the table as his sister and daughter rose, 'why you and Vee shouldn't discuss this little affair – whatever it is – without bothering me.'

It was the first time this controversy had become triangular, for all three of them were shy by habit.

He stopped in mid-sentence, and Ann Veronica opened the door for her aunt. The air was thick with feelings. Her aunt went out of the room with dignity and a rustle, and upstairs to the fastness of her own room. She agreed entirely with her brother. It distressed and confused her that the girl should not come to her. It seemed to show a want of affection, to be a deliberate and unmerited disregard, to justify the reprisal of being hurt.

When Ann Veronica came into the study she found every evidence of a carefully foreseen grouping about the gas fire. Both arm-chairs had been moved a little so as to face each other on either side of the fender, and in the circular glow of the green-shaded lamp there lay, conspicuously waiting, a thick bundle of blue and white papers tied with pink tape. Her father held some printed document in his hand, and appeared not to observe her entry. 'Sit down,' he said, and perused – 'perused' is the word for it – for some moments. Then he put the paper by. 'And what is it all about, Veronica?' he asked with a deliberate note of irony, looking at her a little quizzically over his glasses.

Ann Veronica looked bright and a little elated, and she disregarded her father's invitation to be seated. She stood on the mat instead, and looked down on him. 'Look here, daddy,' she said in a tone of great reasonableness, 'I *must* go to that dance, you know.'

Her father's irony deepened. 'Why?' he asked suavely.

Her answer was not quite ready. 'Well, because I don't see any reason why I shouldn't.'

'You see, I do.'

'Why shouldn't I go?'

'It isn't a suitable place; it isn't a suitable gathering.'

'But, daddy, what do you know of the place and the gathering?'

'And it's entirely out of order; it isn't right, it isn't correct; it's impossible for you to stay in an hotel in London – the idea is preposterous. I can't imagine what possessed you, Veronica.'

He put his head on one side, pulled down the corners of his mouth, and looked at her over his glasses.

'But why is it preposterous?' asked Ann Veronica, and fiddled with a pipe on the mantel.

'Surely!' he remarked, with an expression of worried appeal.

'You see, daddy, I don't think it *is* preposterous. That's really what I want to discuss. It comes to this – am I to be trusted to take care of myself, or am I not?'

'To judge from this proposal of yours, I should say not.'

'I think I am.'

'As long as you remain under my roof,' he began, and paused.

'You are going to treat me as though I wasn't. Well, I don't think that's fair.'

'Your ideas of fairness,' he remarked, and discontinued that sentence. 'My dear girl,' he said in a tone of patient reasonableness, 'you are a mere child. You know nothing of life, nothing of its dangers, nothing of its possibilities. You think everything is harmless and simple, and so forth. It isn't. It isn't. That's where you go wrong. In some things, in many things, you must trust to your elders, to those who know more of life than you do. Your aunt and I have discussed all this matter. There it is. You can't go.'

The conversation hung for a moment. Ann Veronica tried to keep hold of a complicated situation and not lose her head. She had turned round sideways so as to look down into the fire.

'You see, father,' she said, 'it isn't only this affair of the dance. I want to go to that because it's a new experience, because I think it will be interesting and give me a view of things. You say I know nothing. That's probably true. But how am I to know of things?'

'Some things I hope you may never know,' he said.

'I'm not so sure. I want to know – just as much as I can.'

'Tut!' he said fuming, and put out his hand to the papers in the pink tape.

'Well, I do. It's just that I want to say. I want to be a human being; I want to learn about things and know about things, and not to be protected as something too precious for life, cooped up in one narrow little corner.'

'Cooped up!' he cried. 'Did I stand in the way of your going to college? Have I ever prevented you going about at any reasonable hour? You've got a bicycle!'

'H'm!' said Ann Veronica, and then went on: 'I want to be taken seriously. A girl – at my age – is grown-up. I want to go on with my university work under proper conditions now that I've done the intermediate. It isn't as though I haven't done well. I've never muffed an exam yet. Roddy muffed two. . . .'

Her father interrupted. 'Now look here, Veronica, let us be

plain with each other. You are not going to that infidel Russell's classes. You are not going anywhere but to the Tredgold College. I've thought that out, and you must make up your mind to it. All sorts of considerations come in. While you live in my house you must follow my ideas. You are wrong even about that man's scientific position and his standard of work. There are men in the Lowndean who laugh at him – simply laugh at him. And I have seen work by his pupils myself that struck me as being – well, next door to shameful. There's stories, too, about his demonstrator, Capes. Something or other. The kind of man who isn't content with his science, and writes articles in the monthly reviews. Anyhow, there it is: *you are not going there.*'

The girl received this intimation in silence, but the face that looked down upon the gas fire took an expression of obstinacy that brought out a hitherto latent resemblance between parent and child. When she spoke her lips twitched.

'Then I suppose when I have graduated I am to come home?'

'It seems the natural course.'

'And do nothing?'

'There are plenty of things a girl can find to do at home.'

'Until some one takes pity on me and marries me?'

He raised his eyebrows in mild appeal. His foot tapped impatiently, and he took up the papers.

'Look here, father,' she said, with a change in her voice, 'suppose I won't stand it?'

He regarded her as though this was a new idea.

'Suppose, for example, I go to this dance?'

'You won't.'

'Well' – her breath failed her for a moment. 'How would you prevent it?' she asked.

'But I have forbidden it!' he said, raising his voice.

'Yes, I know. But suppose I go?'

'Now, Veronica! No, no. This won't do. Understand me! I forbid it. I do not want to hear from you even the threat of disobedience.' He spoke loudly. 'The thing is forbidden!'

'I am ready to give up anything that you show to be wrong.'

'You will give up anything I wish you to give up.'

They stared at one another through a pause, and both faces were flushed and obstinate.

She was trying by some wonderful, secret, and motionless gymnastics to restrain her tears. But when she spoke her lips quivered, and they came. 'I mean to go to that dance,' she blubbered. 'I mean to go to that dance. I meant to reason with you, but you won't reason. You're dogmatic.'

At the sight of her tears his expression changed to a mingling of triumph and concern. He stood up, apparently intending to put an arm about her, but she stepped back from him quickly. She produced a handkerchief, and with one sweep of this and a simultaneous gulp had abolished her fit of weeping. His voice now had lost its ironies.

'Now, Veronica,' he pleaded, 'Veronica, this is most unreasonable. All we do is for your good. Neither your aunt nor I have any other thought but what is best for you.'

'Only you won't let me live. Only you won't let me exist!'

Mr Stanley lost patience. He bullied frankly.

'What nonsense is this? What raving! My dear child, you *do* live, you *do* exist! You have this home. You have friends, acquaintances, social standing, brothers and sisters, every advantage! Instead of which, you want to go to some mixed classes or other and cut up rabbits and dance about at nights in wild costumes with casual art student friends and God knows who. That – that isn't living! You are beside yourself. You don't know what you ask, nor what you say. You have neither reason nor logic. I am sorry to seem to hurt you, but all I say is for your good. You *must* not, you *shall* not go. On this I am resolved. I put my foot down like – like adamant. And a time will come, Veronica, mark my words, a time will come when you will bless me for my firmness to-night. It goes to my heart to disappoint you, but this thing must not be.'

He sidled towards her, but she recoiled from him, leaving him in possession of the hearthrug.

'Well,' she said, 'good night, father.'

'What!' he asked; 'Not a kiss?'

She affected not to hear.

The door closed softly upon her. For a long time he remained standing before the fire, staring at the situation. Then he sat down and filled his pipe slowly and thoughtfully. . . .

'I don't see what else I could have said,' he remarked.

Chapter II

Ann Veronica Gathers Points of View

I

'Are you coming to the Fadden dance, Ann Veronica?' asked Constance Widgett.

Ann Veronica considered her answer. 'I mean to,' she replied.

'You are making your dress?'

'Such as it is.'

They were in the elder Widgett girl's bedroom; Hetty was laid up, she said, with a sprained ankle, and a miscellaneous party was gossiping away her tedium. It was a large, littered, self-forgetful apartment, decorated with unframed charcoal sketches by various incipient masters; and an open bookcase, surmounted by plaster casts and the half of a human skull, displayed an odd miscellany of books – Shaw and Swinburne, *Tom Jones, Fabian Essays*, Pope and Dumas, cheek by jowl. Constance Widgett's abundant copper-red hair was bent down over some dimly remunerative work – stencilling in colours upon rough, white material – at a kitchen table she had dragged upstairs for the purpose; while on her bed there was seated a slender lady of thirty or so in a dingy green dress, whom Constance had introduced with a wave of her hand as Miss Miniver. Miss Miniver looked out on the world through large emotional blue eyes that were further magnified by the glasses she wore, and her nose was pinched and pink and her mouth was whimsically petulant. Her glasses moved quickly as her glance travelled from face to face. She seemed bursting with the desire to talk, and watching for her opportunity. On her lapel was an ivory button, bearing the words 'Votes for Women'. Ann Veronica sat at the foot of the sufferer's bed, while Teddy Widgett, being something of an athlete, occupied the only bedroom chair – a decadent piece, essentially a tripod and largely a formality – and smoked cigarettes, and tried to conceal the fact that he was looking all the time at Ann Veronica's eyebrows. Teddy was the hatless young man who had turned Ann Veronica aside from the Avenue two days before. He was the junior of both his sisters, co-educated and much broken in to feminine society. A bowl of roses, just brought by Ann Veronica, adorned the communal dressing-table, and Ann Veronica was particularly trim in preparation for a call she was to make with her aunt later in the afternoon.

Ann Veronica decided to be more explicit. 'I've been,' she said, 'forbidden to come.'

'Hal-*lo*!' said Hetty, turning her head on the pillow; and Teddy remarked with profound emotion: 'My God!'

'Yes,' said Ann Veronica, 'and that complicates the situation.'

'Auntie?' asked Constance, who was conversant with Ann Veronica's affairs.

'No! My father. It's – it's a serious prohibition.'

'Why?' asked Hetty.

'That's the point. I asked him why, and he hadn't a reason.'

'*You asked your father for a reason*!' said Miss Miniver, with great intensity.

'Yes. I tried to have it out with him, but he wouldn't have it out.' Ann Veronica reflected for an instant. 'That's why I think I ought to come.'

'You asked your father for a reason!' Miss Miniver repeated.

'We always have things out with *our* father, poor dear!' said Hetty. 'He's got almost to like it.'

'Men,' said Miss Miniver, '*never* have a reason. Never! And they don't know it! They have no idea of it. It's one of their worst traits, one of their very worst.'

'But I say, Vee,' said Constance, 'if you come and you are forbidden to come there'll be the deuce of a row.'

Ann Veronica was deciding for further confidences. Her situation was perplexing her very much, and the Widgett atmosphere was lax and sympathetic, and provocative of discussion. 'It isn't only the dance,' she said.

'There's the classes,' said Constance, the well-informed.

'There's the whole situation. Apparently I'm not to exist yet. I'm not to study, I'm not to grow. I've got to stay at home and remain in a state of suspended animation.'

'*Dusting*!' said Miss Miniver, in a sepulchral voice.

'Until you marry, Vee,' said Hetty.

'Well, I don't feel like standing it.'

'Thousands of women have married merely for freedom,' said Miss Miniver. 'Thousands! Ugh! And found it a worse slavery.'

'I suppose,' said Constance, stencilling away at bright pink petals, 'it's our lot. But it's very beastly.'

'What's our lot?' asked her sister.

'Slavery! Downtroddenness! When I think of it I feel all over boot marks – men's boots. We hide it bravely, but so it is. Damn! I've splashed.'

Miss Miniver's manner became impressive. She addressed Ann Veronica with an air of conveying great open secrets to her. 'As things are at present,' she said, 'it is true. We live under man-made institutions, and that is what they amount to. Every girl in the world practically, except a few of us who teach or typewrite, and then we're underpaid and sweated – it's dreadful to think how we are sweated!' She had lost her generalization, whatever it was. She hung for a moment, and then went on conclusively: 'Until we have the vote that is how things *will* be.'

'I'm all for the vote,' said Teddy.

'I suppose a girl *must* be underpaid and sweated,' said Ann Veronica. 'I suppose there's no way of getting a decent income – independently.'

'Women have practically *no* economic freedom,' said Miss Miniver, 'because they have no political freedom. Men have seen to that. The one profession, the one decent profession, I mean, for a woman – except the stage – is teaching, and there we trample on one another. Everywhere else – the law, medicine, the Stock Exchange – prejudice bars us.'

'There's art,' said Ann Veronica, 'and writing.'

'Every one hasn't the gift. Even there a woman never gets a fair chance. Men are against her. Whatever she does is minimized. All the best novels have been written by women, and yet see how men sneer at the lady novelist still! There's only one way to get on for a woman, and that is to please men. That is what they think we are for!'

'We're beasts,' said Teddy. 'Beasts!'

But Miss Miniver took no notice of his admission.

'Of course,' said Miss Miniver – she went on in a regularly undulating voice – 'we *do* please men. We have that gift. We can see round them and behind them and through them, and most of us use that knowledge, in the silent way we have, for our great ends. Not all of us, but some of us. Too many. I wonder what men would say if we threw the mask aside – if we really told them what *We* thought of them, really showed them what *We* were.' A flush of excitement crept into her cheeks.

'Maternity,' she said, 'has been our undoing.'

From that she opened out into a long, confused, emphatic discourse on the position of women, full of wonderful statements, while Constance worked at her stencilling and Ann Veronica and Hetty listened, and Teddy contributed sympathetic noises and consumed cheap cigarettes. As she talked she made weak little gestures with her hands, and she thrust her face forward from her bent shoulders; and she peered sometimes at Ann Veronica and sometimes at a photograph of the Axenstrasse, near Flüelen, that hung upon the wall. Ann Veronica watched her face, vaguely sympathizing with her, vaguely disliking her physical insufficiency and her convulsive movements, and the fine eyebrows were knit with a faint perplexity. Essentially the talk was a mixture of fragments of sentences heard, of passages read, or arguments indicated rather than stated, and all of it was served in a sauce of strange enthusiasm, thin yet intense. Ann Veronica had had some training at the Tredgold College in disentangling threads from confused statements, and she had a curious persuasion that in all this fluent muddle there was something – something real, something that signified. But it was very hard to follow. She did not understand the note of hostility to men that ran through it all, the bitter vindictiveness that lit Miss Miniver's cheeks and eyes, the sense of some at last insupportable wrong slowly accumulated. She had no inkling of that insupportable wrong.

'We are the species,' said Miss Miniver, 'men are only incidents. They give themselves airs, but so it is. In all the species of animals the females are more important than the males; the males have to please them. Look at the cock's feathers, look at the competition there is everywhere, except among humans. The stags and oxen and things all have to fight for us, everywhere. Only in man is the male made the most important. And that happens through our maternity; it's our very importance that degrades us. While we were minding the children they stole our rights and liberties. The children made us slaves, and the men took advantage of it. It's – Mrs Shalford says – the accidental conquering the essential. Originally in the first animals there were no males, none at all. It has been proved. Then they appear among the lower things' – she made meticulous gestures to figure the scale of life; she seemed to be holding up specimens, and peering through her glasses at them – 'among crustaceans and things, just as little creatures, ever so inferior to the females. Mere hangers-on. Things you would laugh at. And among human beings, too, women to begin with were the rulers and leaders; they owned all the property, they invented all the arts. The primitive government was the Matriarchate. The Matriarchate! The Lords of Creation just ran about and did what they were told.'

'But is that really so?' said Ann Veronica.

'It has been proved,' said Miss Miniver, and added, 'by American professors.'

'But how did they prove it?'

'By science,' said Miss Miniver, and hurried on, putting out a rhetorical hand that showed a slash of finger through its glove. 'And now, look at us! See what we have become. Toys! Delicate trifles! A sex of invalids. It is we who have become the parasites and toys.'

It was, Ann Veronica felt, at once absurd and extraordinarily right. Hetty, who had periods of lucid expression, put the thing for her from her pillow. She charged boldly into the space of Miss Miniver's rhetorical pause.

'It isn't quite that we're toys. Nobody toys with me. Nobody regards Constance or Vee as a delicate trifle.'

Teddy made some confused noise, a thoracic street row; some remark was assassinated by a rival in his throat and buried hastily under a cough.

'They'd better not,' said Hetty. 'The point is we're not toys, toys isn't the word; we're litter. We're handfuls. We're regarded as inflammable litter that mustn't be left about. We are the species, and maternity is our game; that's all right, but nobody wants that admitted for fear we should all catch fire, and set about fulfilling the purpose of our beings without waiting for further explanations. As if we didn't know! The practical trouble is our ages. They used to marry us off at seventeen, rush us into things before we had time to protest. They don't now. Heaven knows why! They don't marry most of us off now until high up in the twenties. And the age gets higher. We have to hang about in the interval. There's a great gulf opened, and nobody's got any plans what to do with us. So the world is choked with waste and waiting daughters. Hanging about! And they start thinking and asking questions, and begin to be neither one thing nor the other. We're partly human beings and partly females in suspense.'

Miss Miniver followed with an expression of perplexity, her mouth shaped to futile expositions. The Widgett method of thought puzzled her weakly rhetorical mind. 'There is no remedy, girls,' she began breathlessly, 'except the vote. Give us *that*—'

Ann Veronica came in with a certain disregard of Miss Miniver. 'That's it,' she said. 'They have no plans for us. They have no ideas what to do with us.'

'Except,' said Constance, surveying her work with her head on one side, 'to keep the matches from the litter.'

'And they won't let us make plans for ourselves.'

'We will,' said Miss Miniver, refusing to be suppressed, 'if some of us have to be killed to get it.' And she pressed her lips together in white resolution and nodded, and she was manifestly full of that same passion for conflict and self-sacrifice that has given the world martyrs since the beginning of things. 'I wish I could make every woman, every girl, see this as clearly as I see it – just what the vote means to us. Just what it means. . . .'

2

As Ann Veronica went back along the Avenue to her aunt she became aware of a light-footed pursuer running. Teddy overtook her, a little out of breath, his innocent face flushed, his straw-coloured hair disordered. He was out of breath, and spoke in broken sentences.

'I say, Vee. Half a minute, Vee. It's like this: You want freedom. Look here. You know – if you want freedom. Just an idea of mine. You know how those Russian students do? In Russia. Just a formal marriage. Mere formality. Liberates the girl from parental control. See? You marry me. Simply. No further responsibility whatever. Without hindrance – present occupation. Why not? Quite willing. Get a licence. Just an idea of mine. Doesn't matter a bit to me. Do anything to please you, Vee. Anything. Not fit to be dust on your boots. Still – there you are!'

He paused.

Ann Veronica's desire to laugh unrestrainedly was checked by the tremendous earnestness of his expression. 'Awfully good of you, Teddy,' she said.

He nodded silently, too full for words.

'But I don't see,' said Ann Veronica, 'just how it fits the present situation.'

'No! Well, I just suggested it. Threw it out. Of course, if at any time – see reason – alter your opinion. Always at your service. No offence, I hope. All right! I'm off. Due to play hockey. Jackson's. Horrid snorters! So long, Vee! Just suggested it. See? Nothing really. Passing thought.'

'Teddy,' said Ann Veronica, 'you're a dear!'

'Oh, quite!' said Teddy convulsively, and lifted an imaginary hat and left her.

3

The call Ann Veronica paid with her aunt that afternoon had at first much the same relation to the Widgett conversation that a plaster statue of Mr Gladstone would have to a carelessly displayed interior on a dissecting-room table. The Widgetts talked with a remarkable absence of external coverings, the Palsworthys found all the meanings of life on its surfaces. They seemed the most wrapped things in all Ann Veronica's wrappered world. The Widgett mental furniture was perhaps worn and shabby, but there it was before you, undisguised, fading visibly in an almost pitiless sunlight. Lady Palsworthy was the widow of a knight who had won his spurs in the wholesale coal trade; she was of good seventeenth-century attorney blood, a county family, and distantly related to Aunt Mollie's deceased curate. She was the social leader of Morningside Park, and in her superficial and euphuistic* way an extremely kind and pleasant woman. With her lived a Mrs Pramlay, a sister of the Morningside Park doctor, and a very active and useful member of the Committee of the Impoverished Gentlewomen's Aid Society. Both ladies were on easy and friendly terms with all that was best in Morningside Park society; they had an afternoon once a month that was quite well attended, they sometimes gave musical evenings, they dined out and gave a finish to people's dinners, they had a full-size croquet lawn and tennis beyond, and understood the art of bringing people together. And they never talked of anything at all, never discussed, never even encouraged gossip. They were just nice.

Ann Veronica found herself walking back down the Avenue that had just been the scene of her first proposal beside her aunt, and speculating for the first time in her life about that lady's mental attitudes. Her prevailing effect was one of quiet and complete assurance, as though she knew all about everything, and was only restrained by her instinctive delicacy from telling what she knew. But the restraint exercised by her instinctive delicacy was very great; over and above coarse or sexual matters it covered religion and politics and any mention of money matters or crime, and Ann Veronica found herself wondering whether these exclusions represented, after all, anything more than suppressions. Was there anything at all in those locked rooms of her aunt's mind? Were they fully furnished and only a little dusty and cobwebby and in need of an airing, or were they stark vacancy, except, perhaps, for a cockroach or so or the gnawing of a rat? What was the mental equivalent of a rat's gnawing? The image was going astray. But what would her aunt think of Teddy's recent off-hand suggestion of marriage? What would she think of the Widgett conversation? Suppose she was to tell her aunt quietly but firmly about the parasitic males of degraded crustacea. The girl suppressed a chuckle that would have been inexplicable.

There came a wild rush of anthropological lore into her brain, a flare of indecorous humour. It was one of the secret troubles of her mind, this grotesque twist her ideas would sometimes take, as though they rebelled and rioted. After all, she found herself reflecting, behind her aunt's complacent visage there was a past as lurid as any one's – not, of course, her aunt's own personal past, which was apparently just that curate and almost incredibly jejune, but an ancestral past with all sorts of scandalous things in it: fire and slaughterings, exogamy, marriage by capture, corrobo-rees, cannibalism! Ancestresses with perhaps dim anticipatory likenesses to her aunt, their hair less neatly done, no doubt, their manners and gestures as yet undisciplined, but still ancestresses in the direct line, must have danced through a brief and stirring life in the woady buff. Was there no echo anywhere in Miss Stanley's pacified brain? Those empty rooms, if they were empty, were the equivalents of astoundingly decorated predecessors. Perhaps it was just as well there was no inherited memory.

Ann Veronica was by this time quite shocked at her own thoughts, and yet they would go on with their freaks. Great vistas of history opened, and she and her aunt were near reverting to the primitive and passionate and entirely indecorous arboreal – were swinging from branches by the arms, and really going on quite dreadfully – when their arrival at the Palsworthys' happily checked this play of fancy, and brought Ann Veronica back to the exigencies of the wrappered life again.

Lady Palsworthy liked Ann Veronica because she was never awkward, had steady eyes, and an almost invariable neatness and dignity in her clothes. She seemed just as stiff and shy as a girl ought to be, Lady Palsworthy thought, neither garrulous nor unready, and free from nearly all the heavy aggressiveness, the overgrown, overblown quality, the egotism and want of consideration of the typical modern girl. But then Lady Palsworthy had never seen Ann Veronica running like the wind at hockey. She had never seen her sitting on tables, nor heard her discussing theology, and had failed to observe that the graceful figure was a natural one, and not due to ably chosen stays. She took it for granted Ann Veronica wore stays – mild stays, perhaps, but stays, and thought no more of the matter. She had seen her really only at teas, with the Stanley strain in her uppermost. There are so many girls nowadays who are quite unpresentable at tea, with their untrimmed laughs, their awful dispositions of their legs when they sit down, their slangy disrespect; they no longer smoke, it is true, like the girls of the eighties and nineties, nevertheless to a fine intelligence they have the flavour of tobacco. They have no amenities, they scratch the mellow surface of things almost as if they did it on purpose; and Lady Palsworthy and Mrs Pramlay lived for amenities and the mellowed surfaces of things. Ann Veronica was one of the few young people – and one must have young people just as one must have flowers – one could ask to a little gathering without the risk of a painful discord. Then the distant relationship to Miss Stanley gave them a slight but pleasant sense of proprietorship in the girl. They had their little dreams about her.

Mrs Pramlay received them in the pretty chintz drawing-room, which opened by french windows on the trim garden, with its croquet lawn, its tennis net in the middle distance, and its remote rose alley lined with smart dahlias and flaming sunflowers. Her eye met Miss Stanley's understandingly, and she was if anything a trifle more affectionate in her greeting to Ann Veronica. Then Ann Veronica passed on towards tea in the garden, which was dotted with the élite of Morningside Park society, and there she was pounced upon by Lady Palsworthy and given tea and led about. Across the lawn and hovering indecisively, Ann Veronica saw and immediately affected not to see Mr Manning, Lady Palsworthy's nephew, a tall young man of seven-and-thirty with a handsome, thoughtful, impassive face, a full black moustache, and a certain heavy luxuriousness of gesture. The party resolved itself for Ann Veronica into a game in which she manoeuvred unostentatiously and finally unsuccessfully to avoid talking alone with this gentleman.

Mr Manning had shown on previous occasions that he found Ann Veronica interesting, and that he wished to interest her. He was a civil servant of some standing, and after a previous conversation upon aesthetics of a sententious, nebulous, and sympathetic character, he had sent her a small volume, which he described as the fruits of his leisure and which was as a matter of fact rather carefully finished verse. It dealt with fine aspects of Mr Manning's feelings, and as Ann Veronica's mind was still largely engaged with fundamentals and found no pleasure in metrical forms, she had not as yet cut its pages. So that as she saw him she remarked to herself very faintly but definitely: 'Oh, golly!' and set up a campaign of avoidance that Mr Manning at last broke down by coming directly to her as she talked with the vicar's aunt about some of the details of the alleged smell of the new church lamps. He did not so much cut into the conversation as loom over it, for he was a tall, if rather studiously stooping, man.

The face that looked down upon Ann Veronica was full of amiable intention. 'Splendid you are looking to-day, Miss Stanley,' he said. 'How well and jolly you must be feeling.'

He beamed over the effect of this and shook hands with effusion, and Lady Palsworthy suddenly appeared as his confederate, and disentangled the vicar's aunt.

'I love this warm end of summer more than words can tell,' he said. 'I've tried to make words tell it. It's no good. Mild, you know, and boon. You want music.'

Ann Veronica agreed, and tried to make the manner of her assent cover a possible knowledge of a probable poem.

'Splendid it must be to be a composer. Glorious! The Pastoral. Beethoven; he's the best of them. Don't you think? Tum, tay, tum tay.'

Ann Veronica did.

'What have you been doing since our last talk? Still cutting up rabbits and probing into things? I've often thought of that talk of ours, often.'

He did not appear to require any answer to his question.

'Often,' he repeated a little heavily.

'Beautiful these autumn flowers are,' said Ann Veronica in a wide, uncomfortable pause.

'Do come and see the Michaelmas daisies at the end of the garden,' said Mr Manning, 'they're a dream.' And Ann Veronica found herself being carried off to an isolation even remoter and more conspicuous than the corner of the lawn, with the whole of the party aiding and abetting and glancing at them. 'Damn!' said Ann Veronica to herself, rousing herself for a conflict.

Mr Manning told her he loved beauty, and extorted a similar admission from her; he then expatiated upon his own love of beauty. He said that for him beauty justified life, that he could not imagine a good action that was not a beautiful one, nor any beautiful thing that could be altogether bad. Ann Veronica hazarded an opinion that as a matter of history some very beautiful people had, to a quite considerable extent, been bad, but Mr Manning questioned whether when they were bad they were really beautiful or when they were beautiful bad. Ann Veronica found her attention wandering a little as he told her that he was not ashamed to feel almost slavish in the presence of really beautiful people, and then they came to the Michaelmas daisies. They were really very fine and abundant, with a blaze of perennial sunflowers behind them.

'They make me want to shout,' said Mr Manning with a sweep of the arm.

'They're very good this year,' said Ann Veronica, avoiding controversial matter.

'Either I want to shout,' said Mr Manning, 'when I see beautiful things, or else I want to weep.' He paused and looked at her, and said, with a sudden drop into a confidential undertone: 'Or else I want to pray.'

'When is Michaelmas Day?' said Ann Veronica a little abruptly.

'Heaven knows!' said Mr Manning, and added, 'the twenty-ninth.'

'I thought it was earlier,' said Ann Veronica. 'Wasn't Parliament to reassemble?'

He put out his hand and leaned against a tree and crossed his legs. 'You're not interested in politics?' he asked, almost with a note of protest.

'Well, rather,' said Ann Veronica. 'It seems— It's interesting.'

'Do you think so? I find my interest in that sort of thing decline and decline.'

'I'm curious. Perhaps because I don't know. I suppose an intelligent person *ought* to be interested in political affairs. They concern us all.'

'I wonder,' said Mr Manning, with a baffling smile.

'I think they do. After all, they're history in the making.'

'A sort of history,' said Mr Manning, and repeated, 'a sort of history. But look at these glorious daisies!'

'But don't you think political questions *are* important?'

'I don't think they are this afternoon, and I don't think they are to you.'

Ann Veronica turned her back on the Michaelmas daisies, and faced towards the house with an air of a duty completed.

'Just come to that seat now you are here, Miss Stanley, and look down the other path; there's a vista of just the common sort. Better even than these.'

Ann Veronica walked as he indicated.

'You know I'm old-fashioned, Miss Stanley. I don't think women need to trouble about political questions.'

'I want a vote,' said Ann Veronica.

'Really!' said Mr Manning, in an earnest voice, and waved his hand to the alley of mauve and purple. 'I wish you didn't.'

'Why not?' She turned on him.

'It jars. It jars with all my ideas. Women to me are something to serene, so fine, so feminine, and politics are so dusty, so sordid, so wearisome and quarrelsome. It seems to me a woman's duty to be beautiful, to *be* beautiful and to behave beautifully, and politics are by their very nature ugly. You see I – I am a woman worshipper. I worshipped women long before I found any woman I might ever hope to worship. Long ago. And – the idea of committees, of hustings, of agenda papers!'

'I don't see why the responsibility of beauty should all be shifted on to the women,' said Ann Veronica, suddenly remembering a part of Miss Miniver's discourse.

'It rests with them by the nature of things. Why should you who are queens come down from your thrones? If you can afford it, *we* can't. We can't afford to turn our women, our Madonnas, our Saint Catherines, our Mona Lisas, our goddesses and angels and fairy princesses, into a sort of man. Womanhood is sacred to me. My politics in that matter wouldn't be to give women votes. I'm a Socialist, Miss Stanley.'

'*What?*' said Ann Veronica, startled.

'A Socialist of the order of John Ruskin. Indeed I am! I would make this country a collective monarchy, and all the girls and women in it should be the queen. They should never come into contact with politics or economics – or any of those things. And we men would work for them and serve them in loyal fealty.'

'That's rather the theory now,' said Ann Veronica. 'Only so many men neglect their duties.'

'Yes,' said Mr Manning, with an air of emerging from an elaborate demonstration, 'and so each of us must, under existing conditions, being chivalrous indeed to all women, choose for himself his own particular and worshipful queen.'

'So far as one can judge from the system in practice,' said Ann Veronica, speaking in a loud, common-sense, detached tone, and beginning to walk slowly but resolutely towards the lawn, 'it doesn't work.'

'Every one must be experimental,' said Mr Manning, and glanced round hastily for further horticultural points of interest in secluded corners. None presented themselves to save him from that return.

'That's all very well when one isn't the material experimented upon,' Ann Veronica had remarked.

'Women would – they *do* have far more power than they think, as influences, as inspirations.'

Ann Veronica said nothing in answer to that.

'You say you want a vote,' said Mr Manning abruptly.

'I think I ought to have one.'

'Well, I have two,' said Mr Manning, 'one in Oxford University and one in Kensington.' He caught up and went on with a sort of clumsiness: 'Let me present you with them and be your voter.'

There followed an instant's pause, and then Ann Veronica had decided to misunderstand.

'I want a vote for myself,' she said. 'I don't see why I should take it second-hand. Though it's very kind of you. And rather unscrupulous. Have you ever voted, Mr Manning? I suppose there's a sort of place like a ticket office. And a ballot box—' Her face assumed an expression of intellectual conflict. 'What is a ballot box like, exactly?' she asked, as though it was very important to her.

Mr Manning regarded her thoughtfully for a moment and stroked his moustache. 'A ballot box, you know,' he said, 'is very largely just a box.' He made quite a long pause, and went on with a sigh. 'You have a voting paper given you—'

They emerged into the publicity of the lawn.

'Yes,' said Ann Veronica, 'yes,' to his explanation, and saw across the lawn Lady Palsworthy talking to her aunt and both of them staring frankly across at her and Mr Manning as they talked.

Chapter III

The Morning of the Crisis

I

Two days after came the day of the Crisis, the day of the Fadden dance. It would have been a crisis anyhow, but it was complicated in Ann Veronica's mind by the fact that a letter lay on the breakfast table from Mr Manning, and that her aunt focused a brightly tactful disregard upon this throughout the meal. Ann Veronica had come down thinking of nothing in the world but her inflexible resolution to go to the dance in the teeth of all opposition. She did not know Mr Manning's handwriting, and opened his letter and read some lines before its import appeared. Then for a time she forgot the Fadden affair altogether. With a well-simulated unconcern and a heightened colour she finished her breakfast.

She was not obliged to go to the Tredgold College, because as yet the college had not settled down for the session. She was supposed to be reading at home, and after breakfast she strolled into the vegetable garden, and having taken up a position upon the staging of a disused greenhouse that had the double advantage of being hidden from the windows of the house and secure from the sudden appearance of any one, she resumed the reading of Mr Manning's letter.

Mr Manning's handwriting had an air of being clear without being easily legible; it was large and rather roundish, with a lack of definition about the letters and a disposition to treat the large ones as liberal-minded people nowadays treat opinions, as all amounting to the same thing really – a years-smoothed boyish rather than an adult hand. And it filled seven sheets of note-paper, each written only on one side.

'MY DEAR MISS STANLEY,' it began, '*I hope you will forgive my bothering you with a letter, but I have been thinking very much over our conversation at Lady Palsworthy's, and I feel there are things I want to say to you so much that I cannot wait until we meet again. It is the worst of talk under such social circumstances that it is always getting cut off so soon as it is beginning; and I went home that afternoon feeling I had said nothing – literally nothing – of the things I had meant to say to you and that were coursing through my head. They were things I had meant very much to talk to you about, so that I went home vexed and disappointed, and only relieved myself a little by writing a few verses. I wonder if you will mind very much when I tell you they were suggested by you. You must forgive the poet's licence I take. Here is one verse. The metrical irregularity is intentional, because I want, as it were, to put you apart: to change the lilt and the mood altogether, when I speak of you.*

"A Song of Ladies and My Lady

"*Saintly white and a lily is Mary,*
  Margaret's violets, sweet and shy;
Green and dewy is Nellie-bud fairy,
  Forget-me-nots live in Gwendolen's eye.
Annabel shines like a star in the darkness,
  Rosamund queens it a rose, deep rose;
But the lady I love is like sunshine in April weather,
  She gleams and gladdens, she warms – and goes."

'*Crude, I admit. But let that verse tell my secret. All bad verse – originally the epigram was Lang's, I believe – is written in a state of emotion.*

'*My dear Miss Stanley, when I talked to you the other afternoon of work and politics and suchlike things, my mind was all the time resenting it beyond measure. There we were discussing whether you should have a vote, and I remembered the last occasion we met it was about your prospects of success in the medical profession or as a Government official such as a number of women now are, and all the time my heart was crying out within me: "Here is the queen of your career." I wanted as I have never wanted before, to take you up, to make you mine, to carry you off and set you apart from all the strain and turmoil of life. For nothing will ever convince me that it is not the man's share in life to shield, to protect, to lead and toil and watch and battle with the world at large. I want to be your knight, your servant, your protector, your – I dare scarcely write the word – your husband. So I come suppliant. I am five-and-thirty, and I have knocked about in the world and tasted the quality of life. I had a hard fight to begin with to win my way into the Upper Division – I was third on a list of forty-seven – and since then I have found myself promoted almost yearly in a widening sphere of social service. Before I met you I never met any one whom I felt I could love, but you have discovered depths in my own nature I had scarcely suspected. Except for a few early ebullitions of passion, natural to a warm and romantic disposition, and leaving no harmful after-effects – ebullitions that by the standards of the higher truth I feel no one can justly cast a stone at, and of which I for one am by no means ashamed – I come to you a pure and unencumbered man. I love you. In addition to my public salary I have a certain private property and further expectations through my aunt, so that I can offer you a life of wide and generous refinement, travel, books, discussion, and easy relations with a circle of clever and brilliant and thoughtful people with whom my literary work has brought me into contact, and of which, seeing me only as you have done alone in Morningside Park, you can have no idea. I have a certain standing not only as a singer but as a critic, and I belong to one of the most brilliant causerie dinner clubs of the day, in which successful Bohemianism, politicians, men of affairs, artists, sculptors, and cultivated noblemen generally, mingle together in the easiest and most delightful intercourse. That is my real milieu, and one that I am convinced you would not only adorn but delight in.*

'I find it very hard to write this letter. There are so many things I want to tell you, and they stand on such different levels, that the effect is necessarily confusing and discordant, and I find myself doubting if I am really giving you the thread of emotion that should run through all this letter. For although I must confess it reads very much like an application or a testimonial or some such thing as that, I can assure you I am writing this in fear and trembling with a sinking heart. My mind is full of ideas and images that I have been cherishing and accumulating – dreams of travelling side by side, of lunching quietly together in some jolly restaurant, of moonlight and music and all that side of life, of seeing you dressed like a queen and shining in some brilliant throng – mine; of your looking at flowers in some old-world garden, our garden – there are splendid places to be got down in Surrey, and a little runabout motor is quite within my means. You know they say, as, indeed, I have just quoted already, that all bad poetry is written in a state of emotion, but I have no doubt that this is true of bad offers of marriage. I have often felt before that it is only when one has nothing to say that one can write easy poetry. Witness Browning. And how can I get into one brief letter

the complex accumulated desires of what is now, I find on reference to my diary, nearly sixteen months of letting my mind run on you – ever since that jolly party at Surbiton, where we raced and beat the other boat. You steered and I rowed stroke. My very sentences stumble and give way. But I do not even care if I am absurd. I am a resolute man, and hitherto when I have wanted a thing I have got it; but I have never yet wanted anything in my life as I have wanted you. It isn't the same thing. I am afraid because I love you, so that the mere thought of failure hurts. If I did not love you so much I believe I could win you by sheer force of character, for people tell me I am naturally of the dominating type. Most of my successes in life have been made with a sort of reckless vigour.

'Well, I have said what I had to say, stumblingly and badly, and baldly. But I am sick of tearing up letters and hopeless of getting what I have to say better said. It would be easy enough for me to write an eloquent letter about something else. Only I do not care to write about anything else. Let me put the main question to you now that I could not put the other afternoon. Will you marry me, Ann Veronica?*

'Very sincerely yours,
'HUBERT MANNING.'

Ann Veronica read this letter through with grave, attentive eyes. Her interest grew as she read, a certain distaste disappeared. Twice she smiled, but not unkindly. Then she went back and mixed up the sheets in a search for particular passages. Finally she fell into reflection.

'Odd!' she said. 'I suppose I shall have to write an answer. It's so different from what one has been led to expect.'

She became aware of her aunt, through the panes of the greenhouse, advancing with an air of serene unconsciousness from among the raspberry canes.

'No, you don't!' said Ann Veronica, and walked out at a brisk and business-like pace towards the house.

'I'm going for a long tramp, auntie,' she said.

'Alone, dear?'

'Yes, aunt. I've got a lot of things to think about.'

Miss Stanley reflected as Ann Veronica went towards the house. She thought her niece very hard and very self-possessed and self-confident. She ought to be softened and tender and confidential at this phase of her life. She seemed to have no idea whatever of the emotional states that were becoming to her age and position. Miss Stanley walked round the garden thinking, and presently house and garden reverberated to Ann Veronica's slamming of the front door.

'I wonder!' said Miss Stanley.

For a long time she surveyed a row of towering hollyhocks, as though they offered an explanation. Then she went in and upstairs, hesitated on the landing, and finally, a little breathless and with an air of great dignity, opened the door, and walked into Ann Veronica's room. It was a neat, efficient-looking room, with a writing-table placed with a business-like regard to the window, and a bookcase surmounted by a pig's skull, a dissected frog in a sealed bottle, and a pile of shiny, black-covered note-books. In the corner of the room were two hockey sticks and a tennis racket, and upon the walls Ann Veronica, by means of autotypes, had indicated her proclivities in art. But Miss Stanley took no notice of these things. She walked straight across to the wardrobe and opened it. There, hanging among Ann Veronica's more normal clothing, was a skimpy dress of red canvas, trimmed with cheap and tawdry braid, and short – it could hardly reach below the knee. On the same peg and evidently belonging to it was a black velvet zouave jacket. And then! a garment that was conceivably a secondary skirt.

Miss Stanley hesitated, and took first one and then another of the constituents of this costume off its peg and surveyed it.

The third item she took with a trembling hand by its waist-belt. As she raised it, its lower portion fell apart into two baggy crimson masses.

'*Trousers!*' she whispered.

Her eyes travelled about the room as if in appeal to the very chairs.

Tucked under the writing table a pair of yellow and gold Turkish slippers of a highly meretricious quality caught her eye. She walked over to them, still carrying the trousers in her hand, and stooped to examine them. They were ingenious disguises of gilt paper destructively gummed, it would seem, to Ann Veronica's best dancing slippers.

Then she reverted to the trousers.

'How *can* I tell him?' whispered Miss Stanley.

2

Ann Veronica carried a light but business-like walking stick. She walked with an easy quickness down the Avenue and through the proletarian portion of Morningside Park, and crossing these fields came into a pretty overhung lane that led towards Caddington and the Downs. And then her pace slackened. She tucked her stick under her arm and re-read Manning's letter.

'Let me think,' said Ann Veronica.

'I wish this hadn't turned up to-day of all days.'

She found it difficult to begin thinking, and indeed she was anything but clear what it was she had to think about. Practically it was most of the chief interests in life that she proposed to settle in this pedestrian meditation. Primarily it was her own problem, and in particular the answer she had to give to Mr Manning's letter; but in order to get data for that she found that she, having a logical and ordered mind, had to decide upon the general relations of men to women, the objects and conditions of marriage and its bearing upon the welfare of the race, the purpose of the race, the purpose, if any, of everything. . . .

'Frightful lot of things aren't settled,' said Ann Veronica.

In addition, the Fadden dance business, all out of proportion, occupied the whole foreground of her thoughts and threw a colour of rebellion over everything. She kept thinking she was thinking about Mr Manning's proposal of marriage and finding she was thinking of the dance.

For a time her efforts to achieve a comprehensive concentration were dispersed by the passage of the village street of Caddington, the passing of a goggled car-load of motorists, and the struggles of a stable lad mounted on one recalcitrant horse and leading another. When she got back to her questions again in the monotonous high road that led up the hill, she found the image of Mr Manning central in her mind. He stood there, large and dark, enunciating, in his clear voice from beneath his large moustache, clear flat sentences, deliberately kindly. He proposed, he wanted to possess her! He loved her.

Ann Veronica felt no repulsion at the prospect. That Mr Manning loved her presented itself to her bloodlessly, stilled from any imaginative quiver or thrill of passion or disgust. The relationship seemed to have almost as much to do with blood and body as a mortgage. It was something that would create a mutual claim, a relationship. It was in another world from that in which men will die for a kiss, and touching hands lights fires that burn up lives – the world of romance, the world of passionately beautiful things.

But that other world, in spite of her resolute exclusion of it, was always looking round corners and peeping through chinks and crannies, and rustling and raiding into the order in which she chose to live, shining out of pictures at her, echoing in lyrics and music; it invaded her dreams, it wrote up broken and enigmatical sentences upon the passage walls of her mind. She was aware of it now as if it were a voice shouting outside a house, shouting passionate verities in a hot sunlight, a voice that cries while people talk insincerely in a darkened room and pretend not to hear. Its shouting now did in some occult manner convey a protest that Mr Manning would on no account do though he was tall and dark and handsome and kind, and thirty-five and adequately prosperous, and all that a husband should be. But there was, it insisted, no mobility in his face, no movement, nothing about him that warmed. If Ann Veronica could have put words to that song they would have been 'Hot-blooded marriage or none!' but she was far too indistinct in this matter to frame any words at all.

'I don't love him,' said Ann Veronica, getting a gleam. 'I don't see that his being a good sort matters. That really settles about that. . . . But it means no end of a row.'

For a time she sat on a rail before leaving the road for the downland turf. 'But I wish,' she said, 'I had some idea what I was really up to.'

Her thoughts went into solution for a time, while she listened to a lark singing.

'Marriage and mothering,' said Ann Veronica, with her mind crystallizing out again as the lark dropped to the nest in the turf. 'And all the rest of it perhaps is a song.'

3

Her mind got back to the Fadden ball.

She meant to go, she meant to go, she meant to go. Nothing would stop her, and she was prepared to face the consequences. Suppose her father turned her out of doors! She did not care, she meant to go. She would just walk out of the house and go. . . .

She thought of her costume in some detail and with consider-able satisfaction, and particularly of a very jolly property dagger with large glass jewels in the handle, that reposed in a drawer in her room. She was to be a corsair's bride. 'Fancy stabbing a man for jealousy!' she thought. 'You'd have to think how to get in between his bones.'

She thought of her father, and with an effort dismissed him from her mind.

She tried to imagine the collective effect of the Fadden ball; she had never seen a fancy-dress gathering in her life. Mr Manning came into her thoughts again, an unexpected, tall, dark, self-contained presence at the Fadden. One might suppose him turning up; he knew a lot of clever people, and some of them might belong to the class. What would he come as?

Presently she roused herself with a guilty start from the task of dressing and re-dressing Mr Manning in fancy costume, as though he was a doll. She had tried him as a Crusader, in which guise he seemed plausible but heavy – 'There *is* something heavy about him; I wonder if it's his moustache?' and as a hussar, which made him preposterous, and as a Black Brunswicker, which was better, and as an Arab sheik. Also she had tried him as a dragoman and as a *gendarme*, which seemed the most suitable of all to his severely handsome, immobile profile. She felt he would tell people the way, control traffic, and refuse admission to public buildings with invincible correctness and the very finest explicit feelings possible. For each costume she had devised a suitable form of matrimonial refusal. 'Oh, Lord!' she said, discovering what she was up to, and dropped lightly from the fence upon the turf and went on her way towards the crest.

'I shall never marry,' said Ann Veronica resolutely. 'I'm not the sort. That's why it's so important I should take my own line now.'

4

Ann Veronica's ideas of marriage were limited and unsystematic. Her teachers and mistresses had done their best to stamp her mind with an ineradicable persuasion that it was tremendously import-ant, and on no account to be thought about. Her first intimations of marriage as a fact of extreme significance in a woman's life had come with the marriage of Alice and the elopement of her second sister, Gwen.

These convulsions occurred when Ann Veronica was about twelve. There was a gulf of eight years between her and the youngest of her brace of sisters, an impassable gulf inhabited chaotically by two noisy brothers. These sisters moved in a grown-up world inaccessible to Ann Veronica's sympathies, and to a large extent remote from her curiosity. She got into rows through meddling with their shoes and tennis rackets, and had moments of carefully concealed admiration when she was privileged to see them just before her bedtime, rather radiantly dressed in white or pink or amber, and prepared to go out with her mother. She thought Alice a bit of a sneak, an opinion her brothers shared, and Gwen rather a snatch at meals. She saw nothing of their love-making, and came home from her boarding school in a state of decently suppressed curiosity for Alice's wedding.

Her impressions of this cardinal ceremony were rich and confused, complicated by a quite transitory passion that awakened no reciprocal fire for a fat curly-headed cousin in black velveteen and a lace collar, who assisted as a page. She followed him about persistently, and succeeded, after a brisk unchivalrous struggle (in which he pinched and asked her to 'cheese it'), in kissing him among the raspberries behind the greenhouse. Afterwards her brother Roddy, also strange in velveteen, feeling rather than knowing of this relationship, punched this Adonis's head.

A marriage in the house proved to be exciting, but extremely disorganizing. Everything seemed designed to unhinge the mind and make the cat wretched. All the furniture was moved, all the meals were disarranged, and everybody, Ann Veronica included, appeared in new, bright costumes. She had to wear cream and a brown sash and a short frock and her hair down, and Gwen cream and a brown sash and a long skirt and her hair up. And her mother, looking unusually alert and hectic, wore cream and brown also, made up in a more complicated manner.

Ann Veronica was much impressed by a mighty trying on and altering and fussing about Alice's 'things' – Alice was being re-costumed from garret to cellar, with a walking dress, and walking boots to measure, and a bride's costume of the most ravishing description, and stockings and suchlike beyond the dreams of avarice – and a constant and increasing dripping into the house of irrelevant remarkable objects, such as:

Real lace bedspread;

Gilt travelling clock;

Ornamental pewter plaque;

Salad bowl (silver mounted) and servers;

Madgett's *English Poets* (twelve volumes), bound purple morocco;

Etc. etc.

Through all this flutter of novelty there came and went a solicitous, preoccupied, almost depressed figure. It was Dr Ralph, formerly the partner of Dr Stickell in the Avenue, and now with a thriving practice of his own in Wamblesmith. He had shaved his side whiskers and come over in flannels, but he was still indisputably the same person who had attended Ann Veronica for the measles and when she swallowed the fish-bone. But his role was altered, and he was now playing the bridegroom in this remarkable drama. Alice was going to be Mrs Ralph. He came in apologetically; all the old 'Well, and how *are* we?' note gone; and once he asked Ann Veronica, almost furtively: 'How's Alice getting on, Vee?' Finally, on the day, he appeared like his old professional self transfigured, in the most beautiful light grey trousers Ann Veronica had ever seen and a new shiny silk hat with a most becoming roll. . . .

It was not simply that all the rooms were rearranged and everybody dressed in unusual fashions, and all the routines of life abolished and put away; people's tempers and emotions also seemed strangely disturbed and shifted about. Her father was distinctly irascible, and disposed more than ever to hide away among the petrological things – the study was turned out. At table he carved in a gloomy but resolute manner. On the Day he had trumpet-like outbreaks of cordiality, varied by a watchful preoccupation. Gwen and Alice were fantastically friendly, which seemed to annoy him, and Mrs Stanley was throughout enigmatical, with an anxious eye on her husband and Alice.

There was a confused impression of livery carriages and whips with white favours, people fussily wanting other people to get in before them, and then the church. People sat in unusual pews, and a wide margin of hassocky emptiness intervened between the ceremony and the walls.

Ann Veronica had a number of fragmentary impressions of Alice strangely transfigured in bridal raiment. It seemed to make her sister downcast beyond any precedent. The bridesmaids and pages got rather jumbled in the aisle, and she had an effect of

Alice's white back and sloping shoulders and veiled head receding towards the altar. In some incomprehensible way that back view made her feel sorry for Alice. Also she remembered very vividly the smell of orange blossom, and Alice, drooping and spiritless, mumbling responses, facing Dr Ralph, while the Rev. Edward Bribble stood between them with an open book. Dr Ralph looked kind and large, and listened to Alice's responses as though he was listening to symptoms and thought that on the whole she was progressing favourably.

And afterwards her mother and Alice kissed long and clung to each other. And Dr Ralph stood by looking considerate. He and her father shook hands manfully.

Ann Veronica had got quite interested in Mr Bribble's rendering of the service – he had the sort of voice that brings out things – and was still teeming with ideas about it when finally a wild outburst from the organ made it clear that, whatever snivelling there might be down in the chancel, that excellent wind instrument was, in its Mendelssohnian way, as glad as ever it could be. 'Pump, pump, per-um-pump, Pum, Pump, Per-um. . . .'

The wedding breakfast was for Ann Veronica a spectacle of the unreal consuming the real; she liked that part very well, until she was carelessly served against her expressed wishes with mayonnaise. She was caught by an uncle, whose opinion she valued, making faces at Roddy because he had exulted at this.

Of the vast mass of these impressions Ann Veronica could make nothing at the time; there they were – Fact! She stored them away in a mind naturally retentive, as a squirrel stores away nuts, for further digestion. Only one thing emerged with any reasonable clarity in her mind at once, and that was that unless she was saved from drowning by an unmarried man, in which case the ceremony is unavoidable, or totally destitute of underclothing, and so driven to get a trousseau, in which hardship a trousseau would certainly be 'ripping', marriage was an experience to be strenuously evaded.

When they were going home she asked her mother why she and Gwen and Alice had cried.

'Ssh!' said her mother, and then added: 'A little natural feeling, dear.'

'But didn't Alice want to marry Dr Ralph?'

'Oh, ssh, Vee!' said her mother, with an evasion as patent as an advertisement board. 'I am sure she will be very happy indeed with Dr Ralph.'

But Ann Veronica was by no means sure of that until she went over to Wamblesmith and saw her sister, very remote and domestic and authoritative, in a becoming tea gown, in command of Dr Ralph's home. Dr Ralph came in to tea and put his arm around Alice and kissed her, and Alice called him 'Squiggles', and stood in the shelter of his arms for a moment with an expression of satisfied proprietorship. She *had* cried, Ann Veronica knew. There had been fusses and scenes dimly apprehended through half-open doors. She had heard Alice talking and crying at the same time, a painful noise. Perhaps marriage hurt. But now it was all over, and Alice was getting on well. It reminded Ann Veronica of having a tooth stopped.

And after that Alice became remoter than ever, and, after a time, ill. Then she had a baby and became as old as any really grown-up person, or older, and very dull. Then she and her husband went off to a Yorkshire practice, and had four more babies, none of whom photographed well, and so she passed beyond the sphere of Ann Veronica's sympathies altogether.

5

The Gwen affair happened when she was away at school at Marticombe-on-Sea, a term before she went to the high school, and was never very clear to her.

Her mother missed writing for a week, and then she wrote in an unusual key. 'My dear,' the letter ran, 'I have to tell you that your sister Gwen has offended your father very much. I hope you will always love her, but I want you to remember she has offended your father and married without his consent. Your father is very angry, and will not have her name mentioned in his hearing. She has married someone he could not approve of, and gone right away. . . .'

When the next holidays came Ann Veronica's mother was ill, and Gwen was in the sick-room when Ann Veronica returned home. She was in one of her old walking dresses, her hair was done in an unfamiliar manner, she wore a wedding-ring, and she looked as if she had been crying.

'Hallo, Gwen!' said Ann Veronica, trying to put every one at their ease. 'Been and married? . . . What's the name of the happy man?'

Gwen owned to 'Fortescue.'

'Got a photograph of him or anything?' said Ann Veronica, after kissing her mother.

Gwen made an inquiry, and, directed by Mrs Stanley, produced a portrait from its hiding-place in the jewel drawer under the mirror. It presented a clean-shaven face, with a large Corinthian nose, hair tremendously waving off the forehead, and more chin and neck than is good for a man.

'*Looks* all right,' said Ann Veronica, regarding him with her head first on one side and then on the other, and trying to be agreeable. 'What's the objection?'

'I suppose she ought to know?' said Gwen to her mother, trying to alter the key of the conversation.

'You see, Vee,' said Mrs Stanley, 'Mr Fortescue is an actor, and your father does not approve of the profession.'

'Oh!' said Ann Veronica. 'I thought they made knights of actors?'

'They may of Hal some day,' said Gwen. 'But it's a long business.'

'I suppose this makes you an actress?' said Ann Veronica.

'I don't know whether I shall go on,' said Gwen, a novel note of languorous professionalism creeping into her voice. 'The other women don't much like it if husband and wife work together, and I don't think Hal would like me to act away from him.'

Ann Veronica regarded her sister with a new respect, but the traditions of family life are strong. 'I don't suppose you'll be able to do it much,' said Ann Veronica.

Later Gwen's trouble weighed so heavily on Mrs Stanley in her illness that her husband consented to receive Mr Fortescue in the drawing-room, and actually shake hands with him in an entirely hopeless manner and hope everything would turn out for the best.

The forgiveness and reconciliation was a cold and formal affair, and afterwards her father went off gloomily to his study, and Mr Fortescue rambled round the garden with soft, propitiatory steps, the Corinthian nose upraised and his hands behind his back, pausing to look long and hard at the fruit-trees against the wall.

Ann Veronica watched him from the dining-room window, and after some moments of maidenly hesitation rambled out into the garden in a reverse direction to Mr Fortescue's steps, and encountered him with an air of artless surprise.

'Hallo!' said Ann Veronica, with arms akimbo and a careless, breathless manner. 'You Mr Fortescue?'

'At your service. You Ann Veronica?'

'Rather! I say – did you marry Gwen?'

'Yes.'

'Why?'

Mr Fortescue raised his eyebrows and assumed a light-comedy expression. 'I suppose I fell in love with her, Ann Veronica.'

'Rum,' said Ann Veronica. 'Have you got to keep her now?'

'To the best of my ability,' said Mr Fortescue with a bow.

'Have you much ability?' asked Ann Veronica.

Mr Fortescue tried to act embarrassment in order to conceal reality, and Ann Veronica went on to ask a string of questions about acting, and whether her sister would act, and was she beautiful enough for it, and who would make her dresses, and so on.

As a matter of fact Mr Fortescue had not much ability to keep her sister, and a little while after her mother's death Ann Veronica met Gwen suddenly on the staircase coming from her father's study, shockingly dingy in dusty mourning and tearful and resentful. And after that Gwen receded from the Morningside Park world, and not even the begging letters and distressful communications that her father and aunt received, but only a vague intimation of dreadfulness, a leakage of incidental comment, flashes of paternal anger at 'that blackguard', came to Ann Veronica's ears.

6

These were Ann Veronica's leading cases in the question of marriage. They were the only real marriages she had seen clearly. For the rest, she derived her ideas of the married state from the observed behaviour of married women, which impressed her in Morningside Park as being tied and dull and inelastic in comparison with the life of the young and from a remarkably various reading among books. As a net result she had come to think of all married people much as one thinks of insects that have lost their wings, and of her sisters as new hatched creatures who had scarcely for a moment had wings. She evolved a dim image of herself cooped up in a house under the benevolent shadow of Mr

Manning. Who knows? – on the analogy of 'Squiggles' she might come to call him 'Mangles!'

'I don't think I can ever marry any one,' she said, and fell suddenly into another set of considerations that perplexed her for a time. Had romance to be banished from life? . . .

It was hard to part with romance, but she had never thirsted so keenly to go on with her university work in her life as she did that day. She had never felt so acutely the desire for free initiative, for a life unhampered by others. At any cost! Her brothers had it practically – at least they had it far more than it seemed likely she would unless she exerted herself with quite exceptional vigour. Between her and the fair, far prospect of freedom and self-development manoeuvred Mr Manning, her aunt and father, neighbours, customs, traditions, forces. They seemed to her that morning to be all armed with nets and prepared to throw them over her directly her movements became in any manner truly free.

She had a feeling as though something had dropped from her eyes, as though she had just discovered herself for the first time – discovered herself as a sleep-walker might do, abruptly among dangers, hindrances, and perplexities, on the verge of a cardinal crisis.

The life of a girl presented itself to her as something happy and heedless and unthinking, yet really guided and controlled by others, and going on amidst unsuspected screens and concealments. And in its way it was very well. Then suddenly with a rush came reality, came 'growing up'; a hasty imperative appeal for seriousness, for supreme seriousness. The Ralphs and Mannings and Fortescues came down upon the raw inexperience, upon the blinking ignorance of the new-comer; and before her eyes were fairly open, before she knew what had happened, a new set of guides and controls, a new set of obligations and responsibilities and limitations, had replaced the old. 'I want to be a Person,' said Ann Veronica to the downs and the open sky; 'I will not have this happen to me, whatever else may happen in its place.'

Ann Veronica had three things very definitely settled by the time when, a little after midday, she found herself perched up on a gate between a bridle-path and a field that commanded the whole wide stretch of country between Chalking and Waldersham. Firstly, she did not intend to marry at all, and particularly she did not mean to marry Mr Manning; secondly, by some measure or other, she meant to go on with her studies, not at the Tredgold Schools, but at the Imperial College; and, thirdly, she was, as an immediate and decisive act, a symbol of just exactly where she stood, a declaration of free and adult initiative, going that night to the Fadden ball.

But the possible attitude of her father she had still to face. So far she had the utmost difficulty in getting on to that vitally important matter. The whole of that relationship persisted in remaining obscure. What would happen when next morning she returned to Morningside Park?

He couldn't turn her out of doors. But what he could do or might do she could not imagine. She was not afraid of violence, but she was afraid of something mean, some secondary kind of force. Suppose he stopped all her allowance, made it imperative that she should either stay ineffectually resentful at home or earn a living for herself at once. . . . It appeared highly probable to her that he would stop her allowance.

What can a girl do?

Somewhere at this point Ann Veronica's speculations were interrupted and turned aside by the approach of a horse and rider. Mr Ramage, that iron-grey man of the world, appeared dressed in a bowler hat and a suit of hard grey, astride of a black horse. He pulled rein at the sight of her, saluted, and regarded her with his rather too protuberant eyes. The girl's gaze met his in interested inquiry.

'You've got my view,' he said, after a pensive second. 'I always get off here and lean over that rail for a bit. May I do so to-day?'

'It's your gate,' she said amiably, 'you got it first. It's for you to say, if I may sit on it.'

He slipped off the horse. 'Let me introduce you to Caesar,' he said; and she patted Caesar's neck, and remarked how soft his nose was, and secretly deplored the ugliness of equine teeth. Ramage tethered the horse to the further gate-post, and Caesar blew heavily and began to investigate the hedge.

Ramage leant over the gate at Ann Veronica's side, and for a moment there was silence.

He made some obvious comments on the wide view warming towards its autumnal blaze that spread itself in hill and valley, wood and village below.

'It's as broad as life,' said Mr Ramage, regarding it and putting a well-booted foot up on the bottom rail.

7

'And what are you doing here, young lady,' he said, looking up at her face, 'wandering alone so far from home?'

'I like long walks,' said Ann Veronica, looking down on him.

'Solitary walks?'

'That's the point of them. I think over all sorts of things.'

'Problems?'

'Sometimes quite difficult problems.'

'You're lucky to live in an age when you can do so. Your mother, for instance, couldn't. She had to do her thinking at home – under inspection.'

She looked down on him thoughtfully, and he let his admiration of her free young poise show in his face.

'I suppose things have changed?' she said.

'Never was such an age of transition.'

She wondered what to. Mr Ramage did not know. 'Sufficient unto me is the change thereof,' he said, with all the effect of an epigram.

'I must confess,' he said, 'the New Woman* and the New Girl intrigue me profoundly. I am one of those people who are interested in women, more interested than I am in anything else. I don't conceal it. And the change, the change of attitude! The way all the old clingingness has been thrown aside is amazing. And all the old – the old trick of shrinking up like a snail at a touch. If you had lived twenty years ago you would have been called a Young Person, and it would have been your chief duty in life not to know, never to have heard of, and never to understand.'

'There's quite enough still,' said Ann Veronica smiling, 'that one doesn't understand.'

'Quite. But your role would have been to go about saying: "I beg your pardon," in a reproving tone to things you understood quite well in your heart and saw no harm in. That terrible Young Person! she's vanished. Lost, stolen, or strayed, the Young Person!
. . . I hope we may never find her again.'

He rejoiced over this emancipation. 'While that lamb was about every man of any spirit was regarded as a dangerous wolf. We wore invisible chains and invisible blinkers. Now, you and I can gossip at a gate, and *Honi soit qui mal y pense*. The change has given man one good thing he never had before,' he said. 'Girl friends. And I am coming to believe the best as well as the most beautiful friends a man can have are girl friends.'

He paused, and went on after a keen look at her:

'I had rather gossip to a really intelligent girl than to any man alive.'

'I suppose we *are* more free than we were?' said Ann Veronica, keeping the question general.

'Oh, there's no doubt of it! Since the girls of the eighties broke bounds and sailed away on bicycles – my young days go back to the very beginnings of that – it's been one triumphant relaxation.'

'Relaxation perhaps. But are we any more free?'

'Well?'

'I mean we've long strings to tether us, but we are bound all the same. A woman isn't much freer – in reality.'

Mr Ramage demurred.

'One runs about,' said Ann Veronica.

'Yes.'

'But it's on condition one doesn't do anything.'

'Do what?'

'Oh! – anything.'

He looked interrogation with a faint smile.

'It seems to me it comes to earning one's living in the long run,' said Ann Veronica, colouring faintly. 'Until a girl can go away as a son does and earn her independent income, she's still on a string. It may be a long string, long enough if you like to tangle up all sorts of people; but there it is! If the paymaster pulls, home she must go. That's what I mean.'

Mr Ramage admitted the force of that. He was a little impressed by Ann Veronica's metaphor of the string, which, indeed, she owed to Hetty Widgett. '*You* wouldn't like to be independent?' he asked abruptly. 'I mean *really* independent. On your own. It isn't such fun as it seems.'

'Every one wants to be independent,' said Ann Veronica. 'Every one. Man or woman.'

'And you?'

'Rather!'

'I wonder why?'

'There's no why. It's just to feel – one owns oneself.'

'Nobody does that,' said Ramage, and kept silence for a moment.

'But a boy – a boy goes out into the world and presently stands on his own feet. He buys his own clothes, chooses his own company, makes his own way of living.'

'You'd like to do that?'

'Exactly.'

'Would you like to be a boy?'

'I wonder! It's out of the question, anyway.'

Ramage reflected. 'Why don't you?'

'Well, it might mean rather a row.'

'I know—' said Ramage, with sympathy.

'And besides,' said Ann Veronica, sweeping that aspect aside, 'what could I do? A boy sails out into a trade or profession. But – it's one of the things I've just been thinking over. Suppose – suppose a girl did want to start in life, start in life for herself—' She looked him frankly in the eyes. 'What ought she to do?'

'Suppose you—'

'Yes, suppose I—'

He felt that his advice was being asked. He became a little more personal and intimate. 'I wonder what you could do?' he said. 'I should think *you* could do all sorts of things. . . .'

'What ought you to do?' He began to produce his knowledge of the world for her benefit, jerkily and allusively, and with a strong, rank flavour of *savoir faire*. He took an optimist view of her chances. Ann Veronica listened thoughtfully, with her eyes on the turf, and now and then she asked a question, or looked up to discuss a point. In the meanwhile, as he talked, he scrutinized her face, ran his eyes over her careless, gracious poise, wondered hard about her. He described her privately to himself as a splendid girl. It was clear she wanted to get away from home, that she was impatient to get away from home. Why? While the front of his mind was busy warning her not to fall into the hopeless miseries of underpaid teaching, and his explaining his idea that for women of initiative, quite as much as for men, the world of business had by far the best chances, the back chambers of his brain were busy with the problem of that 'Why?'

His first idea as a man of the world was to explain her unrest by a lover, some secret or forbidden or impossible lover. But he dismissed that because then she would ask her lover and not him all these things. Restlessness, then, was the trouble, simple restlessness; home bored her. He could quite understand the daughter of Mr Stanley being bored and feeling limited. But was that enough? Dim, formless suspicions of something more vital wandered about his mind. Was the young lady impatient for experience? Was she adventurous? As a man of the world he did not think it becoming to accept maidenly calm as anything more than a mask. Warm life was behind that always, even if it slept. If it was not an actual personal lover, it still might be the lover not yet incarnate, not yet perhaps suspected. . . .

He had diverged only a little from the truth when he said that his chief interest in life was women. It wasn't so much women as Woman that engaged his mind. His was the Latin turn of thinking; he had fallen in love at thirteen, and he was still capable – he prided himself – of falling in love. His invalid wife and her money had been only the thin thread that held his life together; beaded on that permanent relation had been an interweaving series of other feminine experiences, disturbing, absorbing, interesting, memorable affairs. Each one had been different from the others, each had had a quality all its own, a distinctive freshness, a distinctive beauty. He could not understand how men could live ignoring this one predominant interest, this wonderful research into personality and the possibilities of pleasing, these complex, fascinating expeditions that began in interest and mounted to the supremest, most passionate intimacy. All the rest of his existence was subordinate to this pursuit; he lived for it, worked for it, kept himself in training for it.

So while he talked to this girl of work and freedom, his slightly protuberant eyes were noting the gracious balance of her limbs and body across the gate, the fine lines of her chin and neck. Her grave fine face, her warm clear complexion, had already aroused his curiosity as he had gone to and fro in Morningside Park, and here suddenly he was near to her and talking freely and intimately. He had found her in a communicative mood, and he used the accumulated skill of years in turning that to account.

She was pleased and a little flattered by his interest and sympathy. She became eager to explain herself, to show herself, in the right light. He was manifestly exerting his mind for her, and she found herself fully disposed to justify his interest.

She, perhaps, displayed herself rather consciously as a fine person unduly limited. She even touched lightly on her father's unreasonableness.

'I wonder,' said Ramage, 'that more girls don't think as you do and want to strike out in the world.'

And then he speculated. 'I wonder if you will?'

'Let me say one thing,' he said. 'If ever you do and I can help you in any way, by advice or inquiry or recommendation— You see, I'm no believer in feminine incapacity, but I do perceive there is such a thing as feminine inexperience. As a sex you're a little undertrained – in affairs. I'd take it – forgive me if I seem a little urgent – as a sort of proof of friendliness. I can imagine nothing more pleasant in life than to help you, because I know it would pay to help you. There's something about you, a little flavour of Will, I suppose, that makes one feel – good luck about you and success. . . .'

And while he talked and watched her as he talked, she answered, and behind her listening watched and thought about him. She liked the animated eagerness of his manner.

His mind seemed to be a remarkably full one; his knowledge of detailed reality came in just where her own mind was most weakly equipped. Through all he said ran one quality that pleased her – the quality of a man who feels that things can be done, that one need not wait for the world to push one before one moved. Compared with her father and Mr Manning and the men in 'fixed' positions generally that she knew, Ramage, presented by himself, had a fine suggestion of freedom, of power, of deliberate and sustained adventure. . . .

She was particularly charmed by his theory of friendship. It was really very jolly to talk to a man in this way – who saw the woman in her and did not treat her as a child. She was inclined to think that perhaps for a girl the converse of his method was the case; an older man, a man beyond the range of anything 'nonsensical', was, perhaps, the most interesting sort of friend one could meet. But in that reservation it may be she went a little beyond the converse of his view. . . .

They got on wonderfully well together. They talked for the better part of an hour, and at last walked together to the junction of high road and the bridle path. There, after protestations of friendliness and helpfulness that were almost ardent, he mounted a little clumsily and rode off at an amiable pace, looking his best, making a leg with his riding gaiters, smiling and saluting, while Ann Veronica turned northward and so came to Micklechesil. There, in a little tea and sweet-stuff shop, she bought and consumed slowly and absentmindedly the insufficient nourishment that is natural to her sex on such occasions.

Chapter IV

The Crisis

I

We left Miss Stanley with Ann Veronica's fancy dress in her hands and her eyes directed to Ann Veronica's pseudo-Turkish slippers.

When Mr Stanley came home at a quarter to six – an earlier train by fifteen minutes than he affected – his sister met him in the hall with a hushed expression. 'I'm so glad you're here, Peter,' she said. 'She means to go.'

'Go!' he said. 'Where?'

'To that ball.'

'What ball?' The question was rhetorical. He knew.

'I believe she's dressing upstairs – now.'

'Then tell her to undress, confound her!' The City had been thoroughly annoying that day, and he was angry from the outset. Miss Stanley reflected on this proposal for a moment.

'I don't think she will,' she said.

'She must,' said Mr Stanley, and went into his study. His sister followed. 'She can't go now. She'll have to wait for dinner' he said uncomfortably.

'She's going to have some sort of meal with the Widgetts down the Avenue, and go up with them.'

'She told you that?'

'Yes.'

'When?'

'At tea.'

'But why didn't you prohibit once for all the whole thing? How dared she tell you that?'

'Out of defiance. She just sat and told me that was her arrangement. I've never seen her quite so sure of herself.'

'What did you say?'

'I said: "My dear Veronica! how can you think of such things?"'

'And then?'

'She had two more cups of tea and some cake and told me of her walk.'

'She'll meet somebody one of these days – walking about like that.'

'She didn't say she'd met any one.'

'But didn't you say some more about that ball?'

'I said everything I could say as soon as I realized she was trying to avoid the topic. I said: "It is no use your telling me about this walk and pretend I've been told about the ball, because you haven't. Your father has forbidden you to go!" '

'Well?'

'She said: "I hate being horrid to you and father, but I feel it my duty to go to that ball!" '

'Felt it her duty!'

' "Very well," I said, "then I wash my hands of the whole business. Your disobedience be upon your own head." '

'But this is flat rebellion!' said Mr Stanley, standing on the hearthrug with his back to the unlit gas-fire. 'You ought at once – you ought at once to have told her that. What duty does a girl owe to any one before her father? Obedience to him, that is surely the first law? What *can* she put before that?' His voice began to rise. 'One would think I had said nothing about the matter. One would think I had agreed to her going. I suppose this is what she learns in her infernal London colleges. I suppose this is the sort of damned rubbish—'

'Oh! Ssh, Peter!' cried Miss Stanley.

He stopped abruptly. In the pause a door could be heard opening and closing on the landing upstairs. Then light footsteps became audible, descending the staircase with a certain deliberation, and a faint rustle of skirts.

'Tell her,' said Mr Stanley, with an imperious gesture, 'to come in here.'

2

Miss Stanley emerged from the study and stood watching Ann Veronica descend.

The girl was flushed with excitement, bright-eyed, and braced for a struggle; her aunt had never seen her looking so fine or so pretty. Her fancy dress, save for the green-grey stockings, the pseudo-Turkish slippers, and baggy silk trousered ends natural to a corsair's bride, was hidden in a large black-silk-hooded opera cloak. Beneath the hood it was evident that her rebellious hair was bound up with red silk, and fastened by some device in her ears (unless she had had them pierced, which was too dreadful a thing to suppose!) were long brass filigree ear-rings.

'I'm just off, aunt,' said Ann Veronica.

'Your father is in the study and wishes to speak to you.'

Ann Veronica hesitated, and then stood in the open doorway and regarded her father's stern presence. She spoke with an entirely false note of cheerful off-handedness. 'I'm just in time to say good-bye before I go, father. I'm going up to London with the Widgetts to that ball.'

'Now look here, Ann Veronica,' said Mr Stanley, 'just a moment. You are *not* going to that ball!'

Ann Veronica tried a less genial, more dignified note.

'I thought we had discussed that, father.'

'You are not going to that ball. You are not going out of this house in that get-up.'

Ann Veronica tried yet more earnestly to treat him, as she would treat any man, with an insistence upon her due of masculine respect. 'You see,' she said very gently, 'I *am* going. I am sorry to seem to disobey you, but I am. I wish' – she found she had embarked on a bad sentence – 'I wish we needn't have quarrelled.'

She stopped abruptly, and turned about towards the front door. In a moment he was beside her. 'I don't think you can have heard me, Vee,' he said with intensely controlled fury. 'I said you were' – he shouted – '*n o t t o g o!*'

She made, and overdid, an immense effort to be a princess. She tossed her head, and, having no further words, moved towards the door. Her father intercepted her, and for a moment she and he struggled with their hands upon the latch. A common rage flushed their faces. 'Let go!' she gasped at him, a blaze of anger.

'Veronica!' cried Miss Stanley warningly, and 'Peter!'

For a moment they seemed on the verge of an altogether desperate scuffle. Never for a moment had violence come between these two since long ago he had, in spite of her mother's protest in the background, carried her kicking and squalling to the nursery for some forgotten crime. With something near to horror they found themselves thus confronted.

The door was fastened by a catch and a latch with an inside key, to which at night a chain and two bolts were added. Carefully abstaining from thrusting against each other, Ann Veronica and her father began an absurdly desperate struggle, the one to open the door, the other to keep it fastened. She seized the key, and he grasped her hand and squeezed it roughly and painfully between the handle and the ward as she tried to turn it. His grip twisted her wrist. She cried out with the pain of it.

A wild passion of shame and self-disgust swept over her. Her spirit awoke in dismay to an affection in ruins, to the immense undignified disaster that had come to them.

Abruptly she desisted, recoiled, and turned and fled upstairs.

She made noises between weeping and laughter as she went. She gained her room, and slammed her door and locked it as though she feared violence and pursuit.

'O God!' she cried, 'O God!' and flung aside her opera cloak, and for a time walked about the room – a corsair's bride at a crisis of emotion. 'Why can't he reason with me,' she said again and again, 'instead of doing this?'

3

There presently came a phase in which she said: 'I *won't* stand it even now. I will go to-night.'

She went as far as her door, then turned to the window. She opened this and scrambled out – a thing she had not done for five long years of adolescence – upon the leaded space above the built-out bathroom on the first floor. Once upon a time she and Roddy had descended thence by the drain-pipe.

But things that a girl of sixteen may do in short skirts are not things to be done by a young lady of twenty-one in fancy dress and an opera cloak, and just as she was coming unaided to an adequate realization of this, she discovered Mr Pragmar, the wholesale druggist, who lived three gardens away, and who had been mowing his lawn to get an appetite for dinner, standing in a fascinated attitude beside the forgotten lawn-mower and watching her intently.

She found it extremely difficult to infuse an air of quiet correctitude into her return through the window, and when she was safely inside she waved clenched fists and executed a noiseless dance of rage.

When she reflected that Mr Pragmar probably knew Mr Ramage, and might describe the affair to him, she cried 'Oh!' with renewed vexation, and repeated some steps of her dance in a new and more ecstatic measure.

4

At eight that evening Miss Stanley tapped at Ann Veronica's bedroom door.

'I've brought you up some dinner, Vee,' she said.

Ann Veronica was lying on her bed in a darkling room staring at the ceiling. She reflected before answering. She was frightfully hungry. She had eaten little or no tea, and her midday meal had been worse than nothing.

She got up and unlocked the door.

Her aunt did not object to capital punishment or war, or the industrial system or casual wards, or flogging of criminals or the Congo Free State, because none of these things really got hold of her imagination; but she did object, she did not like, she could not bear to think of people not having and enjoying their meals. It was her distinctive test of an emotional state, its interference with a kindly normal digestion. Any one very badly moved choked down a few mouthfuls; the symptom of supreme distress was not to be able to touch a bit. So that the thought of Ann Veronica upstairs had been extremely painful for her through all the silent dinner time that night. As soon as dinner was over she went into the kitchen and devoted herself to compiling a tray – not a tray merely of half-cooled dinner things, but a specially prepared 'nice' tray, suitable for tempting any one. With this she now entered.

Ann Veronica found herself in the presence of the most disconcerting fact in human experience, the kindliness of people you believe to be thoroughly wrong. She took the tray with both hands, gulped, and gave way to tears.

Her aunt leaped unhappily to the thought of penitence.

'My dear,' she began, with an affectionate hand on Ann Veronica's shoulder, 'I do so wish you would realize how it grieves your father.'

Ann Veronica flung away from the hand, and the pepper pot on the tray upset, sending a puff of pepper into the air and instantly filling them both with an intense desire to sneeze.

'I don't think you see,' she replied, with tears on her cheeks and her brows knitting, 'how it shames and, ah! – disgraces me – ah tishu!'

She put down the tray with a concussion on her toilet table.

'But dear! think! He is your father. Shooh!'

'That's no reason,' said Ann Veronica, speaking through her handkerchief and stopping abruptly.

Niece and aunt regarded each other for a moment over their pocket handkerchiefs with watery but antagonistic eyes, each far too profoundly moved to see the absurdity of the position.

'I hope,' said Miss Stanley with dignity, and turned door-ward with features in civil warfare. 'Better state of mind,' she gasped. . . .

Ann Veronica stood in the twilight room staring at the door that had slammed upon her aunt, her pocket handkerchief rolled tightly in her hand. Her soul was full of the sense of disaster. She had made her first fight for dignity and freedom as a grown-up and independent Person, and this was how the universe had treated her. It had neither succumbed to her nor wrathfully overwhelmed her. It had thrust her back with an undignified scuffle, with vulgar comedy, with an unendurable, scornful grin.

'By God!' said Ann Veronica for the first time in her life. 'But I will. I will!'

Chapter V

The Flight to London

I

Ann Veronica had an impression that she did not sleep at all that night, and at any rate she got through an immense amount of feverish feeling and thinking.

What was she going to do?

One main idea possessed her; she must get away from home, she must assert herself at once or perish. 'Very well,' she would say, 'then I must go.' To remain, she felt, was to concede everything. And she would have to go to-morrow. It was clear it must be to-morrow. If she delayed a day she would delay two days, if she delayed two days she would delay a week, and after a week things would be adjusted to submission for ever. 'I'll go,' she vowed to the night, 'or I'll die!' She made plans and estimated means and resources. These and her general preparations had perhaps a certain disproportion. She had a gold watch, a very good gold watch that had been her mother's, a pearl necklace that was also pretty good, some unpretending rings, some silver bangles and a few other such inferior trinkets, three pounds thirteen shillings unspent of her dress and book allowance, and a few good saleable books. So equipped, she proposed to set up a separate establishment in the world.

And then she would find work.

For most of a long and fluctuating night she was fairly confident that she would find work; she knew herself to be strong, intelligent, and capable by the standards of most of the girls she knew. She was not quite clear how she should find it, but she felt she would. Then she would write and tell her father what she had done, and put their relationship on a new footing.

That was how she projected it, and in general terms it seemed plausible and possible. But in between these wider phases of comparative confidence were gaps of disconcerting doubt, when the universe was presented as making sinister and threatening faces at her, defying her to defy, preparing a humiliating and shameful overthrow. 'I don't care,' said Ann Veronica to the darkness; 'I'll fight it.'

She tried to plan her proceedings in detail. The only difficulties that presented themselves clearly to her were the difficulties of getting away from Morningside Park, and not the difficulties at the other end of the journey. These were so outside her experience that she found it possible to thrust them almost out of sight by saying they would be 'all right' in confident tones to herself. But still she knew they were not right, and at times they became a horrible obsession as of something waiting for her round the corner. She tried to imagine herself 'getting something,' to project herself as sitting down at a desk and writing, or as returning after her work to some pleasantly equipped and free and independent flat. For a time she furnished the flat. But even with that furniture it remained extremely vague, the possible good and the possible evil as well! The possible evil! 'I'll go,' said Ann Veronica for the hundredth time. 'I'll go. I don't care *what* happens.'

She awoke out of a doze as though she had never been sleeping. It was time to get up.

She sat on the edge of her bed and looked about her, at her room, at the row of black-covered books and the pig's skull. 'I must take them,' she said, to help herself over her own incredulity. 'How shall I get my luggage out of the house? . . . '

The figure of her aunt, a little distant, a little propitiatory, behind the coffee things, filled her with a sense of almost catastrophic adventure. Perhaps she might never come back to that breakfast-room again. Never! Perhaps some day, quite soon, she might regret that breakfast-room. She helped herself to the remainder of the slightly congealed bacon, and reverted to the problem of getting her luggage out of the house. She decided to call in the help of Teddy Widgett, or, failing him, of one of his sisters.

2

She found the younger generation of the Widgetts engaged in languid reminiscences, and all, as they expressed it, a 'bit decayed'. Every one became tremendously animated when they heard that Ann Veronica had failed them because she had been, as she expressed it, 'locked in'.

'My God!' said Teddy more impressively than ever.

'But what are you going to do?' asked Hetty.

'What can one do?' asked Ann Veronica. 'Would you stand it? I'm going to clear out.'

'Clear out?' cried Hetty.

'Go to London,' said Ann Veronica.

She had expected sympathetic admiration, but instead the whole Widgett family, except Teddy, expressed a common dismay. 'But how can you?' asked Constance. 'Who will you stop with?'

'I shall go on my own. Take a room!'

'I say!' said Constance. 'But who's going to pay for the room?'

'I've got money,' said Ann Veronica. 'Anything is better than this – this stifled life down here.' And seeing that Hetty and Constance were obviously developing objections, she plunged at once into a demand for help. 'I've got nothing in the world to pack with except a toy size portmanteau. Can you lend me some stuff?'

'You *are* a chap!' said Constance, and warmed only slowly from the idea of dissuasion to the idea of help. But they did what they could for her. They agreed to lend her their hold-all and a large, formless bag which they called the communal trunk. And Teddy declared himself ready to go to the ends of the earth for her, and carry her luggage all the way.

Hetty, looking out of the window – she always smoked her after-breakfast cigarette at the window for the benefit of the less advanced section of Morningside Park society – and trying not to raise objections, saw Miss Stanley going down towards the shops.

'If you must go on with it,' said Hetty, 'Now's your time.' And Ann Veronica at once went back with the hold-all, trying not to hurry indecently but to keep up her dignified air of being a wronged person doing the right thing at a smart trot, to pack. Teddy went round by the garden backs and dropped the bag over the fence. All this was exciting and entertaining. Her aunt returned before the packing was done, and Ann Veronica lunched with an uneasy sense of bag and hold-all packed upstairs and inadequately hidden from chance intruders by the valance of the bed. She went down, flushed and light-hearted, to the Widgetts' after lunch to make some final arrangements, and then, as soon as her aunt had retired to lie down for her usual digestive hour, took the risk of the servants having the enterprise to report her proceedings and carried bag and hold-all to the garden gate, whence Teddy, in a state of ecstatic service, bore them to the railway station. Then she went upstairs again, dressed herself carefully for town, put on her most businesslike-looking hat, and with a wave of emotion she found it hard to control, walked down to catch the 3.17 up train.

Teddy handed her into the second-class compartment her season ticket warranted, and declared she was 'simply splendid'. 'If you want anything,' he said, 'or get into any trouble, wire me. I'd come back from the ends of the earth. I'd do anything, Vee. It's horrible to think of you!'

'You're an awful brick, Teddy!' she said.

'Who wouldn't be – for you?'

The train began to move. 'You're splendid!' said Teddy, with his hair wild in the wind. 'Good luck! Good luck!'

She waved from the window until the bend hid him.

She found herself alone in the train, asking herself what she must do next, and trying not to think of herself as cut off from home or any refuge whatever from the world she had resolved to face. She felt smaller and more adventurous even than she had expected to feel. 'Let me see,' she said to herself, trying to control a slight sinking of the heart, 'I am going to take a room in a lodging-house because that is cheaper. . . . But perhaps I had better get a room in an hotel to-night and look round. . . .

'It's bound to be all right,' she said.

But her heart kept on sinking. What hotel should she go to? If she told a cabman to drive to an hotel, any hotel, what would he do – or say? He might drive to something dreadfully expensive, and not at all the quiet sort of thing she required. Finally she decided that even for an hotel she must look round, and that meanwhile she would 'book' her luggage at Waterloo. She told the porter to take it to the booking-office, and it was only after a disconcerting moment or so that she found she ought to have directed him to go to the cloak-room. But that was soon put right, and she walked out into London with a peculiar exaltation of mind, an exaltation that partook of panic and defiance but was chiefly a sense of vast unexampled release.

She inhaled a deep breath of air – London air.

3

She dismissed the first hotels she passed, she scarcely knew why, mainly perhaps from the mere dread of entering them, and crossed

Waterloo Bridge at a leisurely pace. It was high afternoon, there was no great throng of foot passengers, and many an eye from omnibus and pavement rested gratefully on her fresh, trim presence as she passed, young and erect, with the light of determination shining through the quiet self-possession of her face. She was dressed as English girls do dress for town, without either coquetry or harshness, her collarless blouse confessed a pretty neck, her eyes were bright and steady, and her dark hair waved loosely and graciously over her ears. . . .

It seemed at first the most beautiful afternoon of all time to her, and perhaps the thrill of her excitement did add a distinctive and culminating keenness to the day. The river, the big buildings on the north bank, Westminster, and St Paul's, were rich and wonderful with the soft sunshine of London, the softest, the finest grained, the most penetrating and least emphatic sunshine in the world. The very carts and vans and cabs that Wellington Street poured out incessantly upon the bridge seemed ripe and good in her eyes. A traffic of copious barges slumbered over the face of the river – barges either altogether stagnant or dreaming along in the wake of fussy tugs; and above circled, urbanely voracious, the London seagulls. She had never been there before at that hour, in that light, and it seemed to her as if she came to it all for the first time. And this great mellow place, this London, now was hers, to struggle with, to go where she pleased in, to overcome and live in. 'I am glad,' she told herself, 'I came.'

She marked an hotel that seemed neither opulent nor odd in a little side street opening on the Embankment, made up her mind with an effort, and, returning by Hungerford Bridge to Waterloo, took a cab to this chosen refuge with her two pieces of luggage. There was just a minute's hesitation before they gave her a room. The young lady in the bureau said she would inquire, and Ann Veronica, while she affected to read the appeal on a hospital collecting-box upon the bureau counter, had a disagreeable sense of being surveyed from behind by a small, whiskered gentleman in a frock coat, who came out of the inner office and into the hall among a number of equally observant green porters to look at her and her bags. But the survey was satisfactory, and she found herself presently in Room No. 47, straightening her hat and waiting for her luggage to appear.

'All right so far,' she said to herself. . . .

4

But presently, as she sat on the one antimacassered red silk chair and surveyed her hold-all and bag in that tidy, rather vacant and dehumanized apartment, with its empty wardrobe and desert toilet-table and pictureless walls and stereotyped furnishings a sudden blankness came upon her as though she didn't matter, and had been thrust away into this impersonal corner, she and her gear. . . .

She decided to go out into the London afternoon again and get something to eat in an Aerated Bread shop or some such place, and perhaps find a cheap room for herself. Of course that was what she had to do; she had to find a cheap room for herself, and work! This Room No. 47 was no more than a sort of railway compartment on the way to that.

How does one get work?

She walked along the Strand and across Trafalgar Square, and by the Haymarket to Piccadilly, and so through dignified squares and palatial alleys to Oxford Street; and her mind was divided between a speculative treatment of employment on the one hand, and breezes – zephyr breezes – of the keenest appreciation for London, on the other. The jolly part of it was that for the first time in her life so far as London was concerned, she was not going anywhere in particular; for the first time in her life it seemed to her she was taking London in.

She tried to think how people get work. Ought she to walk into some of these places and tell them what she could do? She hesitated at the window of a shipping office in Cockspur Street and at the Army and Navy Stores, but decided that perhaps there would be some special and customary hour, and that it would be better for her to find this out before she made her attempt. And, besides, she didn't just immediately want to make her attempt.

She fell into a pleasant dream of positions and work. Behind every one of these myriad fronts she passed there must be a career or careers. Her ideas of women's employment and a modern woman's pose in life were based largely on the figure of Vivie Warren* in *Mrs Warren's Profession*. She had seen *Mrs Warren's Profession* furtively with Hetty Widgett from the gallery of a Stage Society performance one Monday afternoon. Most of it had been incomprehensible to her, or comprehensible in a way that checked further curiosity, but the figure of Vivien, hard, capable, successful, and bullying, and ordering about a veritable Teddy in the person of Frank Gardner, appealed to her. She saw herself in very much Vivie's position – managing something.

Her thoughts were deflected from Vivie Warren by the peculiar behaviour of a middle-aged gentleman in Piccadilly. He appeared suddenly from the infinite in the neighbourhood of the Burlington Arcade, crossing the pavement towards her and with his eyes upon her. He seemed to her indistinguishably about her father's age. He wore a silk hat a little tilted, and a morning coat buttoned round a tight, contained figure; and a white slip gave a finish to his costume and endorsed the quiet distinction of his tie. His face was a little flushed perhaps, and his small brown eyes were bright. He stopped on the kerbstone, not facing her, but as if he was on his way to cross the road, and spoke to her suddenly over his shoulder.

'Whither away?' he said very distinctly in a curiously wheedling voice. Ann Veronica stared at his foolish, propitiatory smile, his hungry gaze, through one moment of amazement, then stepped aside and went on her way with a quickened step. But her mind was ruffled, and its mirror-like surface of satisfaction was not easily restored.

Queer old gentleman!

The art of ignoring is one of the accomplishments of every well-bred girl, so carefully instilled that at last she can even ignore her own thoughts and her own knowledge. Ann Veronica could at the same time ask herself what this queer old gentleman could have meant by speaking to her, and know – know in general terms, at least – what that accosting signified. About her, as she had gone day by day to and from the Tredgold College, she had seen and not seen many an incidental aspect of those sides of life about which girls are expected to know nothing, aspects that were extraordinarily relevant to her own position and outlook on the world, and yet by convention ineffably remote. For all that she was of exceptional intellectual enterprise, she had never yet considered these things with unaverted eyes. She had viewed them askance, and without exchanging ideas with any one else in the world about them.

She went on her way now no longer dreaming and appreciative, but disturbed and unwillingly observant behind her mask of serene contentment.

That delightful sense of free, unembarrassed movement was gone.

As she neared the bottom of the dip in Piccadilly she saw a woman approaching her from the opposite direction – a tall woman who at the first glance seemed altogether beautiful and fine. She came along with the fluttering assurance of some tall ship. Then as she drew nearer paint showed upon her face, and a harsh purpose behind the quiet expression of her open countenance, and a sort of unreality in her splendour betrayed itself for which Ann Veronica could not recall the right word – a word, half understood, that lurked and hid in her mind, the word 'meretricious'. Behind this woman and a little to the side of her, walked a man smartly dressed, with desire and appraisal in his eyes. Something insisted that those two were mysteriously linked – that the woman knew the man was there.

It was a second reminder that against her claim to go free and untrammelled there was a case to be made, that after all it was true that a girl does not go alone in the world unchallenged, nor ever has gone freely alone in the world, that evil walks abroad and dangers, and petty insults more irritating than dangers, lurk.

It was in the quiet streets and squares towards Oxford Street that it first came into her head disagreeably that she herself was being followed. She observed a man walking on the opposite side of the way and looking towards her.

'Bother it all!' she swore. 'Bother!' and decided that this was not so, and would not look to right or left again.

Beyond the circus Ann Veronica went into a British Tea Table Company shop to get some tea. And as she was yet waiting for her tea to come she saw this man again. Either it was an unfortunate recovery of a trail, or he had followed her from Mayfair. There was no mistaking his intentions this time. He came down the shop looking for her quite obviously, and took up a position on the other side against a mirror in which he was able to regard her steadfastly.

Beneath the serene unconcern of Ann Veronica's face was a boiling tumult. She was furiously angry. She gazed with a quiet detachment towards the window and the Oxford Street traffic, and in her heart she was busy kicking this man to death. He *had* followed her! What had he followed her for? He must have followed her all the way from beyond Grosvenor Square.

He was a tall man and fair, with bluish eyes that were rather protuberant, and long white hands of which he made a display. He had removed his silk hat, and now sat looking at Ann Veronica over an untouched cup of tea; he sat gloating upon her, trying to catch her eye. Once, when he thought he had done so, he smiled an ingratiating smile. He moved, after quiet intervals, with a quick little movement, and ever and again stroked his small moustache and coughed a self-conscious cough.

'That he should be in the same world with me!' said Ann Veronica, reduced to reading the list of good things the British Tea Table Company had priced for its patrons.

Heaven knows what dim and tawdry conceptions of passion and desire were in that blond cranium, what romance-begotten dreams of intrigue and adventure! but they sufficed, when presently Ann Veronica went out into the darkling street again, to inspire a flitting, dogged pursuit, idiotic, exasperating, indecent.

She had no idea what she should do. If she spoke to a policeman she did not know what would ensue. Perhaps she would have to charge this man and appear in a police court next day.

She became angry with herself. She would not be driven in by this persistent, sneaking aggression. She would ignore him. Surely she could ignore him. She stopped abruptly, and looked in a flower-shop window. He passed, and came loitering back and stood beside her, silently looking into her face.

The afternoon had passed now into twilight. The shops were lighting up into gigantic lanterns of colour, the street lamps were glowing into existence, and she had lost her way. She had lost her sense of direction, and was among unfamiliar streets. She went on from street to street, and all the glory of London had departed. Against the sinister, the threatening, monstrous inhumanity of the limitless city, there was nothing now but this supreme, ugly fact of a pursuit – the pursuit of the undesired, persistent male.

For a second time Ann Veronica wanted to swear at the universe.

There were moments when she thought of turning upon this man and talking to him. But there was something in his face at once stupid and invincible that told her he would go on forcing himself upon her, that he would esteem speech with her a great point gained. In the twilight he had ceased to be a person one could tackle and shame; he had become something more general, a something that crawled and sneaked towards her and would not let her alone . . . .

Then, when the tension was getting unendurable, and she was on the verge of speaking to some casual passer-by and demanding help, her follower vanished. For a time she could scarcely believe he was gone. He had. The night had swallowed him up, but his work on her was done. She had lost her nerve, and there was no more freedom in London for her that night. She was glad to join in the stream of hurrying homeward workers that was now welling out of a thousand places of employment, and to imitate their driven, preoccupied haste. She followed a bobbing white hat and grey jacket until she reached the Euston Road corner of Tottenham Court Road, and there, by the name on a bus and the cries of a conductor, she made a guess of her way. And she did not merely affect to be driven – she felt driven. She was afraid people would follow her, she was afraid of the dark, open doorways she passed, and afraid of the blazes of light; she was afraid to be alone, and she knew not what it was she feared.

It was past seven when she got back to her hotel. She thought then that she had shaken off the man of the bulging blue eyes for ever, but that night she found he followed her into her dreams. He stalked her, he stared at her, he craved her, he sidled slinking and propitiatory and yet relentlessly towards her, until at last she awoke from the suffocating nightmare nearness of his approach, and lay awake in fear and horror listening to the unaccustomed sounds of the hotel.

She came very near that night to resolving that she would return to her home next morning. But the morning brought courage again, and those first intimations of horror vanished completely from her mind.

5

She had sent her father a telegram from the East Strand post office worded thus:

All	is	well	with	me
and	quite	safe	Veronica	

and afterwards she had dined *à la carte* upon a cutlet, and had then set herself to write an answer to Mr Manning's proposal of marriage. But she had found it very difficult.

'DEAR MR MANNING,' she had begun. So far it had been plain sailing, and it had seemed fairly evident to go on: '*I find it very difficult to answer your letter.*'

But after that neither ideas nor phrases had come, and she had fallen thinking of the events of the day. She had decided that she would spend the next morning answering advertisements in the papers that abounded in the writing-room; and so, after half an hour's perusal of back numbers of the *Sketch* in the drawing-room, she had gone to bed.

She found next morning, when she came to this advertisement answering, that it was more difficult than she had supposed. In the first place there were not so many suitable advertisements as she had expected. She sat down by the paper rack with a general feeling of resemblance to Vivie Warren, and looked through the *Morning Post* and *Standard* and *Telegraph*, and afterwards the halfpenny sheets. The *Morning Post* was hungry for governesses and nursery governesses, but held out no other hopes; the *Daily Telegraph* that morning seemed eager only for skirt hands. She went to a writing desk and made some memoranda on a sheet of note-paper, and then remembered that she had no address as yet to which letters could be sent.

She decided to leave this matter until the morrow and devote the morning to settling up with Mr Manning. At the cost of quite a number of torn drafts she succeeded in evolving this:

'DEAR MR MANNING, *I find it very difficult to answer your letter. I hope you won't mind if I say first that I think it does me an extraordinary honour that you should think of any one like myself so highly and seriously, and, secondly, that I wish it had not been written.*'

She surveyed this sentence for some time before going on. 'I wonder,' she said, 'why one writes him sentences like that? It'll have to go,' she decided. 'I've written too many already.' She went on, with a desperate attempt to be easy and colloquial:

'*You see, we were rather good friends, I thought, and now perhaps it will be difficult for us to get back to the old friendly footing. But if that can possibly be done I want it to be done. You see, the plain fact of the case is that I think I am too young and ignorant for marriage. I have been thinking these things over lately, and it seems to me that marriage for a girl is just the supremest thing in life. It isn't just one among a number of important things; for her it is the important thing, and until she knows far more than I know of the facts of life, how is she to undertake it? So please, if you will, forget that you wrote that letter, and forgive this answer. I want you to think of me just as if I was a man, and quite outside marriage altogether.*

'*I do hope you will be able to do this, because I value men friends. I shall be very sorry if I cannot have you for a friend. I think that there is no better friend for a girl than a man rather older than herself.*

'*Perhaps by this time you will have heard of the step I have taken in leaving my home. Very likely you will disapprove highly of what I have done – I wonder? You may, perhaps, think I have done it just in a fit of childish petulance because my father locked me in when I wanted to go to a ball of which he did not approve. But really it is much more than that. At Morningside Park I feel as though all my growing up was presently to stop, as though I was being shut in from the light of life, and, as they say in botany, etiolated. I was just like a sort of dummy that does things as it is told, that is to say, as the strings are pulled. I want to be a person by myself, and to pull my own strings. I had rather have trouble and hardship like that than be taken care of by others. I want to be myself. I wonder if a man can quite understand that passionate feeling? It is quite a passionate feeling. So I am already no longer the girl you knew at Morningside Park. I am a young person seeking employment and freedom and self-development, just as in quite our first talk of all I said I wanted to be.*

'*I do hope you will see how things are, and not be offended with me or frightfully shocked and distressed by what I have done.*

'Very sincerely yours,

'ANN VERONICA STANLEY.'

6

In the afternoon she resumed her search for apartments. The intoxicating sense of novelty had given place to a more business-like mood. She drifted northward from the Strand, and came on some queer and dingy quarters.

She had never imagined life was half so sinister as it looked to her in the beginning of these investigations. She found herself again in the presence of some element in life about which she had been trained not to think, about which she was perhaps instinctively indisposed to think; something which jarred, in spite of all her mental resistance, with all her preconceptions of a clean and courageous girl walking out from Morningside Park as one walks out of a cell into a free and spacious world. One or two landladies refused her with an air of conscious virtue that she found hard to explain. 'We don't let to ladies,' they said.

She drifted, via Theobald's Road, obliquely towards the region about Titchfield Street. Such apartments as she saw were either scandalously dirty or unaccountably dear, or both. And some were adorned with engravings that struck her as being more vulgar and undesirable than anything she had ever seen in her life. Ann Veronica loved beautiful things, and the beauty of undraped loveliness not least among them; but, these were pictures that did but insist coarsely upon the roundness of women's bodies. The windows of these rooms were obscured with draperies, their floors a carpet patchwork; the china ornaments on their mantels were of a class apart. After the first onset several of the women who had apartments to let said she would not do for them, and in effect dismissed her. This also struck her as odd.

About many of these houses hung a mysterious taint as of something weakly and commonly, and dustily evil; the women who negotiated the rooms looked out through a friendly manner as though it was a mask, with hard, defiant eyes. Then one old crone, short-sighted and shaky-handed, called Ann Veronica 'dearie', and made some remark, obscure and slangy, of which the spirit rather than the words penetrated to her understanding.

For a time she looked at no more apartments, and walked through gaunt and ill-cleaned streets, through the sordid under side of life, perplexed and troubled, ashamed of her previous obtuseness. She had something of the feeling a Hindoo must experience who has been into surroundings or touched something that offends his caste. She passed people in the streets and regarded them with a quickening apprehension; once or twice came girls dressed in slatternly finery, going towards Regent Street from out these places. It did not occur to her that they at least had found a way of earning a living, and had that much economic superiority to herself. It did not occur to her that save for some accidents of education and character they had souls like her own.

For a time Ann Veronica went on her way gauging the quality of sordid streets. At last, a little way to the northward of Euston Road, the moral cloud seemed to lift, the moral atmosphere to change; clean blinds appeared in the windows, clean doorsteps

before the doors, a different appeal in the neatly placed cards
bearing the word:

APARTMENTS

in the clear bright windows. At last in a street near the Hampstead
Road she hit upon a room that had an exceptional quality of space
and order, and a tall woman with a kindly face to show it. 'You're
a student perhaps?' said the tall woman. 'At the Tredgold
Women's College,' said Ann Veronica. She felt it would save
explanations if she did not state she had left her home and was
looking for employment. The room was papered with green,
large-patterned paper that was at worst a trifle dingy, and the
arm-chair and the seats of the other chairs were covered with the
unusual brightness of a large-patterned chintz, which also sup-
plied the window curtain. There was a round table covered, not
with the usual 'tapestry' cover, but with a plain green cloth that
went passably with the wall-paper. In the recess beside the fire-
place were some open bookshelves. The carpet was a quiet
drugget and not excessively worn, and the bed in the corner was
covered by a white quilt. There were neither texts nor rubbish on
the walls, but only a stirring version of Belshazzar's feast, a steel
engraving in the early Victorian manner that had some satisfactory blacks. And the woman who showed this room was tall, with
an understanding eye and the quiet manner of the well-trained
servant.

Ann Veronica brought her luggage in a cab from the hotel; she
tipped the hotel porter sixpence and overpaid the cabman
eighteenpence, unpacked some of her books and possessions, and
so made the room a little homelike, and then sat down in a by no
means uncomfortable arm-chair before the fire. She had arranged
for a supper of tea, a boiled egg, and some tinned peaches. She
had discussed the general question of supplies with the helpful
landlady. 'And now,' said Ann Veronica, surveying her apartment
with an unprecedented sense of proprietorship, 'what is the next
step?'

She spent the evening in writing – it was a little difficult – to
her father and and – which was easier – to the Widgetts. She was
greatly heartened by doing this. The necessity of defending herself
and assuming a confident and secure tone did much to dispel the
sense of being exposed and indefensible in a huge dingy world

that abounded in sinister possibilities. She addressed her letters, meditated on them for a time, and then took them out and posted them. Afterwards she wanted to get her letter to her father back in order to read it over again, and, if it tallied with her general impression of it, re-write it.

He would know her address to-morrow. She reflected upon that with a thrill of terror that was also, somehow, in some faint remote way, gleeful.

'Dear old daddy,' she said, 'he'll make a fearful fuss. Well, it had to happen somewhen. . . . Somehow. I wonder what he'll say?'

Chapter VI

Expostulations

I

The next morning opened calmly, and Ann Veronica sat in her own room, her very own room, and consumed an egg and marmalade, and read the advertisements in the *Daily Telegraph*. Then began expostulations, preluded by a telegram and headed by her aunt. The telegram reminded Ann Veronica that she had no place for interviews except her bed-sitting-room, and she sought her landlady and negotiated hastily for the use of the ground-floor parlour, which very fortunately was vacant. She explained she was expecting an important interview, and asked that her visitor should be duly shown in. Her aunt arrived about half-past ten, in black and with an unusually thick spotted veil. She raised this with the air of a conspirator unmasking, and displayed a tear-flushed face. For a moment she remained silent.

'My dear,' she said, when she could get her breath, 'you must come home at once.'

Ann Veronica closed the door quite softly and stood still.

'This has almost killed your father. . . . After Gwen!'

'I sent a telegram.'

'He cares so much for you. He did so care for you.'

'I sent a telegram to say I was all right.'

'All right! And I never dreamt anything of the sort was going on. I had no idea!' She sat down abruptly and threw her wrists limply upon the table. 'Oh, Veronica!' she said, 'to leave your home!'

She had been weeping. She was weeping now. Ann Veronica was overcome by this amount of emotion.

'Why did you do it?' her aunt urged. 'Why could you not confide in us?'

'Do what?' said Ann Veronica.

'What you have done.'

'But what have I done?'

'Elope! Go off in this way. We had no idea. We had such a pride in you, such hope in you. I had no idea you were not the happiest girl. Everything I could do! Your father sat up all night. Until at last I persuaded him to go to bed. He wanted to put on his overcoat and come after you and look for you – in London. We made sure – it was just like Gwen. Only Gwen left a letter – on the pincushion. You didn't even do that, Vee; not even that.'

'I sent a telegram, aunt,' said Ann Veronica.

'Like a stab. You didn't even put the twelve words.'

'I said I was all right.'

'Gwen said she was happy. Before that came your father didn't even know you were gone. He was just getting cross about your being late for dinner – you know his way – when it came. He opened it – just off-hand, and then when he saw what it was he hit at the table and sent his soup spoon flying and splashing on to the table-cloth. "My God!" he said, "I'll go after them and kill him. I'll go after them and kill him." For the moment I thought it was a telegram from Gwen.'

'But what did father imagine?'

'Of course he imagined! Any one would! "What has happened, Peter?" I asked. He was standing up with the telegram crumpled in his hand. He used a most awful word! Then he said: "It's Ann Veronica, gone to join her sister!" "Gone!" I said. "Gone!" he said. "Read that," and threw the telegram at me, so that it went into the tureen. He swore when I tried to get it out with the ladle, and told me what it said. Then he sat down again in a chair and said that people who wrote novels ought to be strung up. It was as much as I could do to prevent him flying out of the house there and then and coming after you. Never since I was a girl have I seen your father so moved. "Oh! little Vee!" he cried, "little Vee!" and put his face between his hands and sat still for a long time before he broke out again.'

Ann Veronica had remained standing while her aunt spoke.

'Do you mean, aunt,' she asked, 'that my father thought I had gone off – with some man?'

'What else *could* he think? Would any one *dream* you would be so mad as to go off alone?'

'After – after what had happened the night before?'

'Oh, why raise up old scores? If you could see him this morning, his poor face as white as a sheet and all cut about with shaving! He was for coming up by the very first train and looking for you, but I said to him: "Wait for the letters," and there, sure enough, was yours. He could hardly open the envelope, he trembled so.

Then he threw the letter at me. "Go and fetch her home," he said; "it isn't what we thought! It's just a practical joke of hers." And with that he went off to the City, stern and silent, leaving his bacon on his plate – a great slice of bacon hardly touched. No breakfast he's had; no dinner, hardly a mouthful of soup – since yesterday at tea.'

She stopped. Aunt and niece regarded each other silently.

'You must come home to him at once,' said Miss Stanley.

Ann Veronica looked down at her fingers on the claret-coloured table-cloth. Her aunt had summoned up an altogether too vivid picture of her father as the masterful man, over-bearing, emphatic, sentimental, noisy, aimless. Why on earth couldn't he leave her to grow in her own way? Her pride rose at the bare thought of return. 'I don't think I *can* do that,' she said. She looked up and said a little breathlessly: 'I'm sorry, aunt, but I don't think I can.'

2

Then it was the expostulations really began.

From first to last, on this occasion, her aunt expostulated for about two hours. 'But, my dear,' she began, 'it is impossible! It is quite out of the question. You simply can't.' And to that, through vast rhetorical meanderings, she clung. It reached her only slowly that Ann Veronica was standing to her resolution. 'How will you live?' she appealed. 'Think of what people will say!' That became a refrain. 'Think of what Lady Palsworthy will say! Think of what' – So-and-so – 'will say! What are we to tell people?

'Besides, what am I to tell your father?'

At first it had not been at all clear to Ann Veronica that she would refuse to return home; she had had some dream of a capitulation that should leave her an enlarged and defined freedom, but as her aunt put this aspect and that of her flight to her, as she wandered illogically and inconsistently from one urgent consideration to another, as she mingled assurance and aspects and emotions, it became clearer and clearer to the girl that there could be little or no change in the position of things if she returned. 'And what will Mr Manning think?' said her aunt.

'I don't care what any one thinks,' said Ann Veronica.

'I can't imagine what has come over you,' said her aunt. 'I can't conceive what you want. You foolish girl!'

Ann Veronica took that in silence. At the back of her mind, dim and yet disconcerting, was the perception that she herself did not know what she wanted. And yet she knew it was not fair to call her a foolish girl.

'Don't you care for Mr Manning?' said her aunt.

'I don't see what he has to do with my coming to London.'

'He – he worships the ground you tread on. You don't deserve it, but he does. Or at least he did the day before yesterday. And here you are!'

Her aunt opened all the fingers of her gloved hand in a rhetorical gesture. 'It seems to me all madness – madness! Just because your father – wouldn't let you disobey him!'

3

In the afternoon the task of expostulation was taken up by Mr Stanley in person. Her father's ideas of expostulation were a little harsh and forcible, and over the claret-coloured table-cloth and under the gas chandelier, with his hat and umbrella between them like the mace in Parliament, he and his daughter contrived to have a violent quarrel. She had intended to be quietly dignified, but he was in a smouldering rage from the beginning, and began by assuming, which alone was more than flesh and blood could stand, that the insurrection was over and that she was coming home submissively. In his desire to be emphatic and to avenge himself for his overnight distresses, he speedily became brutal, more brutal than she had ever known him before.

'A nice time of anxiety you've given me, young lady,' he said as he entered the room. 'I hope you're satisfied.'

She was frightened – his anger always did frighten her – and in her resolve to conceal her fright she carried a queen-like dignity to what she felt even at the time was a preposterous pitch. She said she hoped she had not distressed him by the course she had felt obliged to take, and he told her not to be a fool. She tried to keep her side up by declaring that he had put her into an impossible position, and he replied by shouting: 'Nonsense! Nonsense! Any father in my place would have done what I did.'

Then he went on to say: 'Well, you've had your little adventure, and I hope now you've had enough of it. So go upstairs and get your things together while I look out for a hansom.'

To which the only possible reply seemed to be: 'I'm not coming home.'

'Not coming home!'

'No!' And, in spite of her resolve to be a Person, Ann Veronica began to weep with terror at herself. Apparently she was always doomed to weep when she talked to her father. But he was always forcing her to say and do such unexpectedly conclusive things. She feared he might take her tears as a sign of weakness. So she said: 'I won't come home. I'd rather starve!'

For a moment the conversation hung upon that declaration. Then Mr Stanley, putting his hands on the table in the manner rather of a barrister than a solicitor, and regarding her balefully through his glasses with quite undisguised animosity, asked: 'And may I presume to inquire, then, what you mean to do? – how do you propose to live?'

'I shall live,' sobbed Ann Veronica. 'You needn't be anxious about that! I shall contrive to live.'

'But I *am* anxious,' said Mr Stanley, 'I am anxious. Do you think it's nothing to me to have my daughter running about London looking for odd jobs and disgracing herself?'

'Shan't get odd jobs,' said Ann Veronica, wiping her eyes.

And from that point they went on to a thoroughly embittering wrangle. Mr Stanley used his authority, and commanded Ann Veronica to come home, to which, of course, she said she wouldn't; and then he warned her not to defy him, warned her very solemnly, and then commanded her again. He then said that if she would not obey him in this course she should 'never darken his doors again', and was, indeed, frightfully abusive. This threat terrified Ann Veronica so much that she declared with sobs and vehemence that she would never come home again, and for a time both talked at once and very wildly. He asked her whether she understood what she was saying, and went on to say still more precisely that she should never touch a penny of his money until she came home again – not one penny. Ann Veronica said she didn't care.

Then abruptly Mr Stanley changed his key. 'You poor child!' he said; 'don't you see the infinite folly of these proceedings? Think! Think of the love and affection you abandon! Think of your aunt, a second mother to you. Think if your own mother was alive!'

He paused, deeply moved.

'If my own mother was alive,' sobbed Ann Veronica, 'she would understand.'

The talk became more and more inconclusive and exhausting. Ann Veronica found herself incompetent, undignified, and detestable, holding on desperately to a hardening antagonism to her father, quarrelling with him, wrangling with him, thinking of repartees – almost as if he was a brother. It was horrible, but what could she do? She meant to live her own life, and he meant, with contempt and insults, to prevent her. Anything else that was said she now regarded only as an aspect of or diversion from that.

In the retrospect she was amazed to think how things had gone to pieces, for at the outset she had been quite prepared to go home again upon terms. While waiting for his coming she had stated her present and future relations with him with what had seemed to her the most satisfactory lucidity and completeness. She had looked forward to an explanation. Instead had come this storm, this shouting, this weeping, this confusion of threats and irrelevant appeals. It was not only that her father had said all sorts of inconsistent and unreasonable things, but that by some incomprehensible infection she herself had replied in the same vein. He had assumed that her leaving home was the point at issue, that everything turned on that, and that the sole alternative was obedience, and she had fallen in with that assumption until rebellion seemed a sacred principle. Moreover, atrociously and inexorably, he allowed it to appear ever and again in horrible gleams that he suspected there was some man in the case. . . . Some man!

And to conclude it all was the figure of her father in the doorway, giving her a last chance, his hat in one hand, his umbrella in the other, shaken at her to emphasize his point.

'You understand, then,' he was saying, 'you understand?'

'I understand,' said Ann Veronica, tear-wet and flushed with a reciprocal passion, but standing up to him with an equality that amazed even herself, 'I understand.' She controlled a sob. 'Not a penny – not one penny – and never darken your doors again!'

4

The next day her aunt came again and expostulated, and was just saying it was 'an unheard-of-thing' for a girl to leave her home as Ann Veronica had done, when her father arrived, and was shown in by the pleasant-faced landlady.

Her father had determined on a new line. He put down his hat and umbrella, rested his hands on his hips, and regarded Ann Veronica firmly.

'Now,' he said quietly, 'it's time we stopped this nonsense.'

Ann Veronica was about to reply, when he went on, with a still more deadly quiet: 'I am not here to bandy words with you. Let us have no more of this humbug. You are to come home.'

'I thought I explained—'

'I don't think you can have heard me,' said her father; 'I have told you to come home.'

'I thought I explained—'

'Come home!'

Ann Veronica shrugged her shoulders.

'Very well,' said her father.

'I think this ends the business,' he said, turning to his sister. 'It's not for us to supplicate any more. She must learn wisdom – as God pleases.'

'But, my dear Peter!' said Miss Stanley.

'No,' said her brother conclusively, 'it's not for a parent to go on persuading a child.'

Miss Stanley rose and regarded Ann Veronica fixedly. The girl stood with her hands behind her back, sulky, resolute, and intelligent, a strand of her black hair over one eye and looking more than usually delicate-featured, and more than ever like an obdurate child.

'She doesn't know.'

'She does.'

'I can't imagine what makes you fly out against everything like this,' said Miss Stanley to her niece.

'What is the good of talking?' said her brother. 'She must go her own way. A man's children nowadays are not his own. That's the fact of the matter. Their minds are turned against him. . . . Rubbishy novels and pernicious rascals. We can't even protect them from themselves.'

An immense gulf seemed to open between father and daughter as he said these words.

'I don't see,' gasped Ann Veronica, 'why parents and children . . . shouldn't be friends.'

'Friends!' said her father. 'When we see you going through disobedience to the devil! Come, Molly, she must go her own way. I've tried to use my authority. And she defies me. What more is there to be said? She defies me!'

It was extraordinary. Ann Veronica felt suddenly an effect of tremendous pathos; she would have given anything to have been able to frame and make some appeal, some utterance that should bridge this bottomless chasm that had opened between her and her father, and she could find nothing whatever to say that was in the least sincere and appealing.

'Father,' she cried, 'I have to live!'

He misunderstood her. 'That,' he said grimly, with his hand on the door handle, 'must be your own affair, unless you choose to live at Morningside Park.'

Miss Stanley turned to her. 'Vee,' she said, 'come home. Before it is too late.'

'Come, Molly,' said Mr Stanley at the door.

'Vee!' said Miss Stanley, 'you hear what your father says!'

Miss Stanley struggled with emotion. She made a curious movement towards her niece, then suddenly, convulsively, she dabbed down something lumpy on the table and turned to follow her brother. Ann Veronica stared for a moment in amazement at this dark green object that clashed as it was put down. It was a purse. She made a step forward. 'Aunt!' she said, 'I can't—'

Then she caught a wild appeal in her aunt's blue eye, halted, and the door clicked upon them.

There was a pause, and then the front door slammed. . . .

Ann Veronica realized that she was alone with the world. And this time the departure had a tremendous effect of finality. She had to resist an impulse of sheer terror, to run out after them and give in.

'Gods,' she said at last, 'I've done it this time!'

'Well!' She took up the neat morocco purse, opened it, and examined the contents.

It contained three sovereigns, six and fourpence, two postage stamps, a small key, and her aunt's return half ticket to Morningside Park.

5

After the interview Ann Veronica considered herself formally cut off from home. If nothing else had clenched that, the purse had. Nevertheless there came a residuum of expostulations. Her brother Roddy, who was in the motor line, came to expostulate; her sister Alice wrote. And Mr Manning called.

Her sister Alice seemed to have developed a religious sense away there in Yorkshire, and made appeals that had no meaning for Ann Veronica's mind. She exhorted Ann Veronica not to become one of 'those unsexed intellectuals, neither man nor woman'.

Ann Veronica meditated over that phrase. 'That's *him*,' said Ann Veronica in sound idiomatic English. 'Poor old Alice!'

Her brother Roddy came to her and demanded tea, and asked her to state a case. 'Bit thick on the old man, isn't it?' said Roddy, who had developed a bluff, straightforward style in the motor shop.

'Mind my smoking?' said Roddy. 'I don't see quite what your game is, Vee, but I suppose you've got a game on somewhere.

'Rummy lot we are!' said Roddy. 'Alice – Alice gone dotty, and all over kids. Gwen – I saw Gwen the other day, and the paint's thicker than ever. Jim is up to the neck in Mahatmas and Theosophy and Higher Thought and rot, writes letters worse than Alice. And now *you*'re on the warpath. I believe I'm the only sane member of the family left. The G.V.'s as mad as any of you, in spite of all his respectability; not a bit of him straight anywhere, not one bit.'

'Straight?'

'Not a bit of it! He's been out after eight per cent since the beginning. Eight per cent! He'll come a cropper one of these days, if you ask me. He's been near it once or twice already. That's got his nerves to rags. I suppose we're all human beings really, but what price the sacred Institution of the Family! Us as a bundle! Eh? . . . I don't half disagree with you, Vee, really; only thing is, I don't see how you're going to pull it off. A home *may* be a sort of cage, but still – it's a home. Gives you a right to hang on to the old man until he busts – practically. Jolly hard life for a girl, getting a living. Not *my* affair.'

He asked questions and listened to her views for a time.

'I'd chuck this lark right off if I were you, Vee,' he said. 'I'm five years older than you, and no end wiser, being a man. What you're after is too risky. It's a damned hard thing to do. It's all very handsome starting out on your own, but it's too damned hard. That's my opinion, if you ask me. There's nothing a girl can do that isn't sweated to the bone. You square the G.V., and go home before you have to. That's my advice. If you don't eat humble pie now you may live to fare worse later. *I* can't help you a cent. Life's hard enough nowadays for an unprotected male. Let alone a girl. You got to take the world as it is, and the only possible trade for a girl that isn't sweated is to get hold of a man and make him do it for her. It's no good flying out at that, Vee; *I* didn't arrange it. It's Providence. That's how things are; that's the order of the world. Like appendicitis. It isn't pretty, but we're made so. Rot, no doubt; but we can't alter it. You go home and live on the G.V., and get some other man to live on as soon as possible. It isn't sentiment, but it's horse sense. All this Woman-who-Diddery* – no damn good. After all old P. – Providence I mean – *has* arranged it so that men will keep you, more or less. He made the universe on those lines. You've got to take what you can get.'

That was the quintessence of her brother Roddy.

He played variations on this theme for the better part of an hour.

'You go home,' he said at parting; 'you go home. It's all very fine and all that, Vee, this freedom, but it isn't going to work. The world isn't ready for girls to start out on their own yet; that's the plain fact of the case. Babies and females have got to keep hold of somebody or go under – anyhow, for the next few generations. You go home and wait a century, Vee, and then try again. Then you *may* have a bit of a chance. Now you haven't the ghost of one – not if you play the game fair.'

6

It was remarkable to Ann Veronica how completely Mr Manning, in his entirely different dialect, endorsed her brother Roddy's view of things. He came along, he said, just to call, with large, loud apologies, radiantly kind and good. Miss Stanley, it was manifest, had given him Ann Veronica's address. The kind-faced landlady had failed to catch his name, and said he was a tall, handsome gentleman with a great black moustache. Ann Veronica, with a sigh at the cost of hospitality, made a hasty negotiation for an extra tea and for a fire in the ground-floor apartment, and preened herself carefully for the interview. In the little apartment, under the gas chandelier, his inches and his stoop were certainly very effective. In the bad light he looked at once military and sentimental and studious, like one of Ouida's* guardsmen revised by Mr Haldane* and the London School of Economics and finished in the Keltic school*.

'It's unforgivable of me to call, Miss Stanley,' he said, shaking hands in a peculiar, high, fashionable manner; 'but you know you said we might be friends.

'It's dreadful for you to be here,' he said, indicating the yellow presence of the first fog of the year without, 'but your aunt told me something of what had happened. It's just like your Splendid Pride to do it. Quite!'

He sat in the arm-chair ad took tea and consumed several of the extra cakes which she had sent out for, and talked to her and expressed himself, looking very earnestly at her with his deep-set eyes, and carefully avoiding any crumbs on his moustache the while. Ann Veronica sat firelit by her tea-tray with, quite unconsciously, the air of an expert hostess.

'But how is it all going to end?' said Mr Manning.

'Your father, of course,' he said, 'must come to realize just how Splendid you are! He doesn't understand. I've seen him, and he doesn't a bit understand. *I* didn't understand before that letter. It makes me want to be just everything I *can* be to you. You're like some splendid Princess in Exile in these Dreadful Dingy apartments!'

'I'm afraid I'm anything but a princess when it comes to earning a salary,' said Ann Veronica. 'But, frankly, I mean to fight this through if I possibly can.'

'My God!' said Manning in a stage aside. 'Earning a salary!

'You're like a Princess in Exile!' he repeated, overruling her. 'You come into these sordid surroundings – you mustn't mind my calling them sordid – and it makes them seem as though they didn't matter. . . . I don't think they do matter. I don't think any surroundings could throw a shadow on you.'

Ann Veronica felt a slight embarrassment. 'Won't you have some more tea, Mr Manning?' she asked.

'You know,' said Mr Manning, relinquishing his cup without answering her question, 'when I hear you talk of earning a living it's as if I heard of an archangel going on the Stock Exchange – or Christ selling doves. . . . Forgive my daring. I couldn't help the thought.'

'It's a very good image,' said Ann Veronica.

'I knew you wouldn't mind.'

'But does it correspond with the facts of the case? You know, Mr Manning, all this sort of thing is very well as sentiment, but does it correspond with the realities? Are women truly such angelic things and men so chivalrous? You men have, I know, meant to make us queens and goddesses, but in practice – well, look, for example, at the stream of girls one meets going to work of a morning, round-shouldered, cheap, and underfed! They aren't queens, and no one is treating them as queens. And look, again, at the women one finds letting lodgings. . . . I was looking for rooms last week. It got on my nerves – the women I saw. Worse than any men. Everywhere I went and rapped at a door I found behind it another dreadful dingy woman – another fallen queen, I suppose – dingier than the last, dirty, you know, in grain. Their poor hands!'

'I know,' said Mr Manning, with entirely suitable emotion.

'And think of the ordinary wives and mothers, with their anxiety, their limitations, their swarms of children!'

Mr Manning displayed distress. He fended these things off from him with the rump of his fourth piece of cake. 'I know that our social order is dreadful enough,' he said, 'and sacrifices all that is best and most beautiful in life. I don't defend it.'

'And besides, when it comes to the idea of queens,' Ann Veronica went on, 'there's twenty-one and a half million women to twenty million men. Suppose our proper place is a shrine. Still, that leaves over a million shrines short, not reckoning widows who re-marry. And more boys die than girls, so that the real disproportion among adults is even greater.'

'I know,' said Mr Manning, 'I know these Dreadful Statistics. I know there's a sort of right in your impatience at the slowness of Progress. But tell me one thing I don't understand – tell me one thing. How can *you* help it by coming down into the battle and the mire? That's the thing that concerns me.'

'Oh, I'm not trying to help it,' said Ann Veronica. 'I'm only arguing against your position of what a woman should be, and trying to get it clear in my own mind. I'm in this apartment and looking for work because – Well, what else can I do, when my father practically locks me up?'

'I know,' said Mr Manning, 'I know. Don't think I can't sympathize and understand. Still, here we are in this dingy, foggy city. Ye gods! what a wilderness it is! Every one trying to get the better of every one, every one regardless of every one – it's one of those days when every one bumps against you – every one pouring coal smoke into the air and making confusion worse confounded, motor omnibuses clattering and smelling, a horse down in the

Tottenham Court Road, an old woman at the corner coughing dreadfully – all the painful sights of a great city, and here you come into it to take your chances. It's too valiant, Miss Stanley, too valiant altogether!'

Ann Veronica meditated. She had had two days of employment-seeking now. 'I wonder if it is.'

'It isn't,' said Mr Manning, 'that I mind courage in a woman – I love and admire courage. What could be more splendid than a beautiful girl facing a great, glorious tiger? Una and the Lion again and all that! But this isn't that sort of thing; this is just a great, ugly, endless wilderness of selfish, sweating, vulgar competition!'

'That you want to keep me out of?'

'Exactly,' said Mr Manning.

'In a sort of beautiful garden close – wearing lovely dresses and picking beautiful flowers?'

'Ah! If one could!'

'While those other girls trudge to business and those other women let lodgings. And in reality even that magic garden close resolves itself into a villa at Morningside Park and my father being more and more cross and overbearing at meals – and a general feeling of insecurity and futility.'

Mr Manning relinquished his cup and looked meaningly at Ann Veronica. 'There,' he said, 'you don't treat me fairly, Miss Stanley. My garden close would be a better thing than that.'

Chapter VII

Ideals and a Reality

I

And now for some weeks Ann Veronica was to test her market value in the world. She went about in a negligent November London that had become very dark and foggy and greasy and forbidding indeed, and tried to find that modest but independent employment she had so rashly assumed. She went about, intent-looking, and self-possessed, trim and fine, concealing her emotions whatever they were, as the realities of her position opened out before her. Her little bed-sitting-room was like a lair, and she went out from it into this vast, dun world, with its smoke-grey houses, its glaring streets of shops, its dark streets of homes, its orange-lit windows, under skies of dull copper or muddy grey or black, much as an animal goes out to seek food. She would come back and write letters, carefully planned and written letters, or read some book she had fetched from Mudie's – she had invested a half-guinea with Mudie's – or sit over her fire and think.

Slowly and reluctantly she came to realize that Vivie Warren was what is called an 'ideal'.* There were no such girls and no such positions. No work that offered was at all of the quality she had vaguely postulated for herself. With such qualifications as she possessed, two chief channels of employment lay open, and neither attracted her, neither seemed really to offer a conclusive escape from that subjection to mankind against which, in the person of her father, she was rebelling. One main avenue was for her to become a sort of salaried accessory wife or mother, to be a governess or an assistant school-mistress, or a very high type of governess-nurse. The other was to go into a business – into a photographer's reception room, for example, or a costumier's or hat shop. The first set of occupations seemed to her to be altogether too domestic and restricted; for the latter she was dreadfully handicapped by her want of experience. And also she didn't like them. She didn't like the shops, she didn't like the other women's faces; she thought the smirking men in frock coats who dominated these establishments the most intolerable persons she had ever had to face. One called her very distinctly 'My dear!'

Two secretarial posts did indeed seem to offer themselves in which, at least, there was no specific exclusion of womanhood; one was under a Radical member of Parliament, and the other under a Harley Street doctor, and both men declined her proffered services with the utmost civility and admiration and terror. There was also a curious interview at a big hotel with a middle-aged, white-powdered woman, all covered with jewels and reeking of scent, who wanted a companion. She did not think Ann Veronica would do as her companion.

And nearly all these things were fearfully ill-paid. They carried no more than bare subsistence wages, and they demanded all her time and energy. She had heard of women journalists, women writers, and so forth; but she was not even admitted to the presence of the editors she demanded to see, and by no means sure that if she had been she could have done any work they might have given her. One day she desisted from her search and went unexpectedly to the Tredgold College. Her place was not filled; she had been simply noted as absent, and she did a comforting day of admirable dissection upon the tortoise. She was so interested, and this was such a relief from the trudging anxiety of her search for work, that she went on for a whole week as if she was still living at home. Then a third secretarial opening occurred and renewed her hopes again; a position as amanuensis – with which some of the lighter duties of a nurse were combined – to an infirm gentleman of means living in Twickenham, and engaged upon a great literary research to prove that the *Faery Queen* was really a treatise upon molecular chemistry written in a peculiar and picturesquely handled cipher.

2

Now, while Ann Veronica was taking these soundings in the industrial sea, and measuring herself against the world as it is, she was also making extensive explorations among the ideas and attitudes of a number of human beings who seemed to be largely concerned with the world as it ought to be. She was drawn first by Miss Miniver, and then by her own natural interest, into a curious stratum of people who are busied with dreams of world progress, of great and fundamental changes, of a New Age that is to replace all the stresses and disorders of contemporary life.

Miss Miniver learnt of her flight and got her address from the Widgetts. She arrived about nine o'clock the next evening in a state of tremulous enthusiasm. She followed the landlady half-way upstairs, and called up to Ann Veronica, 'May I come up? It's me! You know – Nettie Miniver!' She appeared before Ann Veronica could clearly recall who Nettie Miniver might be.

There was a wild light in her eye, and her straight hair was out demonstrating and suffragetting upon some independent notions of its own. Her fingers were bursting through her gloves, as if to get at once into touch with Ann Veronica. 'You're Glorious!' said Miss Miniver in tones of rapture, holding a hand in each of hers and peering up into Ann Veronica's face. 'Glorious! You're so calm, dear, and so resolute, so serene!

'It's girls like you who will show them what We are,' said Miss Miniver; 'girls whose spirits have not been broken!'

Ann Veronica sunned herself a little in this warmth.

'I was watching you at Morningside Park, dear,' said Miss Miniver. 'I am getting to watch all women. I thought then perhaps you didn't care, that you were like so many of them. *Now* it's just as though you had grown up suddenly.'

She stopped, and then suggested: 'I wonder – I should love – if it was anything *I* said.'

She did not wait for Ann Veronica's reply. She seemed to assume that it must certainly be something she had said. 'They all catch on,' she said. 'It spreads like wildfire. This is such a grand time! Such a glorious time! There never was such a time as this! Everything seems so close to fruition, so coming on and leading on! The Insurrection of Women! They spring up everywhere. Tell me all that happened, one sister woman to another.'

She chilled Ann Veronica a little by that last phrase, and yet the magnetism of her fellowship and enthusiasm was very strong; and it was pleasant to be made out a heroine after so much expostulation and so many secret doubts.

But she did not listen long; she wanted to talk. She sat, crouched together, by the corner of the hearthrug under the bookcase that supported the pig's skull, and looked into the fire and up at Ann Veronica's face, and let herself go. 'Let us put the lamp out,' she said; 'the flames are ever so much better for talking,' and Ann Veronica agreed. 'You are coming right out into life – facing it all.'

Ann Veronica sat with her chin on her hand, red-lit and saying little, and Miss Miniver discoursed. As she talked, the drift and significance of what she was saying shaped itself slowly to Ann Veronica's apprehension. It presented itself in the likeness of a great, grey, dull world, a brutal, superstitious, confused, and wrong-headed world, that hurt people and limited people unac-countably. In remote times and countries its evil tendencies had expressed themselves in the form of tyrannies, massacres, wars, and what not; but just at present in England they shaped as commercialism and competition, silk hats, suburban morals, the sweating system, and the subjection of women. So far the thing was acceptable enough. But over against the world Miss Miniver assembled a small but energetic minority, the Children of Light – people she described as 'being in the van', or 'altogether in the van', about whom Ann Veronica's mind was disposed to be more sceptical.

Everything, Miss Miniver said, was 'working up', everything was 'coming on' – the Higher Thought, the Simple Life, Socialism, Humanitarianism, it was all the same really. She loved to be there, taking part in it all, breathing it, being it. Hitherto in the world's history there had been precursors of this Progress at great inter-vals, voices that had spoken and ceased, but now it was all coming on together in a rush. She mentioned, with familiar respect, Christ and Buddha and Shelley and Nietzsche and Plato. Pioneers all of them. Such names shone brightly in the darkness, with black spaces of unilluminated emptiness about them, as stars shine in the night; but now – now it was different; now it was dawn – the real dawn.

'The women are taking it up,' said Miss Miniver; 'the women and the common people, all pressing forward, all roused.'

Ann Veronica listened with her eyes on the fire.

'Everybody is taking it up,' said Miss Miniver. '*You* had to come in. You couldn't help it. Something drew you. Something draws everybody. From suburbs, from country towns – every-where. I see all the movements. As far as I can, I belong to them all. I keep my finger on the pulse of things.'

Ann Veronica said nothing.

'The dawn!' said Miss Miniver, with her glasses reflecting the fire like pools of blood-red flame.

'I came to London,' said Ann Veronica, 'rather because of my own difficulty. I don't know that I understand altogether.'

'Of course you don't,' said Miss Miniver, gesticulating trium-phantly with her thin hand and thinner wrist, and patting Ann Veronica's knee. 'Of course you don't. That's the wonder of it. But you will, you will. You must let me take you to things – to meetings and things, to conferences and talks. Then you will begin to see. You will begin to see it all opening out. I am up to the ears in it all – every moment I can spare. I throw up work – everything! I just teach in one school, one good school, three days a week. All the rest – movements! I can live now on fourpence a day. Think how free that leaves me to follow things up! I must take you everywhere. I must take you to the suffrage people, and the Tolstoyans, and the Fabians.'*

'I have heard of the Fabians,' said Ann Veronica.

'It's *the* society!' said Miss Miniver. 'It's the centre of the intellectuals. Some of the meetings are wonderful! Such earnest, beautiful women! Such deep-browed men! . . . And to think that there they are making history! There they are putting together the plans of a new world. Almost light-heartedly. There is Shaw, and Webb, and Wilkins the author, and Toomer, and Dr Tumpany – the most wonderful people! There you see them discussing, decid-ing, planning! Just think – *they are making a new world!*'

'But *are* these people going to alter everything?' said Ann Veronica.

'What else can happen?' asked Miss Miniver, with a little weak gesture at the glow. 'What else can possibly happen – as things are going now?'

3

Miss Miniver let Ann Veronica into her peculiar levels of the world with so enthusiastic a generosity that it seemed ingratitude to remain critical. Indeed, almost insensibly Ann Veronica became habituated to the peculiar appearance and the peculiar manners of the people 'in the van'. The shock of their intellectual attitude was over, usage robbed it of the first quaint effect of deliberate unrea-son. They were in many respects so right; she clung to that, and shirked more and more the paradoxical conviction that they were also somehow, and even in direct relation to that rightness, absurd.

Very central in Miss Miniver's universe were the Goopes. The Goopes were the oddest little couple conceivable, following a fruitarian career upon an upper floor in Theobald's Road. They were childless and servantless, and they had reduced simple living to the finest of fine arts. Mr Goopes, Ann Veronica gathered, was a mathematical tutor, and visited schools, and his wife wrote a weekly column in *New Ideas* upon vegetarian cookery, vivisection, degeneration, the lacteal secretion, appendicitis, and the Higher Thought generally, and assisted in the management of a fruit shop in the Tottenham Court Road. Their very furniture had mysteriously a high-browed quality, and Mr Goopes when at home dressed simply in a pyjama-shaped suit of canvas sacking tied with brown ribbons, while his wife wore a purple djibbah with a richly embroidered yoke. He was a small, dark, reserved man, with a large inflexible-looking convex forehead, and his wife was very pink and high-spirited, with one of those chins that pass insensibly into a full, strong neck. Once a week, every Saturday, they had a little gathering from nine till the small hours, just talk and perhaps reading aloud and fruitarian refreshments – chestnut sandwiches buttered with nutter, and so forth – and lemonade and unfermented wine; and to one of these symposia Miss Miniver, after a good deal of preliminary solicitude, conducted Ann Veronica.

She was introduced, perhaps a little too obviously for her taste, as a girl who was standing out against her people, to a gathering that consisted of a very old lady with an extremely wrinkled skin and a deep voice, who was wearing what appeared to Ann Veronica's inexperienced eye to be an antimacassar upon her head, a shy, blond young man with a narrow forehead and glasses, two undistinguished women in plain skirts and blouses, and a middle-aged couple, very fat and alike in black, Mr and Mrs Alderman Dunstable, of the Borough Council of Marylebone. These were seated in an imperfect semicircle about a very copper-adorned fire-place, surmounted by a carved wood inscription:

DO IT NOW

And to them were presently added a roguish-looking young man, with reddish hair, an orange tie, and a fluffy tweed suit, and others who, in Ann Veronica's memory, in spite of her efforts to recall details, remained obstinately just 'others'.

The talk was animated, and remained always brilliant in form even when it ceased to be brilliant in substance. There were moments when Ann Veronica rather more than suspected the chief speakers to be, as schoolboys say, showing off at her.

They talked of a new substitute for dripping in vegetarian cookery that Mrs Goopes was convinced exercised an exceptionally purifying influence on the mind. And then they talked of Anarchism and Socialism, and whether the former was the exact opposite of the latter or only a higher form. The reddish-haired young man contributed allusions to the Hegelian philosophy that momentarily confused the discussion. Then Alderman Dunstable, who had hitherto been silent, broke out into speech and went off at a tangent, and gave his personal impressions of quite a number of his fellow councillors. He continued to do this for the rest of the evening intermittently, in and out, among other topics. He addressed himself chiefly to Goopes, and spoke as if in reply to long-sustained inquiries on the part of Goopes into the personnel of the Marylebone Borough Council. 'If you were to ask me,' he would say, 'I should say Blinders is straight. An ordinary type, of course –'

Mrs Dunstable's contributions to the conversation were entirely in the form of nods; whenever Alderman Dunstable praised or blamed she nodded twice or thrice, according to the requirements of his emphasis. And she seemed always to keep one eye on Ann Veronica's dress. Mrs Goopes disconcerted the alderman a little by abruptly challenging the roguish-looking young man in the orange tie (who, it seemed, was the assistant editor of *New Ideas*) upon a critique of Nietzsche and Tolstoy that had appeared in his paper, in which doubts had been cast upon the perfect sincerity of the latter. Everybody seemed greatly concerned about the sincerity of Tolstoy.

Miss Miniver said that if once she lost her faith in Tolstoy's sincerity, nothing she felt would really matter much any more, and she appealed to Ann Veronica whether she did not feel the same; and Mr Goopes said that we must distinguish between sincerity and irony, which was often indeed no more than sincerity at the sublimated level.

Alderman Dunstable said that sincerity was often a matter of opportunity, and illustrated the point to the fair young man with an anecdote about Blinders on the Dust Destructor Committee, during which the young man in the orange tie succeeded in giving the whole discussion a daring and erotic flavour by questioning whether any one could be perfectly sincere in love.

Miss Miniver thought that there was no true sincerity except in love, and appealed to Ann Veronica, but the young man in the orange tie went on to declare that it was quite possible to be sincerely in love with two people at the same time, although perhaps on different planes with each individual, and deceiving them both. But that brought Mrs Goopes down on him with the lesson Titian teaches so beautifully in his 'Sacred and Profane Love', and she became quite eloquent upon the impossibility of any deception in the former.

Then they discoursed on love for a time, and Alderman Dunstable, turning back to the shy, blond young man and speaking in undertones of the utmost clearness, gave a brief and confidential account of an unfounded rumour of the bifurcation of the affections of Blinders that had led to a situation of some unpleasantness upon the Borough Council.

The very old lady in the antimacassar touched Ann Veronica's arm suddenly, and said in a deep arch voice:

'Talking of love again; spring again, love again. Oh! you young people!'

The young man with the orange tie, in spite of Sisyphus-like efforts on the part of Goopes to get the topic on to a higher plane, displayed great persistence in speculating upon the possible distribution of the affections of highly developed modern types.

The old lady in the antimacassar said abruptly: 'Ah! you young people, you young people, if you only *knew*!' and then laughed and then mused in a marked manner; and the young man with the narrow forehead and glasses cleared his throat and asked the young man in the orange tie whether he believed that Platonic love was possible. Mrs Goopes said she believed in nothing else, and with that she glanced at Ann Veronica, rose a little abruptly, and directed Goopes and the shy young man in the handing of refreshments.

But the young man with the orange tie remained in his place, disputing whether the body had not something or other which he called its legitimate claims. And from that they came back by way of the *Kreutzer Sonata* and *Resurrection* to Tolstoy again.

So the talk went on. Goopes, who had at first been a little reserved, resorted presently to the Socratic method to restrain the young man with the orange tie, and bent his forehead over him, and brought out at last very clearly from him that the body was only illusion and everything nothing but just spirit and molecules of thought. It became a sort of duel at last between them, and all the others sat and listened – every one, that is, except the alder-

man, who had got the blond young man into a corner by the
green-stained dresser with the aluminium things, and was sitting
with his back to every one else, holding one hand over his mouth
for greater privacy, and telling him, with an accent of confidential
admission, in whispers of the chronic struggle between the natural
modesty and general inoffensiveness of the Borough Council and
the social evil in Marylebone.

So the talk went on, and presently they were criticizing novelists, and certain daring essays of Wilkins got their due share of
attention, and then they were discussing the future of the theatre.
Ann Veronica intervened a little in the novelists discussion with
a defence of *Esmond* and a denial that the *Egoist* was obscure,
and when she spoke every one else stopped talking and listened.
Then they deliberated whether Bernard Shaw ought to go into
Parliament. And that brought them to vegetarianism and teeto-
talism, and the young man in the orange tie and Mrs Goopes had
a great set-to about the sincerity of Chesterton and Belloc that
was ended by Goopes showing signs of resuming the Socratic
method.

And at last Ann Veronica and Miss Miniver came down the
dark staircase and out into the foggy space of the London squares,
and crossed Russell Square, Woburn Square, Gordon Square,
making an oblique route to Ann Veronica's lodging. They trudged
along a little hungry, because of the fruitarian refreshments, and
mentally very active. And Miss Miniver fell discussing whether
Goopes or Bernard Shaw or Tolstoy or Dr. Tumpany or Wilkins
the author* had the more powerful and perfect mind in existence
at the present time. She was clear there were no other minds like
them in all the world.

4

Then one evening Ann Veronica went with Miss Miniver into the
back seats of the gallery at Essex Hall, and heard and saw the
giant leaders of the Fabian Society who are remaking the world;
Bernard Shaw and Toomer and Dr. Tumpany and Wilkins the
author, all displayed upon a platform. The place was crowded,
and the people about her were almost equally made up of very
good-looking and enthusiastic young people and a great variety
of Goopes-like types. In the discussion there was the oddest

mixture of things that were personal and petty with an idealist devotion that was fine beyond dispute. In nearly every speech she heard was the same implication of great and necessary changes in the world – changes to be won by effort and sacrifice indeed, but surely to be won. And afterwards she saw a very much larger and more enthusiastic gathering, a meeting of the advanced section of the woman movement in Caxton Hall, where the same note of vast changes in progress sounded; and she went to a soirée of the Dress Reform Association and visited a Food Reform Exhibition, where imminent change was made even alarmingly visible. The women's meeting was much more charged with emotional force than the Socialists'. Ann Veronica was carried off her intellectual and critical feet by it altogether, and applauded and uttered cries that subsequent reflection failed to endorse. 'I knew you would feel it,' said Miss Miniver, as they came away flushed and heated. 'I knew you would begin to see how it all falls into place together.'

It did begin to fall into place together. She became more and more alive, not so much to a system of ideas as to a big diffused impulse towards change, to a great discontent with and criticism of life as it is lived, to a clamorous confusion of ideas for reconstruction – reconstruction of the methods of business, of economic development, of the rules of property, of the status of children, of the clothing and feeding and teaching of every one; she developed a quite exaggerated consciousness of a multitude of people going about the swarming spaces of London with their minds full, their talk and gestures full, their very clothing charged with the suggestion of the urgency of this pervasive project of alteration. Some indeed carried themselves, dressed themselves even, rather as foreign visitors from the land of *Looking Backward* and *News from Nowhere** than as the indigenous Londoners they were. For the most part these were detached people: men practising the plastic arts, young writers, young men in employment, a very large proportion of girls and women – self-supporting women or girls of the student class. They made a stratum into which Ann Veronica was now plunged up to her neck; it had become her stratum.

None of the things they said and did were altogether new to Ann Veronica, but now she got them massed and alive, instead of by glimpses or in books – alive and articulate and insistent. The London backgrounds, in Bloomsbury and Marylebone, against which these people went to and fro, took on, by reason of their grey façades, their implacably respectable windows and window blinds, their reiterated unmeaning iron railings, a stronger and stronger suggestion of the flavour of her father at his most obdurate phase, and of all that she felt herself fighting against.

She was already a little prepared by her discursive reading and discussion under the Widgett influence for ideas and 'movements', though temperamentally perhaps she was rather disposed to resist and criticize than embrace them. But the people among whom she was now thrown through the social exertions of Miss Miniver and the Widgetts – for Teddy and Hetty came up from Morningside Park and took her to an eighteenpenny dinner in Soho and introduced her to some art students, who were also Socialists, and so opened the way to an evening of meandering talk in a studio – carried with them like an atmosphere this implication, not only that the world was in some stupid and even obvious way *wrong*, with which indeed she was quite prepared to agree, but that it needed only a few pioneers to behave as such and be thoroughly and indiscriminately 'advanced', for the new order to achieve itself. When ninety per cent out of the ten or twelve people one meets in a month not only say but feel and assume a thing, it is very hard not to fall into the belief that the thing is so. Imperceptibly almost Ann Veronica began to acquire the new attitude, even while her mind still resisted the felted ideas that went with it. And Miss Miniver began to sway her.

The very facts that Miss Miniver never stated an argument clearly, that she was never embarrassed by a sense of self-contradiction, and had little more respect for consistency of statement than a washerwoman has for wisps of vapour, which made Ann Veronica critical and hostile at their first encounter in Morningside Park, became at last with constant association the secret of Miss Miniver's growing influence. The brain tires of resistance, and when it meets again and again, incoherently active, the same phrases, the same ideas that it has already slain, exposed, and dissected and buried, it becomes less and less energetic to repeat the operation. There must be something, one feels, in ideas that achieve persistently a successful resurrection. What Miss Miniver would have called the Higher Truth supervenes.

Yet through these talks, these meetings and conferences, these movements and efforts, Ann Veronica, for all that she went with her friend, and at times applauded with her enthusiastically, yet went nevertheless with eyes that grew more and more puzzled and fine eyebrows more and more disposed to knit. She was with these movements – akin to them, she felt it at times intensely – and yet something eluded her. Morningside Park had been passive and defective; all this rushed about and was active, but it was still defective. It still failed in something. It did seem germane to the matter that so many of the people 'in the van' were plain people, or faded people, or tired-looking people. It did affect the business that they all argued badly and were egotistical in their manners and inconsistent in their phrases. There were moments when she doubted whether the whole mass of movements and societies and gatherings and talks was not simply one coherent spectacle of failure protecting itself from abjection by the glamour of its own assertions. It happened that at the extremest point of Ann Veronica's social circle from the Widgetts was the family of the Morningside Park horse-dealer, a company of extremely dressy and hilarious young women, with one equestrian brother addicted to fancy waistcoats, cigars, and facial spots. These girls wore hats at remarkable angles and bows to startle and kill: they liked to be right on the spot every time and up to everything that was *it* from the very beginning, and they rendered their conception of Socialists and all reformers by the words 'positively frightening' and 'weird'. Well, it was beyond dispute that these words did convey a certain quality of the Movements in general amidst which Miss Miniver disported herself. They *were* weird. And yet for all that—

It got into Ann Veronica's nights at last and kept her awake, the perplexing contrast between the advanced thought and the advanced thinker. The general propositions of Socialism, for example, struck her as admirable, but she certainly did not extend her admiration to any of its exponents. She was still more stirred by the idea of the equal citizenship of men and women by the realization that a big and growing organization of women, were giving form and a generalized expression to just that personal pride, that aspiration for personal freedom and respect which had brought her to London; but when she heard Miss Miniver discoursing on the next step in the suffrage campaign, or read of women, badgering Cabinet ministers, padlocked to railings, or getting up in a public meeting to pipe out a demand for votes and be carried out kicking and screaming, her soul revolted. She could not part with dignity. Something as yet unformulated within her kept her estranged from all these practical aspects of her beliefs.

'Not for these things, O Ann Veronica, have you revolted,' it said; 'and this is not your appropriate purpose.'

It was as if she faced a darkness in which was something very beautiful and wonderful as yet unimagined. The little pucker in her brows became more perceptible.

5

In the beginning of December Ann Veronica began to speculate privately upon the procedure of pawning. She had decided that she would begin with her pearl necklace. She spent a very disagreeable afternoon and evening – it was raining fast outside, and she had very unwisely left her soundest pair of boots in the boothole of her father's house in Morningside Park – thinking over the economic situation and planning a course of action. Her aunt had secretly sent on to Ann Veronica some new warm underclothing, a dozen pairs of stockings, and her last winter's jacket, but the dear lady had overlooked those boots.

These things illuminated her situation extremely. Finally she decided upon a step that had always seemed reasonable to her, but that hitherto she had, from motives too faint for her to formulate, refrained from taking. She resolved to go into the City to Ramage and ask for his advice. And next morning she attired herself with especial care and neatness, found his address in the directory at a post office, and went to him.

She had to wait some minutes in an outer office, wherein three young men of spirited costume and appearance regarded her with ill-concealed curiosity and admiration. Then Ramage appeared with effusion, and ushered her into his inner apartment. The three young men exchanged expressive glances.

The inner apartment was rather gracefully furnished with a thick, fine Turkish carpet, a good brass fender, a fine old bureau, and on the walls were engravings of two young girls' heads by Greuze, and of some modern picture of boys bathing in a sunlit pool.

'But this is a surprise!' said Ramage. 'This is wonderful. I've been feeling that you had vanished from my world. Have you been away from Morningside Park?'

'I'm not interrupting you?'

'You are. Splendidly. Business exists for such interruptions. There you are, the best clients' chair.'

Ann Veronica sat down, and Ramage's eager eyes feasted on her.

'I've been looking out for you,' he said. 'I confess it.'

She had not, she reflected, remembered how prominent his eyes were.

'I want some advice,' said Ann Veronica.

'Yes?'

'You remember once how we talked – at a gate on the Downs? We talked about how a girl might get an independent living.'

'Yes, yes.'

'Well, you see, something has happened at home.'

She paused.

'Nothing has happened to Mr Stanley?'

'I've fallen out with my father. It was about – a question of what I might do or might not do. He— In fact, he – he locked me in my room. Practically.'

Her breath left her for a moment.

'I *say*!' said Mr Ramage.

'I wanted to go to an art-student ball of which he disapproved.'

'And why shouldn't you?'

'I felt that sort of thing couldn't go on. So I packed up and came to London next day.'

'To a friend?'

'To lodgings – alone.'

'I say, you know, you have some pluck. You did it on your own?'

Ann Veronica smiled. 'Quite on my own,' she said.

'It's magnificent!' He leaned back and regarded her with his head a little on one side. 'By Jove!' he said, 'there is something direct about you. I wonder if I should have locked you up if I'd been your father. Luckily I'm not. And you started out forthwith to fight the world and be a citizen on your own basis?' He came forward again and folded his hands under him on his desk. 'How has the world taken it?' he asked. 'If I was the world I think I should have put down a crimson carpet, and asked you to say what you wanted, and generally walk over me. But the world didn't do that.'

'Not exactly.'

'It presented a large impenetrable back, and went on thinking about something else.'

'It offered from fifteen to two-and-twenty shillings a week – for drudgery.'

'The world has no sense of what is due to youth and courage. It never has had.'

'Yes,' said Ann Veronica. 'But the thing is, I want a job.'

'Exactly! And so you came along to me. And you see, I don't turn my back, and I am looking at you and thinking about you from top to toe.'

'And what do you think I ought to do?'

'Exactly!' He lifted a paper-weight and dabbed it gently down again. 'What ought you to do?'

'I've hunted up all sorts of things.'

'The point to note is that fundamentally you don't want particularly to do it.'

'I don't understand.'

'You want to be free and so forth, yes. But you don't particularly want to do the job that sets you free – for its own sake. I mean that it doesn't interest you in itself.'

'I suppose not.'

'That's one of our differences. We men are like children. We can get absorbed in play, in games, in the business we do. That's really why we do them sometimes rather well and get on. But women – women as a rule don't throw themselves into things like that. As a matter of fact it isn't their affair. And, as a natural consequence, they don't do so well, and they don't get on – and so the world doesn't pay them. They don't catch on to discursive interests, you see, because they are more serious, they are concentrated on the central reality of life, and a little impatient of its – its outer aspects. At least that, I think, is what makes a clever woman's independent career so much more difficult than a clever man's.'

'She doesn't develop a speciality.' Ann Veronica was doing her best to follow him.

'She has one, that's why. Her speciality is the central thing in life, it is life itself, the warmth of life, sex – and love.'

He pronounced this with an air of profound conviction and with his eyes on Ann Veronica's face. He had an air of having told her a deep, personal secret. She winced as he thrust the fact at her, was about to answer, and checked herself. She coloured faintly.

'That doesn't touch the question I asked you,' she said. 'It may be true, but it isn't quite what I have in mind.'

'Of course not,' said Ramage, as one who rouses himself from deep preoccupations. And he began to question her in a business-like way upon the steps she had taken and the inquiries she had made. He displayed none of the airy optimism of their previous talk over the downland gate. He was helpful but gravely dubious. 'You see,' he said, 'from my point of view you're grown up – you're as old as all the goddesses and the contemporary of any man alive. But from the – the economic point of view you're a very young and altogether inexperienced person.'

He returned to and developed that idea. 'You're still,' he said, 'in the educational years. From the point of view of most things in the world of employment which a woman can do reasonably well and earn a living by, you're unripe and half-educated. If you had taken your degree, for example.'

He spoke of secretarial work, but even there she would need to be able to do typing and shorthand. He made it more and more evident to her that her proper course was not to earn a salary but to accumulate equipment. 'You see,' he said, 'you are like an inaccessible gold mine. In all this sort of matter. You're splendid stuff, you know, but you've got nothing ready to sell. That's the flat business situation.'

He thought. Then he slapped his hand on his desk and looked up with the air of a man struck by a brilliant idea. 'Look here,' he said, protruding his eyes; 'why get anything to do at all just yet? Why, if you must be free, why not do the sensible thing? Make yourself worth a decent freedom. Go on with your studies at the Imperial College, for example, get a degree, and make yourself good value. Or become a thorough-going typist and stenographer and secretarial expert.'

'But I can't do that.'

'Why not?'

'You see, if I do go home my father objects to the college, and as for typing—'

'Don't go home.'

'Yes, but you forget; how am I to live?'

'Easily. Easily . . . Borrow. . . . From me.'

'I couldn't do that,' said Ann Veronica sharply.

'I see no reason why you shouldn't.'

'It's impossible.'

'As one friend to another. Men are always doing it, and if you set up to be a man—'

'No, it's absolutely out of the question, Mr Ramage.' Ann Veronica's face was hot.

Ramage pursed his rather loose lips and shrugged his shoulders, with his eyes fixed steadily upon her. 'Well, anyhow – I don't see the force of your objection, you know. That's my advice to you. Here I am. Consider you've got resources deposited with me. Perhaps at the first blush – it strikes you as odd. People are brought up to be so shy about money. As though it was indelicate. It's just a sort of shyness. But here I am to draw upon. Here I am as an alternative either to nasty work – or going home.'

'It's very kind of you—' began Ann Veronica.

'Not a bit. Just a friendly polite suggestion. I don't suggest any philanthropy. I shall charge you five per cent, you know, fair and square.'

Ann Veronica opened her lips quickly and did not speak. But the five per cent certainly did seem to improve the aspect of Ramage's suggestion.

'Well, anyhow, consider it open.' He dabbed with his paper-weight again, and spoke in an entirely indifferent tone. 'And now tell me, please, how you eloped from Morningside Park. How did you get your luggage out of the house? Wasn't it – wasn't it rather in some respects – rather a lark? It's one of my regrets for my lost youth. I never ran away from anywhere with anybody anywhen. And now— I suppose I should be considered too old. I don't feel it. . . . Didn't you feel rather *eventful* – in the train – coming up to Waterloo?'

6

Before Christmas Ann Veronica had gone to Ramage again and accepted this offer she had at first declined.

Many little things had contributed to that decision. The chief influence was her awakening sense of the need of money. She had been forced to buy herself that pair of boots and a walking-skirt, and the pearl necklace at the pawnbroker's had yielded very disappointingly. And also, she wanted to borrow that money. It did seem in so many ways exactly what Ramage said it was – the sensible thing to do. There it was – to be borrowed. It would put the whole adventure on a broader and better footing; it seemed, indeed, almost the only possible way in which she might emerge from her rebellion with anything like success. If only for the sake of her argument with her home, she wanted success. And why, after all, should she not borrow money from Ramage?

It was so true what he said; middle-class people *were* ridiculously squeamish about money. Why should they be?

She and Ramage were friends, very good friends. If she was in a position to help him she would help him; only it happened to be the other way round. He was in a position to help her. What was the objection?

She found it impossible to look her own diffidence in the face. So she went to Ramage and came to the point almost at once.

'Can you spare me forty pounds?' she said.

Mr Ramage controlled his expression and thought very quickly.

'Agreed,' he said, 'certainly,' and drew a cheque book towards him.

'It's best,' he said, 'to make it a good round sum.'

'I won't give you a cheque though— Yes, I will. I'll give you an uncrossed cheque, and then you can get it at the bank here, quite close by. . . . You'd better not have all the money on you; you had better open a small account in the post office and draw it out a fiver at a time. That won't involve references, as a bank account would – and all that sort of thing. The money will last longer, and – it won't bother you.'

He stood up rather close to her and looked into her eyes. He seemed to be trying to understand something very perplexing and elusive. 'It's jolly,' he said, 'to feel you have come to me. It's a sort of guarantee of confidence. Last time – you made me feel snubbed.'

He hesitated and went off at a tangent. 'There's no end of things I'd like to talk over with you. It's just upon my lunch time. Come and have lunch with me.'

Ann Veronica fenced for a moment. 'I don't want to take up your time.'

'We won't go to any of these City places. They're just all men, and no one is safe from scandal. But I know a little place where we'll get a little quiet talk.'

Ann Veronica for some indefinable reason did not want to lunch with him, a reason indeed so indefinable that she dismissed it, and Ramage went through the outer office with her, alert and attentive, to the vivid interest of the three clerks. The three clerks fought for the only window, and saw her whisked into a hansom. Their subsequent conversation is outside the scope of our story.

'Ritter's!' said Ramage to the driver, 'Dean Street.'

It was rare that Ann Veronica used hansoms, and to be in one was itself eventful and exhilarating. She liked the high, easy swing of the thing over its big wheels, the quick clatter-patter of the horse, the passage of the teeming streets. She admitted her pleasure to Ramage.

And Ritter's, too, was very amusing and foreign and discreet; a little rambling room with a number of small tables, with red electric light shades and flowers. It was an overcast day, albeit not foggy, and the electric light shades glowed warmly, and an Italian waiter with insufficient English took Ramage's orders, and waited with an appearance of affection. Ann Veronica thought the whole affair rather jolly. Ritter sold better food than most of his compatriots, and cooked it better, and Ramage, with a fine perception of a feminine palate, ordered *Vero Capri*. It was, Ann Veronica felt, as a sip or so of that remarkable blend warmed her blood, just the sort of thing that her aunt would not approve, to be lunching thus, *tête-à-tête* with a man; and yet at the same time it was a perfectly innocent as well as agreeable proceeding.

They talked across their meal in an easy and friendly manner about Ann Veronica's affairs. He was really very bright and clever, with a sort of conversational boldness that was just within the limits of permissible daring. She described the Goopes and the Fabians to him, and gave him a sketch of her landlady; and he talked in the most liberal and entertaining way of a modern young woman's outlook. He seemed to know a great deal about life. He gave glimpses of possibilities. He roused curiosities. He contrasted wonderfully with the empty showing-off of Teddy. His friendship seemed a thing worth having. . . .

But when she was thinking it over in her room that evening vague and baffling doubts came drifting across this conviction. She doubted how she stood towards him, and what the restrained gleam of his face might signify. She felt that perhaps, in her desire to play an adequate part in the conversation, she had talked rather more freely than she ought to have done, and given him a wrong impression of herself.

7

That was two days before Christmas Eve. The next morning came a compact letter from her father.

'MY DEAR DAUGHTER,' it ran, '*Here, on the verge of the season of forgiveness, I hold out a last hand to you in the hope of a reconciliation. I ask you, although it is not my place to ask you, to return home. This roof is still open to you. You will not be taunted if you return, and everything that can be done will be done to make you happy.*

'*Indeed, I must implore you to return. This adventure of yours has gone on altogether too long; it has become a serious distress to both your aunt and myself. We fail altogether to understand your motives in doing what you are doing, or, indeed, how you are managing to do it, or what you are managing on. If you will think only of one trifling aspect – the inconvenience it must be to us to explain your absence – I think you may begin to realize what it all means for us. I need hardly say that your aunt joins with me very heartily in this request.*

'*Please come home. You will not find me unreasonable with you.*
'*Your affectionate*
'FATHER.'

Ann Veronica sat over her fire with her father's note in her hand. 'Queer letters he writes,' she said. 'I suppose most people's letters are queer. Roof open – like a Noah's ark. I wonder if he really wants me to go home. It's odd how little I know of him, and of how he feels and what he feels.

'I wonder how he treated Gwen.'

Her mind drifted into a speculation about her sister. 'I ought to look up Gwen,' she said. 'I wonder what happened.'

Then she fell to thinking about her aunt. 'I would like to go home,' she cried, 'to please her. She has been a dear. Considering how little he lets her have.'

The truth prevailed. 'The unaccountable thing is that I wouldn't go home to please her. She is, in her way, a dear. One *ought* to want to please her. And I don't. I don't care. I can't even make myself care.'

Presently, as if for comparison with her father's letter, she got out Ramage's cheque from the box that contained her papers. For so far she had kept it uncashed. She had not even endorsed it.

'Suppose I chuck it,' she remarked, standing with the mauve slip in her hand – 'suppose I chuck it, and surrender and go home! Perhaps, after all, Roddy was right!

'Father keeps opening the door and shutting it, but a time will come—'

'I could still go home!'

She held Ramage's cheque as if to tear it across. 'No,' she said at last; 'I'm a human being – not a timid female. What could I do at home? The other's a crumple-up – just surrender. Funk! I'll see it out.'

Chapter VIII

Biology

I

January found Ann Veronica a student in the biological laboratory of the Central Imperial College that towers up from among the back streets in the angle between Euston Road and Great Portland Street. She was working very steadily at the advanced course in comparative anatomy, wonderfully relieved to have her mind engaged upon one methodically developing theme in the place of the discursive uncertainties of the previous two months, and doing her utmost to keep right in the back of her mind and out of sight the facts, firstly, that she had achieved this haven of satisfactory activity by incurring a debt to Ramage of forty pounds, and, secondly, that her present position was necessarily temporary and her outlook quite uncertain.

The biological laboratory had an atmosphere that was all its own. It was at the top of the building, and looked clear over a clustering mass of inferior buildings towards Regent's Park. It was long and narrow, a well-lit, well-ventilated, quiet gallery of small tables and sinks, pervaded by a thin smell of methylated spirit and of a mitigated and sterilized organic decay. Along the inner side was a wonderfully arranged series of displayed specimens that Russell himself had prepared. The supreme effect for Ann Veronica was its surpassing relevance; it made every other atmosphere she knew seem discursive and confused. The whole place and everything in it aimed at one thing – to illustrate, to elaborate, to criticize and illuminate, and make ever plainer and plainer the significance of animal and vegetable structure. It dealt from floor to ceiling and end to end with the theory of the forms of life; the very duster by the blackboard was there to do its share in that work, the very washers in the taps; the room was more simply concentrated in aim even than a church. To that, perhaps, a large part of its satisfyingness was due. Contrasted with the confused movements and presences of a Fabian meeting, or the inexplicable enthusiasm behind the suffrage demand, with the speeches that were partly egotistical displays, partly artful manoeuvres, and partly incoherent cries for unsoundly formulated ends, compared with the comings and goings of audiences and supporters that were like the eddy-driven drift of paper in the street, this long, quiet, methodical chamber shone like a star seen through clouds.

Day after day for a measured hour in the lecture theatre, with elaborate power and patience, Russell pieced together difficulty and suggestion, instance and counter-instance, in the elaborate construction of the family tree of life. And then the students went into the long laboratory and followed out these facts in almost living tissue with microscope and scalpel, probe and microtome, and the utmost of their skill and care, making now and then a raid into the compact museum of illustration next door, in which specimens and models and directions stood in disciplined ranks, under the direction of the demonstrator Capes. There was a couple of blackboards at each end of the aisle of tables, and at these Capes, with quick and nervous speech that contrasted vividly with Russell's slow, definitive articulation, directed the dissection and made illuminating comments on the structures under examination. Then he would come along the laboratory, sitting down by each student in turn, checking the work and discussing its difficulties, and answering questions arising out of Russell's lecture.

Ann Veronica had come to the Imperial College obsessed by the great figure of Russell, by the part he had played in the Darwinian controversies, and by the resolute effect of the grim-lipped, yellow, leonine face beneath the mane of silvery hair. Capes was rather a discovery. Capes was something super-added. Russell burnt like a beacon, but Capes illuminated by darting flashes and threw light, even if it was but momentary light, into a hundred corners that Russell left steadfastly in the shade.

Capes was an exceptionally fair man of two or three and thirty, so ruddily blond that it was a mercy he had escaped light eye-lashes, and with a minor but by no means contemptible reputation of his own. He talked at the blackboard in a pleasant, very slightly lisping voice with a curious spontaneity, and was sometimes very clumsy in his exposition, and sometimes very vivid. He dissected rather awkwardly and hurriedly, but, on the whole, effectively, and drew with an impatient directness that made up in significance what it lacked in precision. Across the blackboard the coloured chalks flew like flights of variously tinted rockets as diagram after diagram flickered into being.

There happened that year to be an unusual proportion of girls and women in the advanced laboratory, perhaps because the class as a whole was an exceptionally small one. It numbered nine, and four of these were women students. As a consequence of its small size, it was possible to get along with the work on a much easier and more colloquial footing than a larger class would have permitted. And a custom had grown up of a general tea at four o'clock, under the auspices of a Miss Garvice, a tall and graceful girl of distinguished intellectual incompetence, in whom the hostess instinct seemed to be abnormally developed.

Capes would come to these teas; he evidently liked to come, and he would appear in the doorway of the preparation room, a pleasing note of shyness in his manner, hovering for an invitation.

From the first, Ann Veronica found him an exceptionally interesting man. To begin with, he struck her as being the most variable person she had ever encountered. At times he was brilliant and masterful, talked around and over every one, and would have been domineering if he had not been extraordinarily kindly; at times he was almost monosyllabic, and defeated Miss Garvice's most skilful attempts to draw him out. Sometimes he was obviously irritable and uncomfortable and unfortunate in his efforts to seem at ease. And sometimes he overflowed with a peculiarly malignant wit that played, with devastating effect, upon any topics that had the courage to face it. Ann Veronica's experiences of men had been among more stable types – Teddy, who was always absurd; her father, who was always authoritative and sentimental; Manning, who was always Manning. And most of the others she had met had, she felt, the same steadfastness. Goopes, she was sure, was always high-browed and slow and Socratic. And Ramage, too – about Ramage there would always be that air of avidity, that air of knowledge and inquiry, the mixture of things in his talk that were rather good with things that were rather poor. But one could not count with any confidence upon Capes.

The five men students were a mixed company. There was a very white-faced youngster of eighteen who brushed back his hair exactly in Russell's manner, and was disposed to be uncomfortably silent when he was near her, and to whom she felt it was only Christian kindness to be consistently pleasant; and a lax young man of five and twenty in navy blue, who mingled Marx and Bebel* with the more orthodox gods of the biological pantheon.

There was a short, red-faced, resolute youth, who inherited an authoritative attitude upon bacteriology from his father; a Japanese student of unassuming manners who drew beautifully and had an imperfect knowledge of English; and a dark, unwashed Scotchman with complicated spectacles, who would come every morning as a sort of volunteer supplementary demonstrator, look very closely at her work and her, tell her that her dissections were 'fairish', or 'very fairish indeed', or 'high above the normal female standard', hover as if for some outbreak of passionate gratitude, and with admiring retrospects that made the faceted spectacles gleam like diamonds, return to his own place.

The women, Ann Veronica thought, were not quite so interesting as the men. There were two schoolmistresses, one of whom – Miss Klegg – might have been a first cousin to Miss Miniver, she had so many Miniver traits; there was a preoccupied girl whose name Ann Veronica never learned, but who worked remarkably well; and Miss Garvice, who began by attracting her very greatly – she moved so beautifully – and ended by giving her the impression that moving beautifully was the beginning and end of her being.

2

The next few weeks were a time of the very liveliest thought and growth for Ann Veronica. The crowding impressions of the previous weeks seemed to run together directly her mind left the chaotic search for employment and came into touch again with a coherent and systematic development of ideas. The advanced work at the Central Imperial College was in the closest touch with living interests and current controversies; it drew its illustrations and material from Russell's two great researches – upon the relation of the brachiopods to the echinodermata and upon the secondary and tertiary mammalian and pseudo-mammalian factors in the free larval forms of various marine organisms. Moreover, a vigorous fire of mutual criticism was going on now between the Imperial College and the Cambridge Mendelians and echoed in the lectures. From beginning to end it was first-hand stuff.

But the influence of the science radiated far beyond its own special field – beyond those beautiful but highly technical problems with which we do not propose for a moment to trouble the naturally terrified reader. Biology is an extraordinarily *digestive*

science. It throws out a number of broad experimental generalizations, and then sets out to bring into harmony or relation with
these an infinitely multifarious collection of phenomena. The little
streaks upon the germinating area of an egg, the nervous movements of an impatient horse, the trick of a calculating boy, the
senses of a fish, the fungus at the root of a garden flower, and the
slime upon a sea-wet rock – ten thousand such things bear their
witness and are illuminated. And not only did these tentacular
generalizations gather all the facts of natural history and comparative anatomy together, but they seemed always stretching out
further and further into a world of interests that lay altogether
outside their legitimate bounds.

It came to Ann Veronica one night after a long talk with Miss
Miniver, as a sudden remarkable thing, as a grotesque, novel
aspect, that this slowly elaborating biological scheme had something more than an academic interest for herself. And not only so,
but that it was, after all, a more systematic and particular method
of examining just the same questions that underlay the discussions
of the Fabian Society, the talk of the West Central Arts Club, the
chatter of the studios, and the deep, the bottomless discussions of
the simple-life homes. It was the same Bios whose nature and drift
and ways and methods and aspects engaged them all. And she,
she in her own person too, was this eternal Bios, beginning again
its recurrent journey to selection and multiplication and failure or
survival.

But this was but a momentary gleam of personal application,
and at this time she followed it up no further.

And now Ann Veronica's evenings were also becoming very
busy. She pursued her interest in the Socialist movement and in the
Suffragist agitation in the company of Miss Miniver. They went to
various central and local Fabian gatherings, and to a number of
suffrage meetings. Teddy Widgett hovered on the fringe of all these
gatherings, blinking at Ann Veronica and occasionally making a
wildly friendly dash at her, and carrying her and Miss Miniver off
to drink cocoa with a choice diversity of other youthful and
congenial Fabians after the meetings. Then Mr Manning loomed
up ever and again into her world, full of a futile solicitude, and
almost always declaring she was splendid, splendid, and wishing
he could talk things out with her. Teas he contributed to the
commissariat of Ann Veronica's campaign – quite a number of
teas. He would get her to come to tea with him, usually in a pleasant

tea room over a fruit shop in Tottenham Court Road, and he would discuss his own point of view and hint at a thousand devotions were she but to command him. And he would express various artistic sensibilities and aesthetic appreciations in carefully punctuated sentences and a large, clear voice. At Christmas he gave her a set of a small edition of Meredith's novels, very prettily bound in flexible leather, being guided in the choice of an author, as he intimated, rather by her preferences than his own.

There was something markedly and deliberately liberal-minded in his manner in all their encounters. He conveyed not only his sense of the extreme want of correctitude in their unsanctioned meetings, but also that, so far as he was concerned, this irregularity mattered not at all, that he had flung – and kept on flinging – such considerations to the wind.

And, in addition, she was now seeing and talking to Ramage almost weekly, on a theory which she took very gravely, that they were exceptionally friends. He would ask her to come to dinner with him in some little Italian or semi-Bohemian restaurant in the district towards Soho, or in one of the more stylish and magnificent establishments about Piccadilly Circus, and for the most part she did not care to refuse. Nor, indeed, did she want to refuse. These dinners, from their lavish display of ambiguous *hors-d' oeuvre* to their skimpy ices in dishes of frilled paper, with their Chianti flasks and Parmesan dishes and their polyglot waiters and polyglot clientele, were very funny and bright; and she really liked Ramage, and valued his help and advice. It was interesting to see how different and characteristic his mode of approach was to all sorts of questions that interested her, and it was amusing to discover this other side to the life of a Morningside Park inhabitant. She had thought that all Morningside Park householders came home before seven at the latest, as her father usually did. Ramage talked always about women or some woman's concern, and very much about Ann Veronica's own outlook upon life. He was always drawing contrasts between a woman's lot and a man's, and treating her as a wonderful new departure in this comparison. Ann Veronica liked their relationship all the more because it was an unusual one.

After these dinners they would have a walk, usually to the Thames Embankment to see the two sweeps of river on either side of Waterloo Bridge, and then they would part at Westminster Bridge, perhaps, and he would go on to Waterloo. Once he suggested they should go to a music hall and see a wonderful new dancer, but Ann Veronica did not feel she cared to see a new dancer. So, instead, they talked of dancing and what it might mean in a human life. Ann Veronica thought it was a spontaneous release of energy expressive of well-being, but Ramage thought that by dancing, men, and such birds and animals as dance, come to feel and think of their bodies.

This intercourse, which had been planned to warm Ann Veronica to a familiar affection with Ramage, was certainly warming Ramage to a constantly deepening interest in Ann Veronica. He felt that he was getting on with her very slowly indeed, but he did not see how he could get on faster. He had, he felt, to create certain ideas and vivify certain curiosities and feelings in her. Until that was done a certain experience of life assured him that a girl is a locked coldness against a man's approach. She had all the fascination of being absolutely perplexing in this respect. On the one hand, she seemed to think plainly and simply, and would talk serenely and freely about topics that most women have been trained either to avoid or conceal; and on the other she was unconscious, or else she had an air of being unconscious – that was the riddle – of all sorts of personal applications that almost any girl or woman, one might have thought, would have made. He was always doing his best to call her attention to the fact that he was a man of spirit and quality and experience, and she a young and beautiful woman, and that all sorts of constructions upon their relationship were possible, trusting her to go on from that to the idea that all sorts of relationships were possible. She responded with an unfaltering appearance of insensibility, and never as a young and beautiful woman conscious of sex; always in the character of an intelligent girl student.

His perception of her personal beauty deepened and quickened with each encounter. Every now and then her general presence became radiantly dazzling in his eyes; she would appear in the street coming towards him, a surprise, so fine and smiling and welcoming was she, so expanded and illuminated and living, in contrast with his mere expectation. Or he would find something – a wave in her hair, a little line in the contour of her brow or neck – that made an exquisite discovery.

He was beginning to think about her inordinately. He would sit in his inner office and compose conversations with her, penetrating, illuminating, and nearly conclusive – conversations that never proved to be of the slightest use at all with her when he met her face to face. And he began also at times to wake at night and think about her.

He thought of her and himself, and no longer in that vein of incidental adventure in which he had begun. He thought, too, of the fretful invalid who lay in the next room to his, whose money had created his business and made his position in the world.

'I've had most of the things I wanted,' said Ramage, in the stillness of the night.

3

For a time Ann Veronica's family had desisted from direct offers of a free pardon; they were evidently waiting for her resources to come to an end. Neither father, aunt, nor brothers made a sign, and then one afternoon in early February her aunt came up in a state between expostulation and dignified resentment, but obviously very anxious for Ann Veronica's welfare. 'I had a dream in the night,' she said. 'I saw you in a sort of sloping, slippery place, holding on by your hands and slipping. You seemed to me to be slipping and slipping, and your face was white. It was really most vivid, most vivid! You seemed to be slipping and just going to tumble and holding on. It made me wake up, and there I lay thinking of you, spending your nights up here all alone, and no one to look after you. I wondered what you could be doing and what might be happening to you. I said to myself at once: "Either this is a coincidence or the caper sauce." But I made sure it was you. I felt I *must* do something anyhow, and up I came just as soon as I could to see you.'

She had spoken rather rapidly. 'I can't help saying it,' she said, with the quality of her voice altering, 'but I do *not* think it is right for an unprotected girl to be in London alone as you are.'

'But I'm quite equal to taking care of myself, aunt.'

'It must be most uncomfortable here. It is most uncomfortable for every one concerned.'

She spoke with a certain asperity. She felt that Ann Veronica had duped her in that dream, and now that she had come up to London she might as well speak her mind.

'No Christmas dinner,' she said, 'or anything nice! One doesn't even know what you are doing.'

'I'm going on working for my degree.'

'Why couldn't you do that at home?'

'I'm working at the Imperial College. You see, aunt, it's the only possible way for me to get a good degree in my subjects, and father won't hear of it. There'd only be endless rows if I was at home. And how could I come home – when he locks me in rooms and all that?'

'I do wish this wasn't going on,' said Miss Stanley after a pause. 'I do wish you and your father could come to some agreement.'

Ann Veronica responded with conviction: 'I wish so too.'

'Can't we arrange something? Can't we make a sort of treaty?'

'He wouldn't keep it. He would get very cross one evening, and no one would dare to remind him of it.'

'How can you say such things?'

'But he would!'

'Still, it isn't your place to say so.'

'It prevents a treaty.'

'Couldn't *I* make a treaty?'

Ann Veronica thought, and could not see any possible treaty that would leave it open for her to have quasi-surreptitious dinners with Ramage or go on walking round the London squares discussing Socialism with Miss Miniver towards the small hours. She had tasted freedom now, and so far she had not felt the need of protection. Still, there certainly was something in the idea of a treaty.

'I don't see at all how you can be managing,' said Miss Stanley, and Ann Veronica hastened to reply: 'I do on very little.' Her mind went back to that treaty.

'And aren't there fees to pay at the Imperial College?' her aunt was saying – a disagreeable question.

'There were a few fees.'

'Then how have you managed?'

'Bother!' said Ann Veronica to herself, and tried not to look guilty. 'I was able to borrow the money.'

'Borrow the money! But who lent you the money?'

'A friend,' said Ann Veronica.

She felt herself getting into a corner. She sought hastily in her mind for a plausible answer to an obvious question that didn't come. Her aunt went off at a tangent. 'But, my dear Ann Veronica, you will be getting into debt!'

Ann Veronica at once, and with a feeling of immense relief,

took refuge in her dignity. 'I think, aunt,' she said, 'you might trust to my self-respect to keep me out of that.'

For the moment her aunt could not think of any reply to this counterstroke, and Ann Veronica followed up her advantage by a sudden inquiry about her abandoned boots.

But in the train going home her aunt reasoned it out.

'If she is borrowing money,' said Miss Stanley, 'she *must* be getting into debt. It's all nonsense. . . .'

4

It was by imperceptible degrees that Capes became important in Ann Veronica's thoughts. But then he began to take steps, and, at last, strides to something more and more like predominance. She began by being interested in his demonstrations and his biological theory, then she was attracted by his character, and then, in a manner, she fell in love with his mind.

One day they were at tea in the laboratory and a discussion sprang up about the question of women's suffrage. The movement was then in its earlier militant phases, and one of the women only, Miss Garvice, opposed it, though Ann Veronica was disposed to be lukewarm. But a man's opposition always inclined her to the suffrage side; she had a curious feeling of loyalty in seeing the more aggressive women through. Capes was irritatingly judicial in the matter, neither absurdly against, in which case one might have smashed him, nor hopefully unde-cided, but tepidly sceptical. Miss Klegg and the youngest girl made a vigorous attack on Miss Garvice, who had said she thought women lost something infinitely precious by mingling in the conflicts of life. The discussion wandered, and was punctu-ated with bread and butter. Capes was inclined to support Miss Klegg until Miss Garvice cornered him by quoting him against himself, and citing a recent paper in the *Nineteenth Century*, in which, following Atkinson,* he had made a vigorous and dam-aging attack on Lester Ward's* case for the primitive matriar-chate and the predominant importance of the female throughout the animal kingdom.

Ann Veronica was not aware of this literary side of her teacher; she had a little tinge of annoyance at Miss Garvice's advantage. Afterwards she hunted up the article in question, and it seemed to her quite delightfully written and argued. Capes had the gift of easy, unaffected writing, coupled with very clear and logical thinking, and to follow his written thought gave her the sensation of cutting things with a perfectly new, perfectly sharp knife. She found herself anxious to read more of him, and the next Wednesday she went to the British Museum and hunted first among the half-crown magazines for his essays and then through various scientific quarterlies for his research papers. The ordinary research paper, when it is not extravagant theorizing, is apt to be rather sawdusty in texture, and Ann Veronica was delighted to find the same easy and confident luminosity that distinguished his work for the general reader. She returned to these latter, and at the back of her mind, as she looked them over again, was a very distinct resolve to quote them after the manner of Miss Garvice at the very first opportunity.

When she got home to her lodgings that evening she reflected with something like surprise upon her half-day's employment, and decided that it showed nothing more nor less than that Capes was a really very interesting person indeed.

And then she fell into a musing about Capes. She wondered why he was so distinctive, so unlike other men, and it never occurred to her for some time that this might be because she was falling in love with him.

5

Yet Ann Veronica was thinking a very great deal about love. A dozen shynesses and intellectual barriers were being outflanked or broken down in her mind. All the influences about her worked with her own predisposition and against all the traditions of her home and upbringing to deal with the facts of life in an unabashed manner. Ramage, by a hundred skilful hints, had led her to realize that the problem of her own life was inseparably associated with, and indeed only one special case of, the problems of any woman's life, and that the problem of a woman's life is love.

'A young man comes into life asking how best he may place himself,' Ramage had said; 'a woman comes into life thinking instinctively how best she may give herself.'

She noted that as a good saying, and it germinated and spread tentacles of explanation through her brain. The biological laboratory, perpetually viewing life as pairing and breeding and selection, and again pairing and breeding, seemed only a translated generalization of that assertion. And all the talk of the Miniver people and the Widgett people seemed always to be like a ship in adverse weather on the lee shore of love. 'For seven years,' said Ann Veronica, 'I have been trying to keep myself from thinking about love. . . .

'I have been training myself to look askance at beautiful things.'

She gave herself permission now to look at this squarely. She made herself a private declaration of liberty. 'This is mere nonsense, mere tongue-tied fear!' she said. 'This is the slavery of the veiled life. I might as well be at Morningside Park. This business of love is the supreme affair in life, it is the woman's one event and crisis that makes up for all her other restrictions, and I cower – as we all cower – with a blushing and paralysed mind until it overtakes me! . . .

'I'll be hanged if I do.'

But she could not talk freely about love, she found, for all that manumission.

Ramage seemed always fencing about the forbidden topic, probing for openings, and she wondered why she did not give him them. But something instinctive prevented that, and with the finest resolve not to be 'silly' and prudish she found that whenever he became at all bold in this matter she became severely scientific and impersonal, almost entomological indeed, in her method; she killed every remark as he made it and pinned it out for examination. In the biological laboratory that was their invincible tone. But she disapproved more and more of her own mental austerity. Here was an experienced man of the world, her friend, who evidently took a great interest in this supreme topic and was willing to give her the benefit of his experiences! Why should not she be at her ease with him? Why should not she know things? It is hard enough anyhow for a human being to learn, she decided, but it is a dozen times more difficult than it need be because of all this locking of the lips and thoughts.

She contrived to break down the barriers of shyness at last in one direction, and talked one night of love and the facts of love with Miss Miniver.

But Miss Miniver was highly unsatisfactory. She repeated phrases of Mrs Goopes's: 'Advanced people,' she said, with an air of great elucidation, 'tend to *generalize* love. "He prayeth best who loveth best – all things both great and small." For my own part I go about loving.'

'Yes, but men,' said Ann Veronica, plunging; 'don't you want the love of men?'

For some seconds they remained silent, both shocked by this question.

Miss Miniver looked over her glasses at her friend almost balefully. 'No!' she said at last, with something in her voice that reminded Ann Veronica of a sprung tennis racket.

'I've been through all that,' she went on after a pause.

She spoke slowly. 'I have never yet met a man whose intellect I could respect.'

Ann Veronica looked at her thoughtfully for a moment, and decided to persist on principle.

'But if you had?' she said.

'I can't imagine it,' said Miss Miniver. 'And think, think' – her voice sank – 'of the horrible coarseness!'

'What coarseness?' said Ann Veronica.

'My dear Vee!' Her voice became very low. 'Don't you know?'

'Oh! I know—'

'Well—' Her face was an unaccustomed pink.

Ann Veronica ignored her friend's confusion.

'Don't we all rather humbug about the coarseness? All we women, I mean,' said she. She decided to go on, after a momentary halt. 'We pretend bodies are ugly. Really they are the most beautiful things in the world. We pretend we never think of everything that makes us what we are.'

'No,' cried Miss Miniver almost vehemently. 'You are wrong! I did not think you thought such things. Bodies! Bodies! Horrible things! We are souls. Love lives on a higher plane. We are not animals. If ever I did meet a man I could love, I should love him' – her voice dropped again – 'Platonically.'

She made her glasses glint. 'Absolutely Platonically,' she said. 'Soul to soul.'

She turned her face to the fire, gripped her hands upon her elbows, and drew her thin shoulders together in a shrug. 'Ugh!' she said.

Ann Veronica watched her and wondered about her.

'We do not want the men,' said Miss Miniver, 'we do not want them, with their sneers and loud laughter. Empty, silly, coarse brutes. Brutes! They are the brute still with us! Science some day may teach us a way to do without them. It is only the women matter. It is not every sort of creature needs – these males. Some have no males.'

'There's green-fly,' admitted Ann Veronica. 'And even then—'

The conversation hung for a thoughtful moment.

Ann Veronica readjusted her chin on her hand. 'I wonder which of us is right,' she said. 'I haven't a scrap – of this sort of aversion.'

'Tolstoy is so good about this,' said Miss Miniver, regardless of her friend's attitude. 'He sees through it all. The Higher Life and the Lower. He sees men all defiled by coarse thoughts, coarse ways of living, cruelties. Simply because they are hardened by – by bestiality, and poisoned by the juices of meat slain in anger and fermented drinks – fancy! drinks that have been swarmed in by thousands and thousands of horrible little bacteria!'

'It's yeast,' said Ann Veronica – 'a vegetable.'

'It's all the same,' said Miss Miniver. 'And then they are swollen up and inflamed and drunken with matter. They are blinded to all fine and subtle things; they look at life with bloodshot eyes and dilated nostrils. They are arbitrary and unjust and dogmatic and brutish and lustful.'

'But do you really think men's minds are altered by the food they eat?'

'I know it,' said Miss Miniver. '*Experte credo*. When I am leading a true life, a pure and simple life, free of all stimulants and excitements, I think – I think – oh! with *pellucid* clearness; but if I so much as take a mouthful of meat – or anything – the mirror is all blurred.'

6

Then, arising she knew not how, like a new-born appetite, came a craving in Ann Veronica for the sight and sound of beauty.

It was as if her aesthetic sense had become inflamed. Her mind turned and accused itself of having been cold and hard. She began to look for beauty and discovered it in unexpected aspects and places. Hitherto she had seen it chiefly in pictures and other works of art, incidentally, and as a thing taken out of life. Now the sense of beauty was spreading to a multitude of hitherto unsuspected aspects of the world about her.

The thought of beauty became an obsession. It interwove with her biological work. She found herself asking more and more curiously: 'Why, on the principle of the survival of the fittest, have I any sense of beauty at all?' That enabled her to go on thinking about beauty when it seemed to her right that she should be thinking about biology.

She was very greatly exercised by the two systems of values – the two series of explanations that her comparative anatomy on the one hand and her sense of beauty on the other, set going in her thoughts. She could not make up her mind which was the finer, more elemental thing, which gave its values to the other. Was it that the struggle of things to survive produced as a sort of necessary by-product these intense preferences and appreciations, or was it that some mystical outer thing, some great force, drove life beautyward, even in spite of expediency, regardless of survival value and all the manifest discretions of life? She went to Capes with that riddle and put it to him very carefully and clearly, and he talked well – he always talked at some length when she took a difficulty to him – and sent her to a various literature upon the markings of butterflies, the incomprehensible elaboration and splendour of birds' of paradise and humming-birds' plumes, the patterning of tigers, and a leopard's spots. He was interesting and inconclusive, and the original papers to which he referred her discursively were at best only suggestive. Afterwards, one afternoon, he hovered about her, and came and sat beside her and talked of beauty and the riddle of beauty for some time. He displayed a quite unprofessional vein of mysticism in the matter. He contrasted with Russell, whose intellectual methods were, so to speak, sceptically dogmatic. Their talk drifted to the beauty of music, and they took that up again at tea time.

But as the students sat about Miss Garvice's tea pot and drank tea or smoked cigarettes, the talk got away from Capes. The Scotchman informed Ann Veronica that your view of beauty necessarily depended on your metaphysical premises, and the young man with the Russell-like hair became anxious to distinguish himself by telling the Japanese student that western art was symmetrical and eastern art asymmetrical, and that among the higher organisms the tendency was towards an external symmetry veiling an internal want of balance. Ann Veronica decided she would have to go on with Capes another day, and, looking up, discovered him sitting on a stool with his hands in his pockets and his head a little on one side, regarding her with a thoughtful expression. She met his eye for a moment in curious surprise.

He turned his eyes and stared at Miss Garvice like one who wakes from a reverie, and then got up and strolled down the laboratory towards his refuge, the preparation room.

i

Then one day a little thing happened that clothed itself in significance.

She had been working upon a ribbon of microtome sections of the developing salamander, and he came to see what she had made of them. She stood up and he sat down at the microscope, and for a time he was busy scrutinizing one section after another. She looked down at him and saw that the sunlight was gleaming from his cheeks, and that all over his cheeks was a fine golden down of delicate hairs. And at the sight something leapt within her. Something changed for her.

She became aware of his presence as she had never been aware of any human being in her life before. She became aware of the modelling of his ear, of the muscles of his neck and the textures of the hair that came off his brow, the soft minute curve of eyelid that she could just see beyond his brow; she perceived all these familiar objects as though they were acutely beautiful things. They *were*, she realized, acutely beautiful things. Her senses followed the shoulders under his coat, down to where his flexible, sensitive-looking hand rested lightly upon the table. She felt him as something solid and strong and trustworthy beyond measure. The perception of him flooded her being.

He got up. 'Here's something rather good,' he said, and with a start and an effort she took his place at the microscope, while he stood beside her and almost leaning over her.

She found she was trembling at his nearness and full of a thrilling dread that he might touch her. She pulled herself together and put her eye to the eye-piece.

'You see the pointer?' he asked.

'I see the pointer,' she said.

'It's like this,' he said, and dragged a stool beside her and sat down with his elbow four inches from hers and made a sketch. Then he got up and left her.

She had a feeling at his departure as of an immense cavity, of something enormously gone; she could not tell whether it was infinite regret or infinite relief. . . .

But now Ann Veronica knew what was the matter with her.

8

And as she sat on her bed that night, musing and half-undressed, she began to run one hand down her arm and scrutinize the soft flow of muscle under her skin. She thought of the marvellous beauty of skin, and all the delightfulness of living texture. On the back of her arm she found the faintest down of hair in the world.

'Etherealized monkey,' she said. She held out her arm straight before her, and turned her hand this way and that.

'Why should one pretend?' she whispered. 'Why should one pretend?

'Think of all the beauty in the world that is covered up and overlaid.'

She glanced shyly at the mirror above her dressing-table, and then about her at the furniture, as though it might penetrate to the thoughts that peeped in her mind.

'I wonder,' said Ann Veronica at last, 'if I *am* beautiful? I wonder if I shall ever shine like a light, like a translucent goddess?—

'I wonder—

'I suppose girls and women have prayed for this, have come to this— In Babylon, in Nineveh.

'Why shouldn't one face the facts of oneself?'

She stood up. She posed herself before her mirror and surveyed herself with gravely thoughtful, gravely critical, and yet admiring eyes. 'And after all, I am just one common person!'

She watched the throb of the arteries in the stem of her neck, and put her hand at last gently and almost timidly to where her heart beat beneath her breast.

9

The realization that she was in love flooded Ann Veronica's mind, and altered the quality of all its topics.

She began to think persistently of Capes, and it seemed to her now that for some weeks at least she must have been thinking persistently of him unawares. She was surprised to find how stored her mind was with impressions and memories of him, how vividly she remembered his gestures and little things that he had said. It occurred to her that it was absurd and wrong to be so continuously thinking of one engrossing topic, and she made a strenuous effort to force her mind to other questions.

But it was extraordinary what seemingly irrelevant things could restore her to the thought of Capes again. And when she went to sleep, then always Capes became the novel and wonderful guest of her dreams.

For a time it really seemed all-sufficient to her that she should love. That Capes should love her seemed beyond the compass of her imagination. Indeed, she did not want to think of him as loving. She wanted to think of him as her beloved person, to be near him and watch him, to have him going about, doing this and that, saying this and that, unconscious of her, while she too remained unconscious of herself. To think of him as loving her would make all that different. Then he would turn his face to her, and she would have to think of herself in his eyes. She would become defensive – what she did would be the thing that mattered. He would require things of her, and she would be passionately concerned to meet his requirements. Loving was better than that. Loving was self-forget-fulness, pure delighting in another human being. She felt that with Capes near to her she would be content always to go on loving.

She went next day to the schools, and her world seemed all made of happiness just worked up roughly into shapes and occasions and duties. She found she could do her microscope work all the better for being in love. She winced when first she heard the preparation room door open and Capes came down the laboratory; but when at last he reached her she was self-possessed. She put a stool for him at a little distance from her own, and after he had seen the day's work he hesitated and then plunged into a resumption of their discussion about beauty.

'I think,' he said, 'I was a little too mystical about beauty the other day.'

'I like the mystical way,' she said.

'Our business here is the right way. I've been thinking, you know— I'm not sure that primarily the perception of beauty isn't just intensity of feeling free from pain; intensity of perception without any tissue destruction.'

'I like the mystical way better,' said Ann Veronica, and thought. 'A number of beautiful things are not intense.'

'But delicacy, for example, may be intensely perceived.'

'But why is one face beautiful and another not?' objected Ann Veronica; 'on your theory any two faces side by side in the sunlight ought to be equally beautiful. One must get them with exactly the same intensity.'

He did not agree with that. 'I don't mean simply intensity of sensation. I said intensity of perception. You may perceive harmony, proportion, rhythm, intensely. They are things faint and slight in themselves, as physical facts, but they are like the detonator of a bomb: they let loose the explosive. There's the internal factor as well as the external. . . . I don't know if I express myself clearly. I mean that the point is that vividness of perception is the essential factor of beauty; but, of course, vividness may be created by a whisper.'

'That brings us back,' said Ann Veronica, 'to the mystery. Why should some things and not others open the deeps?'

'Well, that might, after all, be an outcome of selection – like the preference for blue flowers, which are not nearly so bright as yellow, of some insects.'

'That doesn't explain sunsets.'

'Not quite so easily as it explains an insect alighting on coloured paper. But perhaps if people didn't like clear, bright, healthy eyes – which is biologically understandable – they couldn't like precious stones. One thing may be a necessary collateral of the others. And, after all, a fine clear sky of bright colours is the signal to come out of hiding and rejoice and go on with life.'

'H'm!' said Ann Veronica, and shook her head.

Capes smiled cheerfully, with his eyes meeting hers. 'I throw it out in passing,' he said. 'What I am after is that beauty isn't a special inserted sort of thing; that's my idea. It's just life, pure life, life nascent, running clear and strong.'

He stood up to go on to the next student.

'There's morbid beauty,' said Ann Veronica.

'I wonder if there is!' said Capes, and paused, and then bent down over the boy who wore his hair like Russell.

Ann Veronica surveyed his sloping back for a moment, and then drew her microscope towards her. Then for a time she sat very still. She felt that she had passed a difficult corner, and that now she could go on talking with him again, just as she had been used to do before she understood what was the matter with her. . . .

She had one idea, she found, very clear in her mind – that she would get a research scholarship, and so contrive another year in the laboratory.

'Now I see what everything means,' said Ann Veronica to herself; and it really felt for some days as though the secret of the universe, that had been wrapped and hidden from her so obstinately, was at last altogether displayed.

Chapter IX

Discords

One afternoon, soon after Ann Veronica's great discovery, a telegram came into the laboratory for her. It ran:

Bored	and	nothing	to	do
will	you	dine	with	me
to-night	somewhere	and	talk	I
shall	be	grateful	Ramage	

Ann Veronica was rather pleased by this. She had not seen Ramage for ten or eleven days, and she was quite ready for a gossip with him. And now her mind was so full of the thought that she was in love – in love! – that marvellous state! that I really believe she had some dim idea of talking to him about it. At any rate, it would be good to hear him saying the sort of things he did – perhaps now she would grasp them better – with this world-shaking secret brandishing itself about inside her head within a yard of him.

She was sorry to find Ramage a little disposed to be melancholy. 'I have made over seven hundred pounds in the last week,' he said.

'That's exhilarating,' said Ann Veronica.

'Not a bit of it,' he said; 'it's only a score in a game.'

'It's a score you can buy all sorts of things with.'

'Nothing that one wants.'

He turned to the waiter, who held a wine card. 'Nothing can cheer me,' he said, 'except champagne.' He meditated. 'This,' he said, and then: 'No! Is this sweeter? Very well.

'Everything goes well with me,' he said, folding his arms under him and regarding Ann Veronica with the slightly projecting eyes wide open. 'And I'm not happy. I believe I'm in love.'

He leant back for his soup.

Presently he resumed: 'I believe I must be in love.'

'You can't be that,' said Ann Veronica wisely.

'How do you know?'

'Well, it isn't exactly a depressing state, is it?'

'*You* don't know.'

'One has theories,' said Ann Veronica radiantly.

'Oh, theories! Being in love is a fact.'

'It ought to make one happy.'

'It's an unrest – a longing – What's that?' The waiter had intervened. 'Parmesan – take it away!'

He glanced at Ann Veronica's face, and it seemed to him that she really was exceptionally radiant. He wondered why she thought love made people happy, and began to talk of the smilax and pinks that adorned the table. He filled her glass with champagne. 'You *must*,' he said, 'because of my depression.'

They were eating quails when they returned to the topic of love. 'What made you think,' he said abruptly, with the gleam of avidity in his face, 'that love makes people happy?'

'I know it must.'

'But how?'

He was, she thought, a little too insistent. 'Women know these things by instinct,' she answered.

'I wonder,' he said, 'if women do know things by instinct? I have my doubts about feminine instinct. It's one of our conventional superstitions. A woman is supposed to know when a man is in love with her. Do you think she does?'

Ann Veronica picked among her salad with a judicial expression of face. 'I think she would,' she decided.

'Ah!' said Ramage impressively.

Ann Veronica looked up at him and found him regarding her with eyes that were almost woebegone, and into which, indeed, he was trying to throw much more expression than they could carry. There was a little pause between them, full for Ann Veronica of rapid elusive suspicions and intimations.

'Perhaps one talks nonsense about a woman's instinct,' she said. 'It's a way of avoiding explanations. And girls and women, perhaps, are different. I don't know. I don't suppose a girl can tell if a man is in love with her or not in love with her.' Her mind went off to Capes. Her thoughts took words for themselves. 'She can't. I suppose it depends on her own state of mind. If one wants a thing very much, perhaps, one is inclined to think one can't have it. I suppose if one were to love someone, one would feel doubtful. And if one were to love someone very much, it's just so that one would be blindest, just when one wanted most to see.'

She stopped abruptly, afraid that Ramage might be able to infer Capes from the things she had said, and indeed his face was very eager.

'Yes?' he said.

Ann Veronica blushed. 'That's all,' she said. 'I'm afraid I'm a little confused about these things.'

Ramage looked at her, and then fell into deep reflection as the waiter came to paragraph their talk again.

'Have you ever been to the opera, Ann Veronica?' said Ramage.

'Once or twice.'

'Shall we go now?'

'I think I would like to listen to music. What is there?'

'*Tristan.*'

'I've never heard *Tristan and Isolde.*'

'That settles it. We'll go. There's sure to be a place somewhere.'

'It's rather jolly of you,' said Ann Veronica.

'It's jolly of you to come,' said Ramage.

So presently they got into a hansom together, and Ann Veronica sat back feeling very luxurious and pleasant, and looked at the lights and stir and misty glitter of the street traffic from under slightly drooping eyelids, while Ramage sat closer to her than he need have done, and glanced ever and again at her face, and made to speak and said nothing. And when they got to Covent Garden Ramage secured one of the little upper boxes, and they came into it as the overture began.

Ann Veronica took off her jacket and sat down in the corner chair, and leant forward to look into the great hazy warm brown cavity of the house, and Ramage placed his chair to sit beside her and near her, facing the stage. The music took hold of her slowly as her eyes wandered from the indistinct still ranks of the audience to the little busy orchestra with its quivering violins, its methodical movements of brown and silver instruments, its brightly lit scores and shaded lights. She had never been to the opera before except as one of a congested mass of people in the cheaper seats, and with backs and heads and women's hats for the frame of the spectacle; there was by contrast a fine large sense of space and ease in her present position. The curtain rose out of the concluding bars of the overture and revealed Isolde on the prow of the barbaric ship. The voice of the young seaman came floating down from the masthead, and the story of the immortal lovers had begun. She knew the story only imperfectly, and followed it now with a passionate and deepening interest. The splendid voices sang on from phase to phase of love's unfolding, the ship drove across the sea to the beating rhythm of the rowers. The lovers broke into passionate knowledge of themselves and each other, and then, a jarring intervention, came King Mark amidst the shouts of the sailormen, and stood beside them.

The curtain came festooning slowly down, the music ceased, the lights in the auditorium glowed out, and Ann Veronica woke out of her confused dream of involuntary and commanding love in a glory of sound and colours to discover that Ramage was sitting close beside her with one hand resting lightly on her waist. She made a quick movement, and the hand fell away.

'By God! Ann Veronica,' he said, sighing deeply. 'This stirs one.'

She sat quite still looking at him.

'I wish you and I had drunk that love potion,' he said.

She found no ready reply to that, and he went on: 'This music is the food of love. It makes me desire life beyond measure. Life! Life and love? It makes me want to be always young, always strong, always devoting my life – and dying splendidly.'

'It is very beautiful,' said Ann Veronica in a low tone.

They said no more for a moment, and each was now acutely aware of the other. Ann Veronica was excited and puzzled, with a sense of a strange and disconcerting new light breaking over her relations with Ramage. She had never thought of him at all in that way before. It did not shock her; it amazed her, interested her beyond measure. But also this must not go on. She felt he was going to say something more – something still more personal and intimate. She was curious, and at the same time clearly resolved she must not hear it. She felt she must get him talking upon some impersonal theme at any cost. She snatched about in her mind. 'What is the exact force of a *motif?*' she asked at random. 'Before I heard much Wagnerian music I heard enthusiastic descriptions of it from a mistress I didn't like at school. She gave me an impression of a sort of patched quilt; little bits of patterned stuff coming up again and again.'

She stopped with an air of interrogation.

Ramage looked at her for a long and discriminating interval without speaking. He seemed to be hesitating between two courses of action. 'I don't know much about the technique of music,' he said at last, with his eyes upon her. 'It's a matter of feeling with me.'

He contradicted himself by plunging into an exposition of *motifs*. By a tacit agreement they ignored the significant thing between them, ignored the slipping away of the ground on which they had stood together hitherto. . . .

All through the love music of the second act, until the hunting horns of Mark break in upon the dream, Ann Veronica's consciousness was flooded with the perception of a man close beside her, preparing some new thing to say to her, preparing, perhaps, to touch her, stretching hungry invisible tentacles about her. She tried to think what she should do in this eventuality or that. Her mind had been and was full of the thought of Capes, a huge generalized Capes-lover. And in some incomprehensible way Ramage was confused with Capes; she had a grotesque disposition to persuade herself that this was really Capes who surrounded her, as it were, with wings of desire. The fact that it was her trusted friend making illicit love to her remained, in spite of all her effort, an insignificant thing in her mind. The music confused and distracted her, and made her struggle against a feeling of intoxication. Her head swam. That was the inconvenience of it; her head was swimming. The music throbbed into the warnings that preceded the king's irruption.

Abruptly he gripped her wrist. 'I love you, Ann Veronica. I love you – with all my heart and soul.'

She put her face closer to his. She felt the warm nearness of his. '*Don't!*' she said, and wrenched her wrist from his retaining hand.

'My God! Ann Veronica,' he said, struggling to keep his hold upon her; 'my God! Tell me – tell me now – tell me you love me!'

His expression was as it were rapaciously furtive. She answered in whispers, for there was the white arm of a woman in the next box peeping beyond the partition within a yard of him.

'My hand! This isn't the place!'

He released her hand and talked in eager undertones against an auditory background of urgency and distress.

'Ann Veronica,' he said. 'I tell you this is love. I love the soles of your feet. I love your very breath. I have tried not to tell you – tried to be simply your friend. It is no good. I want you. I worship you.

I would do anything – I would give anything to make you mine. . . . Do you hear me? Do you hear what I am saying? . . . Love!'

He held her arm and abandoned it again at her quick defensive movement. For a long time neither spoke again.

She sat drawn together in her chair in the corner of the box, at a loss what to say or do – afraid, curious, perplexed. It seemed to her that it was her duty to get up and clamour to go home to her room, to protest against his advances as an insult. But she did not in the least want to do that. These sweeping dignities were not within the compass of her will; she remembered she liked Ramage, and owed things to him, and she was interested – she was profoundly interested. He was in love with her. She tried to grasp all the welter of values in the situation simultaneously, and draw some conclusion from their disorder.

He began to talk again in quick undertones that she could not clearly hear.

'I have loved you,' he was saying, 'ever since you sat on that gate and talked. I have always loved you. I don't care what divides us. I don't care what else there is in the world. I want you beyond measure or reckoning. . . .'

His voice rose and fell amidst the music and the singing of Tristan and King Mark, like a voice heard in a badly connected telephone. She stared at his pleading face.

She turned to the stage, and Tristan was wounded in Kurvenal's arms, with Isolde at his feet, and King Mark, the incarnation of masculine force and obligation, the masculine creditor of love and beauty, stood over him, and the second climax was ending in wreaths and reek of melodies; and then the curtain was coming down in a series of short rushes, the music had ended, and the people were stirring and breaking out into applause, and the lights of the auditorium were resuming. The lighting up pierced the obscurity of the box, and Ramage stopped his urgent flow of words abruptly and sat back. This helped to restore Ann Veronica's self-command.

She turned her eyes to him again, and saw her late friend and pleasant and trusted companion, who had seen fit suddenly to change into a lover, babbling interesting inacceptable things. He looked eager and flushed and troubled. His eyes caught at hers with passionate inquiries. 'Tell me,' he said; 'speak to me.' She realized it was possible to be sorry for him – acutely sorry for the situation. Of course this thing was absolutely impossible. But she was disturbed, mysteriously disturbed. She remembered abruptly that she was really living upon his money. She leaned forward and addressed him.

'Mr Ramage,' she said, 'please don't talk like this.'

He made to speak and did not.

'I don't want you to do it, to go on talking to me. I don't want to hear you. If I had known that you had meant to talk like this I wouldn't have come here.'

'But how can I help it? How can I keep silence?'

'Please!' she insisted. 'Please not now.'

'I *must* talk with you. I must say what I have to say!'

'But not now – not here.'

'It came,' he said. 'I never planned it— And now I have begun—'

She felt acutely that he was entitled to explanations, and as acutely that explanations were impossible that night. She wanted to think.

'Mr Ramage,' she said, 'I can't— Not now. Will you please— Not now, or I must go.'

He stared at her, trying to guess at the mystery of her thoughts.

'You don't want to go?'

'No. But I must – I ought—'

'I *must* talk about this. Indeed I must.'

'Not now.'

'But I love you. I love you – unendurably.'

'Then don't talk to me now. I don't want you to talk to me now. There is a place— This isn't the place. You have misunderstood. I can't explain—'

They regarded one another, each blinded to the other. 'Forgive me,' he decided to say at last, and his voice had a little quiver of emotion, and he laid his hand on hers upon her knee. 'I am the most foolish of men. I was stupid – stupid and impulsive beyond measure to burst upon you in this way. I – I am a love-sick idiot, and not accountable for my actions. Will you forgive me – if I say no more?'

She looked at him with perplexed, earnest eyes.

'Pretend,' he said, 'that all I have said hasn't been said. And let us go on with our evening. Why not? Imagine I've had a fit of hysteria – and that I've come round.'

'Yes,' she said, and abruptly she liked him enormously. She felt this was the sensible way out of this oddly sinister situation.

He still watched her and questioned her.

'And let *us* have a talk about this – some other time. Somewhere, where we can talk without interruption. Will you?'

She thought, and it seemed to him she had never looked so self-disciplined and deliberate and beautiful. 'Yes,' she said, 'that is what we ought to do.' But now she doubted again of the quality of the armistice they had just made.

He had a wild impulse to shout. 'Agreed,' he said with queer exaltation, and his grip tightened on her hand. 'And to-night we are friends?'

'We are friends,' said Ann Veronica, and drew her hand quickly away from him.

'To-night we are as we have always been. Except that this music we have been swimming in is divine. While I have been pestering you, have you heard it? At least, you heard the first act. And all the third act is love-sick music. Tristan dying and Isolde coming to crown his death. Wagner had just been in love when he wrote it all. It begins with that queer cor anglais solo. Now I shall never hear it but what this evening will come pouring back over me.'

The lights sank, the prelude to the third act was beginning, the music rose and fell in crowded intimations of lovers separated – lovers separated with scars and memories between them, and the curtain went reefing up to display Tristan lying wounded on his couch and the shepherd crouching with his pipe.

2

They had their explanations the next evening, but they were explanations in quite other terms than Ann Veronica had anticipated, quite other and much more startling and illuminating terms. Ramage came for her at her lodgings, and she met him graciously and kindly as a queen who knows she must needs give sorrow to a faithful liege. She was unusually soft and gentle in her manner to him. He was wearing a new silk hat, with a slightly more generous brim than its predecessor, and it suited his type of face, robbed his dark eyes a little of their aggressiveness, and gave him a solid and dignified and benevolent air. A faint anticipation of triumph showed in his manner and a subdued excitement.

'We'll go to a place where we can have a private room,' he said. 'Then – then we can talk things out.'

So they went this time to the Rococo, in Germain Street, and upstairs to a landing upon which stood a bald-headed waiter with whiskers like a French admiral and discretion beyond all limits in his manner. He seemed to have expected them. He ushered them with an amiable flat hand into a minute apartment with a little gas stove, a silk crimson-covered sofa, and a bright little table, gay with napery and hot-house flowers.

'Odd little room,' said Ann Veronica, dimly apprehending that obtrusive sofa.

'One can talk without undertones, so to speak,' said Ramage. 'It's – private.' He stood looking at the preparations before them with an unusual preoccupation of manner, then roused himself to take her jacket, a little awkwardly, and hand it to the waiter, who hung it in the corner of the room. It appeared he had already ordered dinner and wine, and the whiskered waiter waved in his subordinate with the soup forthwith.

'I'm going to talk of indifferent themes,' said Ramage, a little fussily, 'until these interruptions of the service are over. Then – then we shall be together. . . . How did you like *Tristan?*'

Ann Veronica paused the fraction of a second before her reply came.

'I thought much of it amazingly beautiful.'

'Isn't it? And to think that man got it all out of the poorest little love-story for a respectable titled lady! Have you read of it?'

'Never.'

'It gives in a nutshell the miracle of art and the imagination. You get this queer irascible musician quite impossibly and unfortunately in love with a wealthy patroness, and then out of his brain comes *this*, a tapestry of glorious music, setting out love to lovers, lovers who love in spite of all that is wise and respectable and right.'

Ann Veronica thought. She did not want to seem to shrink from conversation, but all sorts of odd questions were running through her mind. 'I wonder why people in love are so defiant, so careless of other considerations?'

'The very hares grow brave. I suppose because it is the chief thing in life.' He stopped and said earnestly: 'It *is* the chief thing in life, and everything else goes down before it. Everything, my dear, everything! . . . But we have got to talk upon indifferent themes until we have done with this blond young gentleman from Bavaria. . . .'

The dinner came to an end at last, and the whiskered waiter presented his bill and evacuated the apartment and closed the door behind him with an almost ostentatious discretion. Ramage stood up, and suddenly turned the key in the door in an off-hand manner. 'Now,' he said, 'No one can blunder in upon us. We are alone and we can say and do what we please. We two.' He stood still, looking at her.

Ann Veronica tried to seem absolutely unconcerned. The turning of the key startled her, but she did not see how she could make an objection. She felt she had stepped into a world of unknown usages.

'I have waited for this,' he said, and stood quite still, looking at her until the silence became oppressive.

'Won't you sit down,' she said, 'and tell me what you want to say?' Her voice was flat and faint. Suddenly she had become afraid. She struggled not to be afraid. After all, what could happen?

He was looking at her very hard and earnestly. 'Ann Veronica,' he said.

Then before she could say a word to arrest him he was at her side. 'Don't!' she said weakly, as he had bent down and put one arm about her and seized her hands with his disengaged hand and kissed her – kissed her almost upon her lips. He seemed to do ten things before she could think to do one, to leap upon her and take possession.

Ann Veronica's universe, which had never been altogether so respectful to her as she could have wished, gave a shout and whirled head over heels. Everything in the world had changed for her. If hate could kill, Ramage would have been killed by a flash of hate. 'Mr Ramage!' she cried, and struggled to her feet.

'My darling!' he said, clasping her resolutely in his arms, 'my dearest!'

'Mr Ramage!' she began, and his mouth sealed hers and his breath was mixed with her breath. Her eye met his four inches away, and his was glaring, immense, and full of resolution, a stupendous monster of an eye.

She shut her lips hard, her jaw hardened, and she set herself to struggle with him. She wrenched her head away from his grip and got her arm between his chest and hers. They began to wrestle fiercely. Each became frightfully aware of the other as a plastic energetic body, of the strong muscles of neck against cheek, of hands gripping shoulder blade and waist. 'How dare you!' she panted, with her world screaming and grimacing insult at her. 'How dare you!'

They were both astonished at the other's strength. Perhaps Ramage was the more astonished. Ann Veronica had been an ardent hockey player and had had a course of ju-jutsu in the high school. Her defence ceased rapidly to be in any sense ladylike, and became vigorous and effective; a strand of black hair that had escaped its hairpins came athwart Ramage's eyes, and then the knuckles of a small but very hardly clenched fist had thrust itself with extreme effectiveness and painfulness under his jawbone and ear.

'Let go!' said Ann Veronica through her teeth, strenuously inflicting agony, and he cried out sharply and let go and receded a pace.

'*Now*!' said Ann Veronica. 'Why did you dare to do that?'

3

Each of them stared at the other, set in a universe that had changed its system of values with kaleidoscopic completeness. She was flushed, and her eyes were bright and angry; her breath came sobbing, and her hair was all abroad in wandering strands of black. He too was flushed and ruffled; one side of his collar had slipped from its stud and he held a hand to the corner of his jaw.

'You vixen!' said Mr Ramage, speaking the simplest first thought of his heart.

'You had no right—' panted Ann Veronica.

'Why on earth,' he asked, 'did you hurt me like that?'

Ann Veronica did her best to think she had not deliberately attempted to cause him pain. She ignored his question.

'I never dreamt!' she said.

'What on earth did you expect me to do, then?' he asked.

4

Interpretation came pouring down upon her almost blindingly; she understood now the room, the waiter, the whole situation. She understood. She leapt to a world of shabby knowledge, of furtive base realizations. She wanted to cry out upon herself for the uttermost fool in existence.

'I thought you wanted to have a talk to me,' she said.

'I wanted to make love to you.

'You knew it,' he added in her momentary silence.

'You said you were in love with me,' said Ann Veronica; 'I wanted to explain—'

'I said I loved and wanted you.' The brutality of his first astonishment was evaporating. 'I am in love with you. You know I am in love with you. And then you go – and half throttle me. . . . I believe you've crushed a gland or something. It feels like it.'

'I am sorry,' said Ann Veronica. 'What else was I to do?'

For some seconds she stood watching him, and both were thinking very quickly. Her state of mind would have seemed altogether discreditable to her grandmother. She ought to have been disposed to faint and scream at all these happenings; she ought to have maintained a front of outraged dignity to veil the sinking of her heart. I would like to have to tell it so. But indeed that is not at all a good description of her attitude. She was an indignant queen, no doubt; she was alarmed and disgusted within limits; but she was highly excited, and there was something, some low adventurous strain in her being, some element, subtle at least if base, going about the rioting ways and crowded insurgent meeting-places of her mind declaring that the whole affair was after all – they are the only words that express it – a very great lark indeed. At the bottom of her heart she was not a bit afraid of Ramage. She had unaccountable gleams of sympathy with and liking for him. And the grotesquest fact was that she did not so much loathe as experience with a quite critical condemnation this strange sensation of being kissed. Never before had any human being kissed her lips. . . .

It was only some hours after that these ambiguous elements evaporated and vanished and loathing came, and she really began to be thoroughly sick and ashamed of the whole disgraceful quarrel and scuffle.

He, for his part, was trying to grasp the series of unexpected reactions that had so wrecked their *tête-à-tête*. He had meant to be master of his fate that evening and it had escaped him altogether. It had, as it were, blown up at the concussion of his first step. It dawned upon him that he had been abominably used by Ann Veronica.

'Look here,' he said, 'I brought you here to make love to you.'

'I didn't understand – your idea of making love. You had better let me go again.'

'Not yet,' he said. 'I do love you. I love you all the more for the streak of sheer devil in you. . . . You are the most beautiful, the most desirable thing I have ever met in this world. It was good to kiss you, even at the price. But, by Jove! you are fierce! You are like those Roman women who carry stilettos in their hair.'

'I came here to talk reasonably, Mr Ramage. It is abominable—'

'What is the use of keeping up this note of indignation, Ann Veronica? Here I am! I am your lover, burning for you. I mean to have you! Don't frown me off now. Don't go back into Victorian respectability and pretend you don't know and you can't think and all the rest of it. One comes at last to the step from dreams to reality. This is your moment. No one will ever love you as I love you now. I have been dreaming of your body and you night after night. I have been imagining—'

'Mr Ramage, I came here— I didn't suppose for one moment you would dare—'

'Nonsense! That is your mistake! You are too intellectual. You want to do everything with your mind. You are afraid of kisses. You are afraid of the warmth in your blood. It's just because all that side of your life hasn't fairly begun.'

He made a step towards her.

'Mr Ramage,' she said sharply, 'I have to make it plain to you. I don't think you understand. I don't love you. I don't. I can't love you. I love someone else. It is repulsive. It disgusts me that you should touch me.'

He stared in amazement at this new aspect of the situation. 'You love someone else?' he repeated.

'I love someone else. I could not dream of loving you.'

And then he flashed his whole conception of the relations of men and women upon her in one astonishing question. His hand went with an almost instinctive inquiry to his jawbone again. 'Then why the devil,' he demanded, 'do you let me stand you dinners and the opera – and why do you come to a *cabinet particulier* with me?'

He became radiant with anger. 'You mean to tell me,' he said, 'that you have a lover? While I have been keeping you! Yes – keeping you!'

This view of life he hurled at her as if it were an offensive missile. It stunned her. She felt she must fly before it and could no longer do so. She did not think for one moment what interpretation he might put upon the word 'lover'.

'Mr Ramage,' she said, clinging to her one point, 'I want to get out of this horrible little room. It has all been a mistake. I have been stupid and foolish. Will you unlock that door?'

'Never!' he said. 'Confound your lover! Look here! Do you really think I am going to run you while he makes love to you? No fear! I never heard of anything so cool. If he wants you, let him get you. You're mine. I've paid for you and helped you, and I'm going to conquer you somehow – if I have to break you to do it. Hitherto you've seen only my easy, kindly side. But now – confound it! how can you prevent it? I *will* kiss you.'

'You won't!' said Ann Veronica with the clearest note of determination.

He seemed to be about to move towards her. She stepped back quickly, and her hand knocked a wine glass from the table to smash noisily on the floor. She caught at the idea. 'If you come a step nearer to me,' she said, 'I will smash every glass on this table.'

'Then by God!' he said, 'you'll be locked up!'

Ann Veronica was disconcerted for a moment. She had a vision of policemen, reproving magistrates, a crowded court, public disgrace. She saw her aunt in tears, her father white-faced and hard hit. 'Don't come nearer!' she said.

There was a discreet knocking at the door, and Ramage's face changed.

'No,' she said, under her breath, 'you can't face it.' And she knew that she was safe.

He went to the door. 'It's all right,' he said reassuringly to the inquirer without.

Ann Veronica glanced at the mirror to discover a flushed and dishevelled disorder. She began at once a hasty readjustment of her hair, while Ramage parleyed with inaudible interrogations. 'A glass slipped from the table,' he explained. . . . '*Non. Pas du tout. Non. . . . Niente. . . . Bitte! . . . Oui, dans la note.* . . . Presently. Presently.' That conversation ended and he turned to her again.

'I am going,' she said grimly, with three hairpins in her mouth.

She took her hat from the peg in the corner and began to put it on. He regarded that perennial miracle of pinning with wrathful eyes.

'Look here, Ann Veronica,' he began. 'I want a plain word with you about all this. Do you mean to tell me you didn't understand why I wanted you to come here?'

'Not a bit of it,' said Ann Veronica stoutly.

'You didn't expect that I should kiss you?'

'How was I to know that a man would – would think it was possible – when there was nothing – no love?'

'How did I know there wasn't love?'

That silenced her for a moment. 'And what on earth,' he said, 'do you think the world is made of? Why do you think I have been doing things for you? The abstract pleasure of goodness? Are you one of the members of that great white sisterhood that takes and does not give? The good accepting woman! Do you really suppose a girl is entitled to live at free quarters on any man she meets without giving any return?'

'I thought,' said Ann Veronica, 'you were my friend.'

'Friend! What have a man and a girl in common to make them friends? Ask that lover of yours! And even with friends, would you have it all Give on one side and all Take on the other? . . . Does *he* know I keep you? . . . You won't have a man's lips near you, but you'll eat out of his hand fast enough.'

Ann Veronica was stung to helpless anger.

'Mr Ramage,' she cried, 'you are outrageous! You understand nothing. You are – horrible. Will you let me go out of this room?'

'No,' cried Ramage; 'hear me out! I'll have that satisfaction anyhow. You women, with your tricks of evasion, you're a sex of swindlers. You have all the instinctive dexterity of parasites. You make yourself charming for help. You climb by disappointing men. This lover of yours –'

'He doesn't know!' cried Ann Veronica.

'Well, *you* know.'

Ann Veronica could have wept with vexation. Indeed a note of weeping broke her voice for a moment as she burst out: 'You know as well as I do that money was a loan!'

'Loan!'

'You yourself called it a loan!'

'Euphuism*. We both understood that.'

'You shall have every penny of it back.'

'I'll frame it – when I get it.'

'I'll pay you if I have to work at shirt-making at threepence an hour.'

'You'll never pay me. You think you will. It's your way of glossing over the ethical position. It's the sort of way a woman always does gloss over her ethical positions. You're all dependants

– all of you. By instinct. Only you good ones – shirk. You shirk a straightforward and decent return for what you get from us – taking refuge in purity and delicacy and suchlike when it comes to payment.'

'Mr Ramage,' said Ann Veronica, 'I want to go – *now*!'

5

But she did not get away just then.

Ramage's bitterness passed as abruptly as his aggression. 'Oh, Ann Veronica!' he cried, 'I cannot let you go like this! You don't understand. You can't possibly understand!'

He began a confused explanation, a perplexing contradictory apology for his urgency and wrath. He loved Ann Veronica, he said; he was so mad to have her that he defeated himself, and did crude and alarming and senseless things. His vicious abusiveness vanished. He suddenly became eloquent and plausible. He did make her perceive something of the acute, tormenting desire for her that had arisen in him and possessed him. She stood, as it were, directed doorward, with her eyes watching every movement, listening to him, repelled by him and yet dimly understanding.

At any rate he made it very clear that night that there was an ineradicable discord in life, a jarring something that must shatter all her dreams of a way of living for women that would enable them to be free and spacious and friendly with men, and that was the passionate predisposition of men to believe that the love of women can be earned and won and controlled and compelled. He flung aside all his talk of help and disinterested friendship as though it had never been even a disguise between them, as though from the first it was no more than a fancy dress they had put quite understandingly upon their relationship. He had set out to win her, and she had let him start. And at the thought of that other lover – he was convinced that that beloved person was a lover, and she found herself unable to say a word to explain to him that this other person, the person she loved, did not even know of her love – Ramage grew angry and savage once more, and returned suddenly to gibe and insult. Men do services for the love of women, and the woman who takes must pay. Such was the simple code that displayed itself in all his thoughts. He left that arid rule clear of the least mist of refinement or delicacy. That he should pay forty pounds to help this girl who preferred another man was no less in his eyes than a fraud and mockery that made her denial a maddening and outrageous disgrace to him. And this though he was evidently passionately in love with her.

For a while he threatened her. 'You have put all your life in my hands,' he declared. 'Think of that cheque you endorsed. There it is – against you. I defy you to explain it away. What do you think people will make of that? What will this lover of yours make of that?'

At intervals Ann Veronica demanded to go, declaring her undying resolve to repay him at any cost, and made short movements doorwards.

But at last this ordeal was over, and Ramage opened the door. She emerged with a white face and wide-open eyes upon a little, red-lit landing. She went past three keenly observant and ostentatiously preoccupied waiters down the thick-carpeted staircase and out of the Hôtel Rococo, that remarkable laboratory of relationships, past a tall porter in blue and crimson, into a cool, clear night.

6

When Ann Veronica reached her little bed-sitting-room again, every nerve in her body was quivering with shame and self-disgust.

She threw hat and coat on the bed and sat down before the fire.

'And now,' she said, splintering the surviving piece of coal into indignant flame-spirting fragments with one dexterous blow, 'what am I to do?

'I'm in a hole! – mess is a better word, expresses it better. I'm in a mess – a nasty mess! a filthy mess! Oh, no end of a mess! Do you hear, Ann Veronica? – you're in a nasty, filthy, unforgivable mess!

'Haven't I just made a silly mess of things?

'Forty pounds! I haven't got twenty!'

She got up, stamped with her foot, and then, suddenly remembering the lodger below, sat down and wrenched off her boots.

'This is what comes of being a young woman up to date. By Jove! I'm beginning to have my doubts about freedom!

'You silly young woman, Ann Veronica! You silly young woman! The smeariness of the thing!

'The smeariness of this sort of thing! . . . Mauled about!'

She fell to rubbing her insulted lips savagely with the back of her hand. 'Ugh!' she said.

'The young women of Jane Austen's time didn't get into this sort of scrape! At least – one thinks so. . . . I wonder if some of them did – and it didn't get reported. Aunt Jane had her quiet moments. Most of them didn't, anyhow. They were properly brought up, and sat still and straight, and took the luck fate brought them as gentlewomen should. And they had an idea of what men were like behind all their nicety. They knew they were all Bogy in disguise. I didn't! I didn't! After all—'

For a time her mind ran on daintiness and its defensive restraints as though it was the one desirable thing. That world of fine printed cambrics and escorted maidens, of delicate secondary meanings and refined allusiveness, presented itself to her imagination with the brightness of a lost paradise, as indeed for many women it is a lost paradise.

'I wonder if there is anything wrong with my manners,' she said. 'I wonder if I've been properly brought up. If I had been quite quiet and white and dignified, wouldn't it have been different? Would he have dared? . . .'

For some creditable moments in her life Ann Veronica was utterly disgusted with herself, she was wrung with a passionate and belated desire to move gently, to speak softly and ambiguously – to be, in effect, prim.

Horrible details recurred to her.

'Why, among other things, did I put my knuckles in his neck – deliberately to hurt him?'

She tried to sound the humorous note.

'Are you aware, Ann Veronica, you nearly throttled that gentleman?'

Then she reviled her own foolish way of putting it.

'You ass and imbecile, Ann Veronica! You female cad! Cad! Cad! . . . Why aren't you folded up clean in lavender – as every young woman ought to be? What have you been doing with yourself? . . .'

She raked into the fire with the poker.

'All of which doesn't help me in the slightest degree to pay back that money.'

That night was the most intolerable one that Ann Veronica had ever spent. She washed her face with unwonted elaboration before she went to bed. This time, there was no doubt, she did not sleep. The more she disentangled the lines of her situation the deeper grew her self-disgust. Occasionally the mere fact of lying in bed became unendurable, and she rolled out and marched about her room and whispered abuse of herself – usually until she hit against some article of furniture.

Then she would have quiet times, in which she would say to herself: 'Now look here! Let me think it all out!'

For the first time, it seemed to her, she faced the facts of a woman's position in the world – the meagre realities of such freedom as it permitted her, the almost unavoidable obligation to some individual man under which she must labour for even a foothold in the world. She had flung away from her father's support with the finest assumption of personal independence. And here she was – in a mess because it had been impossible for her to avoid leaning upon another man. She had thought – What had she thought? That this dependence of women was but an illusion which needed only to be denied to vanish. She had denied it with vigour, and here she was!

She did not so much exhaust this general question as pass from it to her insoluble individual problem again: 'What am I to do?'

She wanted first of all to fling the forty pounds back into Ramage's face. But she had spent nearly half of it, and had no conception of how such a sum could be made good again. She thought of all sorts of odd and desperate expedients, and with passionate petulance rejected them all.

She took refuge in beating her pillow and inventing insulting epithets for herself. She got up, drew up her blind, and stared out of window at a dawn-cold vision of chimneys for a time, and then went and sat on the edge of her bed. What was the alternative to going home? No alternative appeared in that darkness.

It seemed intolerable that she should go home and admit herself beaten. She did most urgently desire to save her face in Morningside Park, and for long hours she could think of no way of putting it that would not be in the nature of unconditional admission of defeat.

'I'd rather go as a chorus girl,' she said.

She was not very clear about the position and duties of a chorus girl, but it certainly had the air of being a last desperate resort. There sprang from that a vague hope that perhaps she might extort a capitulation from her father by a threat to seek that position, and then with overwhelming clearness it came to her that whatever happened she would never be able to tell her father about her debt. The completest capitulation would not wipe out that trouble. And she felt that if she went home it was imperative to pay. She would always be going to and fro up the Avenue, getting glimpses of Ramage, seeing him in trains. . . .

For a time she promenaded the room.

'Why did I ever take that loan? An idiot girl in an asylum would have known better than that!

'Vulgarity of soul and innocence of mind – the worst of all conceivable combinations. I wish someone would kill Ramage by accident! . . .

'But then they would find that cheque endorsed in his bureau. . . .

'I wonder what he will do?' She tried to imagine situations that might arise out of Ramage's antagonism, for he had been so bitter and savage that she could not believe that he would leave things as they were.

The next morning she went out with her post office savings bank book, and telegraphed for a warrant to draw out all the money she had in the world. It amounted to two-and-twenty pounds. She addressed an envelope to Ramage, and scrawled on a half-sheet of paper: 'The rest shall follow.' The money would be available in the afternoon, and she would send him four five-pound notes. The rest she meant to keep her for her immediate necessities. A little relieved by this step towards reinstatement, she went on to the Imperial College to forget her muddle of problems for a time, if she could, in the presence of Capes.

7

For a time the biological laboratory was full of healing virtue. Her sleepless night had left her languid but not stupefied, and for an hour or so the work distracted her altogether from her troubles.

Then after Capes had been through her work and had gone on, it came to her that the fabric of this life of hers was doomed to almost immediate collapse, that in a little while these studies would cease, and perhaps she would never set eyes on him again. After that consolations fled.

The overnight nervous strain began to tell; she became inattentive to the work before her, and it did not get on. She felt sleepy and unusually irritable. She lunched at a creamery in Great Portland Street, and as the day was full of wintry sunshine, spent the rest of the lunch hour in a drowsy gloom, which she imagined to be thought upon the problems of her position, on a seat in Regent's Park. A girl of fifteen or sixteen gave her a handbill that she regarded as a tract until she saw 'Votes for Women' at the top. That turned her mind to the more generalized aspects of her perplexities again. She had never been so disposed to agree that the position of women in the modern world is intolerable.

Capes joined the students at tea, and displayed himself in an impish mood that sometimes possessed him. He did not notice that Ann Veronica was preoccupied and heavy-eyed. Miss Klegg raised the question of women's suffrage, and he set himself to provoke a duel between her and Miss Garvice. The youth with the hair brushed back and the spectacled Scotchman joined in the fray for and against the women's vote.

Ever and again Capes appealed to Ann Veronica. He liked to draw her in, and she did her best to talk. But she did not talk readily, and in order to say something she plunged a little, and felt she plunged. Capes scored back with an uncompromising vigour that was his way of complimenting her intelligence. But this afternoon it discovered an unusual vein of irritability in her. He had been reading Belfort Bax,* and declared himself a convert. He contrasted the lot of women in general with the lot of men, presented men as patient, self-immolating martyrs, and women as the pampered favourites of nature. A vein of conviction mingled with his burlesque.

For a time he and Miss Klegg contradicted one another.

The question ceased to be a tea-table talk, and became suddenly tragically real for Ann Veronica. There he sat, cheerfully friendly in his sex's freedom – the man she loved, the one man she cared should unlock the way to the wide world for her imprisoned feminine possibilities, and he seemed regardless that she stifled under his eyes; he made a jest of all this passionate insurgence of the souls of women against the fate of their conditions.

Miss Garvice repeated again, and almost in the same words she used at every discussion, her contribution to the great question. She thought that women were not made for the struggle and turmoil of life – their place was the little world, the home; that their power lay not in votes but in influence over men and in making the minds of their children fine and splendid.

'Women should understand men's affairs, perhaps,' said Miss Garvice, 'but to mingle in them is just to sacrifice that power of influencing they can exercise now.'

'There *is* something sound in that position,' said Capes, intervening as if to defend Miss Garvice against a possible attack from Ann Veronica. 'It may not be just and so forth, but, after all, it is how things are. Women are not in the world in the same sense that men are – fighting individuals in a scramble. I don't see how they can be. Every home is a little recess, a niche, out of the world, of business and competition, in which women and the future shelter.'

'A little pit!' said Ann Veronica; 'a little prison!'

'It's just as often a little refuge. Anyhow, that is how things are.'

'And the man stands as the master at the mouth of the den.'

'As sentinel. You forget all the mass of training and tradition and instinct that go to make him a tolerable master. Nature is a mother; her sympathies have always been feminist, and she has tempered the man to the shorn woman.'

'I wish,' said Ann Veronica, with sudden anger, 'that you could know what it is to live in a pit!'

She stood up as she spoke, and put down her cup beside Miss Garvice's. She addressed Capes as though she spoke to him alone.

'I can't endure it,' she said.

Every one turned to her in astonishment.

She felt she had to go on. 'No man can realize,' she said, 'what that pit can be. The way – the way we are led on! We are taught to believe we are free in the world, to think we are queens. . . . Then we find out. We find out no man will treat a woman fairly as man to man – no man. He wants you – or he doesn't; and then he helps some other woman against you. . . . What you say is probably all true and necessary. . . . But think of the disillusionment! Except for our sex we have minds like men, desires like men. We come out into the world, some of us –'

She paused. Her words, as she said them, seemed to her to mean nothing, and there was so much that struggled for expression. 'Women are mocked,' she said. 'Whenever they try to take hold of life a man intervenes.'

She felt, with a sudden horror, that she might weep. She wished she had not stood up. She wondered wildly why she had stood up. No one spoke, and she was impelled to flounder on. 'Think

of the mockery!' she said. 'Think how dumb we find ourselves
and stifled! I know we seem to have a sort of freedom. . . . Have
you ever tried to run and jump in petticoats, Mr Capes? Well,
think what it must be to live in them – soul and mind and body!
It's fun for a man to jest at our position.'

'I wasn't jesting,' said Capes abruptly.

She stood face to face with him, and his voice cut across her
speech and made her stop abruptly. She was sore and over-strung,
and it was intolerable to her that he should stand within three yards
of her unsuspectingly, with an incalculably vast power over her
happiness. She was sore with the perplexities of her preposterous
position. She was sick of herself, of her life, of everything but him;
and for him all her masked and hidden being was crying out.

She stopped abruptly at the sound of his voice, and lost the
thread of what she was saying. In the pause she realized the
attention of the others converged upon her, and that the tears were
brimming over her eyes. She felt a storm of emotion surging up
within her. She became aware of the Scotch student regarding her
with stupendous amazement, a tea cup poised in one hairy hand
and his faceted glasses showing a various enlargement of segments
of his eye.

The door into the passage offered itself with an irresistible
invitation – the one alternative to a public, inexplicable passion
of weeping.

Capes flashed to an understanding of her intention, sprang to
his feet, and opened the door for her retreat.

8

'Why should I ever come back?' she said to herself, as she went
down the staircase.

She went to the post office and drew out and sent off her money
to Ramage. And then she came out into the street, sure only of
one thing – that she could not return directly to her lodgings. She
wanted air – and the distraction of having moving and changing
things about her. The evenings were beginning to draw out, and
it would not be dark for an hour. She resolved to walk across the
park to the Zoological Gardens, and so on by way of Primrose
Hill to Hampstead Heath. There she would wander about in the
kindly darkness. And think things out. . . .

Presently she became aware of footsteps hurrying after her, and glanced back to find Miss Klegg, a little out of breath, in pursuit.

Ann Veronica halted a pace, and Miss Klegg came alongside. 'Do *you* go across the park?'

'Not usually. But I'm going to-day. I want a walk.'

'I'm not surprised at it. I thought Mr Capes most trying.'

'Oh, it wasn't that. I've had a headache all day.'

'I thought Mr Capes most unfair,' Miss Klegg went on in a small, even voice; '*most* unfair! I'm glad you spoke out as you did.'

'I didn't mind that little argument.'

'You gave it him well. What you said wanted saying. After you went he got up and took refuge in the preparation room. Or else *I* would have finished him.'

Ann Veronica said nothing, and Miss Klegg went on: 'He very often *is* – most unfair. He has a way of sitting on people. He wouldn't like it if people did it to him. He jumps the words out of your mouth; he takes hold of what you have to say before you have had time to express it properly.'

Pause.

'I suppose he's frightfully clever,' said Miss Klegg.

'He's a Fellow of the Royal Society, and he can't be much over thirty,' said Miss Klegg.

'He writes very well,' said Ann Veronica.

'He can't be more than thirty. He must have married when he was quite a young man.'

'Married?' said Ann Veronica.

'Didn't you know he was married?' asked Miss Klegg, and was struck by a thought that made her glance quickly at her companion.

Ann Veronica had no answer for a moment. She turned her head away sharply. Some automation within her produced in a quite unfamiliar voice the remark: 'They're playing football.'

'It's too far for the ball to reach us,' said Miss Klegg.

'I didn't know Mr Capes was married,' said Ann Veronica, resuming the conversation with an entire disappearance of her former lassitude.

'Oh, yes,' said Miss Klegg; 'I thought every one knew.'

'No,' said Ann Veronica offhandedly. 'Never heard anything of it.'

'I thought every one knew. I thought every one had heard about it.'

'But why?'

'He's married – and, I believe, living separated from his wife. There was a case, or something, some years ago.'

'What case?'

'A divorce – or something – I don't know. But I have heard that he almost had to leave the schools. If it hadn't been for Professor Russell standing up for him they say he would have had to leave.'

'Was he divorced, do you mean?'

'No, but he got himself mixed up in a divorce case. I forget the particulars, but I know it was something very disagreeable. It was among artistic people.'

Ann Veronica was silent for a while.

'I thought every one had heard,' said Miss Klegg. 'Or I wouldn't have said anything about it.'

'I suppose all men,' said Ann Veronica, in a tone of detached criticism, 'get some such entanglement. And, anyhow, it doesn't matter to us.' She turned abruptly at right angles to the path they followed. 'This is my way back to my side of the park,' she said.

'I thought you were coming right across the park.'

'Oh, no,' said Ann Veronica; 'I have some work to do. I just wanted a breath of air. And they'll shut the gates presently. It's not far from twilight.'

9

She was sitting brooding over her fire about ten o'clock that night when a sealed and registered envelope was brought up to her.

She opened it and drew out a letter, and folded within it were the notes she had sent off to Ramage that day. The letter began:

'MY DEAREST GIRL, *I cannot let you do this foolish thing—*'

She crumpled notes and letter together in her hand, and then with a passionate gesture flung them into the fire. Instantly she seized the poker and made a desperate effort to get them out again. But she was only able to save a corner of the letter. The twenty pounds burnt with avidity.

She remained for some seconds crouching at the fender, poker in hand.

'By Jove!' she said, standing up at last, 'that about finishes it, Ann Veronica!'

Chapter X

The Suffragettes

I

'There is only one way out of all this,' said Ann Veronica, sitting up in her little bed in the darkness and biting at her nails.

'I thought I was just up against Morningside Park and father, but it's the whole order of things – the whole blessed order of things. . . .'

She shivered. She frowned and gripped her hands about her knees very tightly. Her mind developed into savage wrath at the present conditions of a woman's life.

'I suppose all life is an affair of chances. But a woman's life is all chance. It's artificially chance. Find your man, that's the rule. All the rest is humbug and delicacy. He's the handle of life for you. He will let you live if it pleases him. . . .

'Can't it be altered?

'I suppose an actress is free? . . .'

She tried to think of some altered state of affairs in which these monstrous limitations would be alleviated, in which women would stand on their own feet in equal citizenship with men. For a time she brooded on the ideals and suggestions of the Socialists, on the vague intimations of an Endowment of Motherhood, of a complete relaxation of that intense individual dependence for women which is woven into the existing social order. At the back of her mind there seemed always one irrelevant qualifying spectator whose presence she sought to disregard. She would not look at him, would not think of him; when her mind wavered, then she muttered to herself in the darkness so as to keep hold of her generalizations.

'It is true. It is no good waiving the thing; it is true. Unless women are never to be free, never to be even respected, there must be a generation of martyrs. . . . Why shouldn't we be martyrs? There's nothing else for most of us, anyhow. It's a sort of blacklegging to want to have a life of one's own. . . .'

She repeated as if she answered an objector: 'A sort of black-legging.

'A sex of blacklegging clients.'

Her mind diverged to other aspects, and another type of womanhood.

'Poor little Miniver! What can she be but what she is? . . . Because she states her case in a tangle, drags it through swamps of nonsense, it doesn't alter the fact that she is right.'

That phrase about dragging the truth through swamps of nonsense she remembered from Capes. At the recollection that it was his, she seemed to fall through a thin surface, as one might fall through the crust of a lava into glowing depths. She wallowed for a time in the thought of Capes, unable to escape from his image and the idea of his presence in her life.

She let her mind run into dreams of that cloud paradise of an altered world in which the Goopes and Minivers, the Fabians and reforming people believed. Across that world was written in letters of light: 'Endowment of Motherhood'. Suppose in some complex yet conceivable way women were endowed, were no longer economically and socially dependent on men. 'If one was free,' she said, 'one could go to him. . . . This vile hovering to catch a man's eye! . . . One could go to him and tell him one loved him. I want to love him. A little love from him would be enough. It would hurt no one. It would not burthen him with any obligation.'

She groaned aloud and bowed her forehead to her knees. She floundered deep. She wanted to kiss his feet. His feet would have the firm texture of his hands.

Then suddenly her spirit rose in revolt. 'I will not have this slavery,' she said. 'I will not have this slavery.'

She shook her fist ceilingward. 'Do you hear!' she said, 'whatever you are, wherever you are! I will not be slave to the thought of any man, slave to the customs of any time. Confound this slavery of sex! I am a man! I will get this under if I am killed in doing it!'

She scowled into the cold blacknesses about her.

'Manning,' she said, and contemplated a figure of inaggressive persistence. 'No!' Her thoughts had turned in a new direction.

'It doesn't matter,' she said, after a long interval, 'if they are absurd. They mean something. They mean everything that women can mean – except submission. The vote is only the beginning, the necessary beginning. If we do not begin—'

She had come to a resolution. Abruptly she got out of bed, smoothed her sheet and straightened her pillow and lay down, and fell almost instantly asleep.

2

The next morning was as dark and foggy as if it was mid-November instead of early March. Ann Veronica woke rather later than usual, and lay awake for some minutes before she remembered a certain resolution she had taken in the small hours. Then instantly she got out of bed and proceeded to dress.

She did not start for the Imperial College. She spent the morning up to ten in writing a series of unsuccessful letters to Ramage, which she tore up unfinished; and finally she desisted and put on her jacket and went out into the lamp-lit obscurity and slimy streets. She turned a resolute face southward.

She followed Oxford Street into Holborn, and then she inquired for Chancery Lane. There she sought and at last found 107A, one of those heterogeneous piles of offices which occupy the eastern side of the lane. She studied the painted names of firms and persons and enterprises on the wall, and discovered that the Women's Bond of Freedom occupied several contiguous suites on the first floor. She went upstairs and hesitated between four doors with ground-glass panes, each of which professed 'The Women's Bond of Freedom' in neat black letters. She opened one and found herself in a large untidy room set with chairs that were a little disarranged as if by an overnight meeting. On the walls were notice boards bearing clusters of newspaper slips, three or four big posters of monster meetings, one of which Ann Veronica had attended with Miss Miniver, and a series of announcements in purple copying ink, and in one corner was a pile of banners. There was no one at all in this room, but through the half-open door of one of the small apartments that gave upon it she had a glimpse of two very young girls sitting at a littered table and writing briskly.

She walked across to this apartment and, opening the door a little wider, discovered a press section of the movement at work.

'I want to inquire,' said Ann Veronica.

'Next door,' said a spectacled young person of seventeen or eighteen, with an impatient indication of the direction.

In the adjacent apartment Ann Veronica found a middle-aged woman with a tired face under the tired hat she wore, sitting at a desk opening letters while a dusky, untidy girl of eight or nine and twenty hammered industriously at a typewriter. The tired woman looked up in inquiring silence at Ann Veronica's diffident entry.

'I want to know more about this movement,' said Ann Veronica.

'Are you with us?' said the tired woman.

'I don't know,' said Ann Veronica, 'I think I am. I want very much to do something for women. But I want to know what you are doing.'

The tired woman sat still for a moment. 'You haven't come here to make a lot of difficulties?' she asked.

'No,' said Ann Veronica, 'but I want to know.'

The tired woman shut her eyes tightly for a moment, and then looked with them at Ann Veronica. 'What can you do?' she asked.

'Do?'

'Are you prepared to do things for us? Distribute bills? Write letters? Interrupt meetings? Canvass at elections? Face dangers?'

'If I am satisfied—'

'If we satisfy you?'

'Then, if possible, I would like to go to prison.'

'It isn't nice going to prison.'

'It would suit me.'

'It isn't nice getting there.'

'That's a question of detail,' said Ann Veronica.

The tired woman looked quietly at her. 'What are your objections?' she said.

'It isn't objections exactly. I want to know what you are doing; how you think this work of yours really does serve women.'

'We are working for the equal citizenship of men and women,' said the tired woman. 'Women have been and are treated as the inferiors of men; we want to make them their equals,'

'Yes,' said Ann Veronica, 'I agree to that. But –'

The tired woman raised her eyebrows in mild protest.

'Isn't the question more complicated than that?' said Ann Veronica.

'You could have a talk to Miss Kitty Brett this afternoon, if you liked. Shall I make an appointment for you?'

Miss Kitty Brett was one of the most conspicuous leaders of the movement. Ann Veronica snatched at the opportunity, and spent most of the intervening time in the Assyrian Court of the British Museum, reading and thinking over a little book upon the feminist movement the tired woman had made her buy. She got a bun and some cocoa in the little refreshment room, and then wandered through the galleries upstairs, crowded with Polynesian idols and Polynesian dancing garments, and all the simple immodest accessories to life in Polynesia, to a seat among the mummies. She was trying to bring her problems to a head, and her mind insisted upon being even more discursive and atmospheric than usual. It generalized everything she put to it.

'Why should women be dependent on men?' she asked; and the question was at once converted into a system of variations upon the theme of 'Why are things as they are?' – 'Why are human beings viviparous?' – 'Why are people hungry thrice a day?' – 'Why does one faint at danger?'

She stood for a time looking at the dry limbs and still human face of that desiccated unwrapped mummy from the very beginnings of social life. It looked very patient, she thought, and a little self-satisfied. It looked as if it had taken its world for granted and prospered on that assumption – a world in which children were trained to obey their elders and the wills of women overruled as a matter of course. It was wonderful to think this thing had lived, had felt and suffered. Perhaps once it had desired some other human being intolerably. Perhaps someone had kissed the brow that was now so cadaverous, rubbed that sunken cheek with loving fingers, held that stringy neck with passionately living hands. But all of that was forgotten. 'In the end,' it seemed to be thinking, 'they embalmed me with the utmost respect – sound spices chosen to endure – the best! I took my world as I found it. *Things are so!*'

3

Ann Veronica's first impression of Kitty Brett was that she was aggressive and disagreeable; her next that she was a person of amazing persuasive power. She was perhaps three and twenty, and very pink and healthy looking, showing a great deal of white and rounded neck above her business-like but altogether feminine blouse, and a good deal of plump, gesticulating forearm out of her short sleeve. She had animated dark blue-grey eyes under her fine eyebrows, and dark brown hair that rolled back simply and effectively from her broad low forehead. And she was about as capable of intelligent argument as a runaway steam roller. She was a trained being – trained by an implacable mother to one end.

She spoke with fluent enthusiasm. She did not so much deal with Ann Veronica's interpolations as dispose of them with quick and use-hardened repartee, and then she went on with a fine directness to sketch the case for her agitation, for that remarkable rebellion of the women that was then agitating the whole world of politics and discussion. She assumed with a kind of mesmeric force all the propositions that Ann Veronica wanted her to define.

'What do we want? What is the goal?' asked Ann Veronica.

'Freedom! Citizenship! And the way to that – the way to everything – is the Vote.'

Ann Veronica said something about a general change of ideas.

'How can you change people's ideas if you have no power?' said Kitty Brett.

Ann Veronica was not ready enough to deal with that counter-stroke.

'One doesn't want to turn the whole thing into a mere sex antagonism.'

'When women get justice,' said Kitty Brett, 'there will be no sex antagonism. None at all. Until then we mean to keep on hammering away.'

'It seems to me that much of a woman's difficulties are economic.'

'That will follow,' said Kitty Brett. 'That will follow.'

She interrupted as Ann Veronica was about to speak again, with a bright contagious hopefulness. 'Everything will follow,' she said.

'Yes,' said Ann Veronica, trying to think where they were, trying to get things plain again that had seemed plain enough in the quiet of the night.

'Nothing was ever done,' Miss Brett asserted, 'without a certain element of faith. After we have got the vote and are recognized as citizens, then we can come to all these other things.'

Even in the glamour of Miss Brett's assurance it seemed to Ann Veronica that this was, after all, no more than the gospel of Miss Miniver with a new set of resonances. And like that gospel it meant something, something different from its phrases, something elusive, and yet something that in spite of the superficial incoherence of its phrasing, was largely essentially true. There was something holding women down, holding women back, and if it wasn't exactly man-made law, man-made law was an aspect of it. There was something indeed holding the whole species back from the imaginable largeness of life. . . .

'The Vote is the symbol of everything,' said Miss Brett.

She made an abrupt personal appeal.

'Oh! please don't lose yourself in a wilderness of secondary considerations,' she said. 'Don't ask me to tell you all that women can do, all that women can be. There is a new life, different from the old life of dependence, possible. If only we are not divided. If only we work together. This is the one movement that brings women of different classes together for a common purpose. If you could see how it gives them souls, women who have taken things for granted, who have given themselves up altogether to pettiness and vanity. . . .'

'Give me something to do,' said Ann Veronica, interrupting her persuasions at last. 'It has been very kind of you to see me, but I don't want to sit and talk and use your time any longer. I want to do something. I want to hammer myself against all this that pens women in. I feel that I shall stifle unless I can do something – and do something soon.'

4

It was not Ann Veronica's fault that the night's work should have taken upon itself the forms of wild burlesque. She was in deadly earnest in everything she did. It seemed to her the last desperate attack upon the universe that would not let her live as she desired to live, that penned her in and controlled her and directed her and disapproved of her, the same invincible wrappering, the same leaden tyranny of a universe that she had vowed to overcome after that memorable conflict with her father at Morningside Park.

She was listed for the raid – she was informed it was to be a raid upon the House of Commons,* though no particulars were given her – and told to go alone to 14 Dexter Street, Westminister, and not to ask any policeman to direct her. 14 Dexter Street, Westminster, she found was not a house, but a yard in an obscure street, with big gates and the name of Podgers & Carlo, Carriers and Furniture Removers, thereon. She was perplexed by this, and stood for some seconds in the empty street hesitating, until the appearance of another circumspect woman under the street lamp at the corner reassured her. In one of the big gates was a little door, and she rapped at this. It was immediately opened by a man with light eyelashes and a manner suggestive of restrained passion. 'Come right in,' he hissed under his breath with the true conspirator's note, closed the door very softly and pointed, 'Through there!'

By the meagre light of a gas lamp she perceived a cobbled yard with four large furniture vans standing with horses and lamps alight. A slender young man, wearing glasses, appeared from the shadow of the nearest van. 'Are you A, B, C, or D?' he asked.

'They told me D,' said Ann Veronica.

'Through there,' he said, and pointed with the pamphlet he was carrying.

Ann Veronica found herself in a little stirring crowd of excited women, whispering and tittering and speaking in undertones.

The light was poor, so that she saw their gleaming faces dimly and indistinctly. No one spoke to her. She stood among them, watching them and feeling curiously alien to them. The oblique ruddy lighting distorted them oddly, made queer bars and patches of shadow upon their clothes. 'It's Kitty's idea,' said one, 'we are to go in the vans.'

'Kitty is wonderful,' said another.

'Wonderful!'

'I have always longed for prison service,' said a voice, 'always. From the beginning. But it's only now I'm able to do it.'

A little blonde creature close at hand suddenly gave way to a fit of hysterical laughter, and caught up the end of it with a sob.

'Before I took up the suffrage,' a firm, flat voice remarked, 'I could scarcely walk upstairs without palpitations.'

Someone hidden from Ann Veronica appeared to be marshalling the assembly. 'We have to get in, I think,' said a nice little old lady in a bonnet to Ann Veronica, speaking with a voice that quavered a little. 'My dear, can you see in this light? I think I would like to get in. Which is C?'

Ann Veronica, with a curious sinking of the heart, regarded the black cavities of the vans. Their doors stood open, and placards with big letters indicated the section assigned to each. She directed the little old woman and then made her way to van D. A young woman with a white badge on her arm stood and counted the sections as they entered their vans.

'When they tap the roof,' she said in a voice of authority, 'you are to come out. You will be opposite the big entrance in Old Palace Yard. It's the public entrance. You are to make for that, and get into the lobby if you can, and so try and reach the floor of the House, crying "Votes for Women!" as you go.'

She spoke like a mistress addressing school children.

'Don't bunch too much as you come out,' she added.

'All right?' asked the man with the light eyelashes, suddenly appearing in the doorway. He waited for an instant, wasting an encouraging smile in the imperfect light, and then shut the doors of the van, leaving the women in darkness. . . .

The van started with a jerk and rumbled on its way.

'It's like Troy!' said a voice of rapture. 'It's exactly like Troy!'

5

So Ann Veronica, enterprising and a little dubious as ever, mingled with the stream of history and wrote her Christian name upon the police court records of the land.

But out of a belated regard for her father she wrote the surname of someone else.

Some day, when the rewards of literature permit the arduous research required, the Campaign of the Women will find its Carlyle, and the particulars of that marvellous series of exploits by which Miss Brett and her colleagues nagged the whole western world into the discussion of women's position become the material for the most delightful and amazing descriptions. At present the world waits for that writer, and the confused record of the newspapers remains the only resource of the curious. When he comes he will do that raid of the pantechnicons the justice it deserves; he will picture the orderly evening scene about the Imperial Legislature in convincing detail; the coming and going of cabs and motor cabs and broughams through the chill, damp evening into New Palace Yard, the reinforced but untroubled and unsuspecting police about the entries of those great buildings whose square and panelled Victorian Gothic streams up from the glare of the lamps into the murkiness of the night; Big Ben shining overhead, an unassailable beacon, and the incidental traffic of Westminster, cabs, carts, and glowing omnibuses going to and from the bridge. About the Abbey and Abingdon Street stood the outer pickets and detachments of the police, their attention all directed westward to where the women in Caxton Hall, Westminster, hummed like an angry hive. Squads reached to the very portals of that center of disturbance. And through all these defences and into Old Palace Yard, into the very vitals of the defenders' position, lumbered the unsuspected vans.

They travelled past the few idle sightseers who had braved the uninviting evening to see what the Suffragettes might be doing; they pulled up unchallenged within thirty yards of those coveted portals.

And then they disgorged.

Were I a painter of subject pictures, I would exhaust all my skill in proportion and perspective and atmosphere upon the august seat of empire, I would present it grey and dignified and immense and respectable beyond any mere verbal description, and then in vivid black and very small, I would put in those valiantly impertinent vans, squatting at the base of its altitudes and pouring out a swift straggling rush of ominous little black objects, minute figures of determined women at war with the universe.

Ann Veronica was in their very forefront.

In an instant the expectant calm of Westminster was ended, and the very Speaker in the chair blenched at the sound of the policemen's whistles. The bolder members in the House left their places to go lobbyward, grinning. Others pulled hats over their noses, cowered in their seats, and feigned that all was right with the world. In Old Palace Yard everybody ran. They either ran to see or ran for shelter. Even two Cabinet ministers took to their heels, grinning insincerely. At the opening of the van doors and the emergence into the fresh air Ann Veronica's doubt and depression gave place to the wildest exhilaration. That same adventurousness that had already buoyed her through crises that would have overwhelmed any normally feminine girl with shame and horror now became uppermost again. Before her was a great Gothic portal. Through that she had to go.

Past her shot the little old lady in the bonnet, running incredibly fast, but otherwise still alertly respectable, and she was making a strange threatening sound as she ran, such as one would use in driving ducks out of a garden – 'B-r-r-r-r-r—!' and pawing with black-gloved hands. The policemen were closing in from the sides to intervene. The little old lady struck like a projectile upon the resounding chest of the foremost of these, and then Ann Veronica had got past and was ascending the steps.

Then most horribly she was clasped about the waist from behind and lifted from the ground.

At that a new element poured into her excitement, an element of wild disgust and terror. She had never experienced anything so disagreeable in her life as the sense of being held helplessly off her feet. She screamed involuntarily – she had never in her life screamed before, and then she began to wriggle and fight like a frightened animal against the men who were holding her.

The affair passed at one leap from a spree to a nightmare of violence and disgust. Her hair got loose, her hat came over one eye, and she had no arm free to replace it. She felt she must suffocate if these men did not put her down, and for a time they would not put her down. Then with an indescribable relief her feet were on the pavement, and she was being urged along by two policemen, who were gripping her wrists in an irresistible expert manner. She was writhing to get her hands loose and found herself gasping with passionate violence: 'It's damnable! – damnable!' to the manifest disgust of the fatherly policeman on her right.

Then they had released her arms and were trying to push her away. 'You be off, missie,' said the fatherly policeman. 'This ain't no place for you.'

He pushed her a dozen yards along the greasy pavement with flat, well-trained hands that there seemed to be no opposing. Before her stretched blank spaces, dotted with running people coming towards her, and below them railings and a statue. She almost submitted to this ending of her adventure. But at the word 'home' she turned again.

'I won't go home,' she said; 'I won't!' and she evaded the clutch of the fatherly policeman and tried to thrust herself past him in the direction of that big portal. 'Steady on!' he cried.

A diversion was created by the violent struggles of the little old lady. She seemed to be endowed with superhuman strength. A knot of three policemen in conflict with her staggered towards Ann Veronica's attendants and distracted their attention. 'I *will* be arrested! I *won't* go home!' the little old lady was screaming over and over agian. They put her down, and she leapt at them; she smote a helmet to the ground.

'You'll have to take her!' shouted an inspector on horseback, and she echoed his cry: 'You'll have to take me!' They seized upon her and lifted her, and she screamed. Ann Veronica became violently excited at the sight. 'You cowards!' said Ann Veronica, 'put her down!' and tore herself from a detaining hand and battered with her fists upon the big red ear and blue shoulder of the policeman who held the little old lady.

So Ann Veronica also was arrested.

And then came the vile experience of being forced and borne along the street to the police station. Whatever anticipation Ann Veronica had formed of this vanished in the reality. Presently she was going through a swaying, noisy crowd, whose faces grinned and stared pitilessly in the light of the electric standards. 'Go it, miss!' cried one. 'Kick aht at 'em!' though, indeed, she went now with Christian meekness, resenting only the thrusting policemen's hands. Several people in the crowd seemed to be fighting. Insulting cries became frequent and various, but for the most part she could not understand what was said. 'Who'll mind the baby nar?' was one of the night's inspirations, and very frequent. A lean young man in spectacles pursued her for some time, crying 'Courage! Courage!' Somebody threw a dab of mud at her, and some of it got down her neck. Immeasurable disgust possessed her. She felt draggled and insulted beyond redemption. She could not hide her face. She attempted by a sheer act of will to end the scene, to will herself out of it anywhere. She had a horrible glimpse of the once nice little old lady being also borne stationward, still faintly battling and very muddy – one lock of greyish hair straggling over her neck, her face scared, white, but triumphant. Her bonnet dropped off and was trampled into the gutter. A little cockney recovered it, and made ridiculous attempts to get to her and replace it.

'You must arrest me!' she gasped breathlessly, insisting insanely on a point already carried; 'you shall!'

The police station at the end seemed to Ann Veronica like a refuge from unnameable disgraces. She hesitated about her name, and, being prompted, gave it at last as Ann Veronica Smith, 107A Chancery Lane. . . .

Indignation carried her through that night, that men and the world could so entreat her. The arrested women were herded in a passage of the Panton Street police station that opened upon a cell too unclean for occupation, and most of them spent the night standing. Hot coffee and cakes were sent in to them in the morning by some intelligent sympathizer, or she would have starved all day. Submission to the inevitable carried her through the circumstances of her appearance before the magistrate.

He was no doubt doing his best to express the attitude of society towards these wearily heroic defendants, but he seemed to be merely rude and unfair to Ann Veronica. He was not, it seemed, the proper stipendiary at all, and there had been some demur to his jurisdiction that had ruffled him. He resented being regarded as irregular. He felt he was human wisdom prudentially interpolated. . . . 'You silly wimmin,' he said over and over again throughout the hearing, plucking at his blotting pad with busy hands. 'You silly creatures! Ugh! Fie upon you!' The court was crowded with people, for the most part supporters and admirers of the defendants, and the man with the light eyelashes was conspicuously active and omnipresent.

Ann Veronica's appearance was brief and undistinguished. She had nothing to say for herself. She was guided into the dock and prompted by a helpful police inspector. She was aware of the body of the court, of clerks seated at a black table littered with papers, of policemen standing about stiffly with expressions of conscious integrity, and a murmuring background of the heads and shoulders of spectators close behind her. On a high chair behind a raised counter the stipendiary's substitute regarded her malevolently over his glasses. A disagreeable young man, with red hair and a loose mouth, seated at the reporter's table, was only too manifestly sketching her.

She was interested by the swearing of the witnesses, the kissing of the book struck her as particularly odd, and then the policemen gave their evidence in staccato jerks and stereotyped phrases.

'Have you anything to ask the witness?' asked the helpful inspector.

The ribald demons that infested the back of Ann Veronica's mind urged various facetious interrogations upon her, as, for example, where the witness had acquired his prose style. She controlled herself, and answered meekly: 'No.'

'Well, Ann Veronica Smith,' the magistrate remarked when the case was all before him, 'you're a good-looking, strong, respectable gell, and it's a pity you silly young wimmin can't find something better to do with your exuberance. Two and twenty! I can't imagine what your parents can be thinking about to let you get into these scrapes.'

Ann Veronica's mind was filled with confused unutterable replies.

'You are persuaded to come and take part in these outrageous proceedings – many of you I am convinced have no idea whatever of their nature. I don't suppose you could tell me even the

derivation of suffrage if I asked you. No! not even the derivation!
But the fashion's been set and in it you must be.'

The men at the reporters' table lifted their eyebrows, smiled
faintly, and leant back to watch how she took her scolding. One
with the appearance of a bald little gnome yawned agonizingly.
They had got all this down already – they heard the substance of
it now for the fourteenth time. The stipendiary would have done
it all very differently.

She found presently she was out of the dock and confronted
with the alternative of being bound over in one surety for the sum
of forty pounds – whatever that might mean – or a month's
imprisonment. 'Second class,' said someone, but first and second
were all alike to her. She elected to go to prison.

At last, after a long rumbling journey in a stuffy windowless
van, she reached Canongate Prison – for Holloway had its quota
already. It was bad luck to go to Canongate.

Prison was beastly. Prison was bleak without spaciousness,
and pervaded by a faint, oppressive smell; and she had to wait
two hours in the sullenly defiant company of two unclean women
thieves before a cell could be assigned to her. Its dreariness, like
the filthiness of the police cell, was a discovery for her. She had
imagined that prisons were white-tiled places, reeking of limewash and immaculately sanitary. Instead, they appeared to be at
the hygienic level of tramps' lodging-houses. She was bathed in
turbid water that had already been used. She was not allowed to
bathe herself: another prisoner, with a privileged manner,
washed her. Conscientious objectors to that process are not
permitted, she found, in Canongate. Her hair was washed for her
also. Then they dressed her in a dirty dress of coarse serge and a
cap, and took away her own clothes. The dress came to her only
too manifestly unwashed from its former wearer; even the under-
linen they gave her seemed unclean. Horrible memories of things
seen beneath the microscope of the baser forms of life crawled
across her mind and set her shuddering with imagined irritations.
She sat on the edge of the bed – the wardress was too busy with
the flood of arrivals that day to discover that she had it down –
and her skin was shivering from the contact of these garments.
She surveyed accommodation that seemed at first merely austere,
and became more and more manifestly inadequate as the moments fled by. She meditated profoundly through several enormous cold hours on all that had happened and all that she had

done since the swirl of the suffrage movement had submerged
her personal affairs. . . .

Very slowly emerging out of a phase of stupefaction, these
personal affairs and her personal problem resumed possession of
her mind. She had imagined she had drowned them altogether.

Chapter XI

Thoughts in Prison

I

The first night in prison she found it impossible to sleep.

The bed was hard beyond any experience of hers, the bed-clothes coarse and insufficient, the cell at once cold and stuffy. The little grating in the door, the sense of constant inspection, worried her. She kept opening her eyes and looking at it. She was fatigued physically and mentally, and neither mind nor body could rest. She became aware that at regular intervals a light flashed upon her face and a bodiless eye regarded her, and this, as the night wore on, became a torment. . . .

Capes came back into her mind. He haunted a state between hectic dreaming and mild delirium, and she found herself talking aloud to him. All through the night an entirely impossible and monumental Capes confronted her, and she argued with him about men and women. She visualized him as in a policeman's uniform and quite impassive. On some insane score she fancied she had to state her case in verse. 'We are the music and you are the instrument,' she said; 'we are verse and you are prose.'

> For men have reason, women rhyme;
> A man scores always, all the time.

This couplet sprang into her mind from nowhere, and immediately begot an endless series of similar couplets that she began to compose and address to Capes. They came teeming distressfully through her aching brain:

> A man can kick, his skirts don't tear;
> A man scores always, everywhere.

> His dress for no man lays a snare;
> A man scores always, everywhere.

> For breath and teeth they need not care;
> A man scores always, everywhere.

> For hats that fail and hats that flare;

Toppers their universal wear;
A man scores always, everywhere.

Men's waists are neither here nor there;
A man scores always, everywhere.

A man can manage without hair;
A man scores always, everywhere.

A heartening drunk I do not dare;
A man scores always, everywhere.

There are no males at men to stare;
A man scores always, everywhere.

And children must we women bear—

'Oh, damn!' she cried, as the hundred and first couplet or so presented itself in her unwilling brain.

For a time she worried about that compulsory bath and cutaneous diseases.

Then she fell into a fever of remorse for the habit of bad language she had acquired.

A man can smoke, a man can swear;
A man scores always, everywhere.

With curses deep and foulness rare;
A man scores always, everywhere.

She rolled over on her face, and stuffed her fingers in her ears to shut out the rhythm from her mind. She lay still for a long time, and her mind resumed at a more tolerable pace. She found herself talking to Capes in an undertone of rational admission.

'There is something to be said for the ladylike theory after all,' she admitted. 'Women ought to be gentle and submissive persons, strong only in virtue and in resistance to evil compulsion. My dear – I can call you that here, anyhow – I know that. The Victorians overdid it a little, I admit. Their idea of maidenly innocence was just a blank white – the sort of flat white that doesn't shine. But that doesn't alter the fact that there *is* innocence. And I've read, and thought, and guessed, and looked – until *my* innocence – it's smirched.

'Smirched! . . .

'You see, dear, one *is* passionately anxious for something – what is it? One wants to be *clean*. You want me to be clean. You would want me to be clean, if you gave me a thought, that is. . . .

'I wonder if you give me a thought. . . .

'I'm not a good woman. I don't mean I'm not a good woman – I mean that I'm not a *good* woman. My poor brain is so mixed, dear, I hardly know what I am saying. I mean I'm not a good specimen of a woman. I've got a streak of male. Things happen to women – proper women – and all they have to do is to take them well. They've just got to keep white. But I'm always trying to make things happen. And I get myself dirty. . . .

'It's all dirt that washes off, dear, but it's dirt.

'The white unaggressive woman who corrects and nurses and serves, and is worshipped and betrayed – the martyr-queen of men, the white mother. . . . You can't do that sort of thing unless you do it over religion, and there's no religion in me – of that sort – worth a rap.

'I'm not gentle. Certainly not a gentlewoman.

'I'm not coarse – no! But I've got no purity of mind – no real purity of mind. A good woman's mind has angels with flaming swords at the portals to keep out fallen thoughts. . . .

'I wonder if there are any good women really.

'I wish I didn't swear. I do swear. It began as a joke. . . . It developed into a sort of secret and private bad manners. It's got to be at last like tobacco-ash over all my sayings and doings. . . .

' "Go it, missie," they said; "Kick aht!"

'I swore at that policeman – and disgusted him. Disgusted him!

> For men policemen never blush;
> A man in all things scores so much. . . .

'Damn! Things are getting plainer. It must be the dawn creeping in.

> Now here hath been dawning another blue day;
> I'm just a poor woman, please take it away.

'Oh, sleep! Sleep! Sleep! Sleep!'

2

'Now,' said Ann Veronica, after the half-hour of exercise, and sitting on the uncomfortable wooden seat without a back that was her perch by day, 'it's no good staying here in a sort of maze. I've got nothing to do for a month but think. I may as well think. I ought to be able to think things out.

'How shall I put the question? What am I? What have I got to do with myself? . . .

'I wonder if many people *have* thought things out?

'Are we all just seizing hold of phrases and obeying moods?

'It wasn't so with old-fashioned people; they knew right from wrong; they had a clear-cut, religious faith that seemed to explain everything and give a rule for everything. We haven't. I haven't, anyhow. And it's no good pretending there is one when there isn't. . . . I suppose I believe in God. . . . Never really thought about Him – people don't. . . . I suppose my creed is: "I believe rather indistinctly in God the Father Almighty, substratum of the evolutionary process, and, in a vein of vague sentimentality that doesn't give a datum for anything at all, in Jesus Christ, His Son." . . .

'It's no sort of good, Ann Veronica, pretending one does believe when one doesn't. . . .

'And as for praying for faith – this sort of monologue is about as near as any one of my sort ever gets to prayer. Aren't I asking – asking plainly now? . . .

'We've all been mixing our ideas, and we've got intellectual hot coppers – every blessed one of us. . . .

'A confusion of motives – that's what I am. . . .

'There is this absurd craving for Mr Capes – the "Capes crave", they would call it in America. Why do I want him so badly? Why do I want him, and think about him, and fail to get away from him?

'It isn't all of me.

'The first person you love, Ann Veronica, is yourself – get hold of that! The soul you have to save is Ann Veronica's soul. . . .'

She knelt upon the floor of her cell and clasped her hands, and remained for a long time in silence.

'Oh, God,' she said at last, 'how I wish I had been taught to pray!'

3

She had some idea of putting these subtle and difficult issues to the chaplain when she was warned of his advent. But she had not reckoned with the etiquette of Canongate. She got up, as she had been told to do, at his appearance, and he amazed her by sitting down, according to custom, on her stool. He still wore his hat, to show that the days of miracles and Christ being civil to sinners are over for ever. She perceived that his countenance was only composed by a great effort, his features severely compressed. He was ruffled, and his ears were red, no doubt from some adjacent controversy. He classified her as he seated himself.

'Another young woman, I suppose,' he said, 'who knows better than her Maker about her place in the world. Have you anything to ask me?'

Ann Veronica readjusted her mind hastily. Her back stiffened. She produced from the depths of her pride the ugly investigatory note of the modern district visitor. 'Are you a special sort of clergyman,' she said, after a pause, and looking down her nose at him, 'or do you go to the universities?'

'Oh!' he said profoundly.

He panted for a moment with unuttered replies, and then, with a scornful gesture, got up and left the cell.

So that Ann Veronica was not able to get the expert advice she certainly needed upon her spiritual state.

4

After a day or so she thought more steadily. She found herself in a phase of violent reaction against the suffrage movement, a phase greatly promoted by one of those unreasonable objections people of Ann Veronica's temperament take at times – to the girl in the next cell to her own. She was a large, resilient girl, with a foolish smile, a still more foolish expression of earnestness, and a throaty contralto voice. She was noisy and hilarious and enthusiastic, and her hair was always abominably done. In the chapel she sang with an open-lunged gusto that silenced Ann Veronica altogether, and in the exercising yard slouched round with carelessly dispersed feet. Ann Veronica decided that 'hoydenish ragger' was the only phrase to express her. She was always breaking rules, whispering asides, intimating signals. She became at times an embodiment for Ann Veronica of all that made the suffrage movement defective and unsatisfying.

She was always initiating petty breaches of discipline. Her greatest exploit was the howling before the midday meal. This was an imitation of the noises made by the carnivora at the

Zoological Gardens at feeding time; the idea was taken up by prisoner after prisoner until the whole place was alive with barkings, yappings, roarings, pelican chatterings, and feline yowlings, interspersed with shrieks of hysterical laughter. To many in that crowded solitude it came as an extraordinary relief. It was better even than the hymn singing. But it annoyed Ann Veronica.

'Idiots!' she said, when she heard this pandemonium, and with particular reference to this young lady with the throaty contralto next door. 'Intolerable idiots! . . .'

It took some days for this phase to pass, and it left some scars and something like a decision. 'Violence won't do it,' said Ann Veronica. 'Begin violence, and the woman goes under. . . .

'But all the rest of our case is right. . . . Yes.'

As the long, solitary days wore on Ann Veronica found a number of definite attitudes and conclusions in her mind.

One of these was a classification of women into women who are and women who are not hostile to men. 'The real reason why I am out of place here,' she said, 'is because I like men. I can talk with them. I've never found them hostile. I've got no feminine class feeling. I don't want any laws or freedoms to protect me from a man like Mr Capes. I know that in my heart I would take whatever he gave. . . .

'A woman wants a proper alliance with a man, a man who is better stuff than herself. She wants that and needs it more than anything else in the world. It may not be just, it may not be fair, but things are so. It isn't law, nor custom, nor masculine violence settled that. It is just how things happen to be. She wants to be free – she wants to be legally and economically free, so as not to be subject to the wrong man; but only God, who made the world, can alter things to prevent her being slave to the right one.

'And if she can't have the right one?

'We've developed such a quality of preference!'

She rubbed her knuckles into her forehead. 'Oh, but life is difficult!' she groaned. 'When you loosen the tangle in one place you tie a knot in another. . . . Before there is any change, any real change, I shall be dead – dead – dead and finished – two hundred years! . . .'

5

One afternoon, while everything was still, the wardress heard her cry out suddenly and alarmingly, and with great and unmistakable passion: 'Why in the name of goodness did I burn that twenty pounds?'

6

She sat regarding her dinner. The meat was coarse and disagreeably served.

'I suppose someone makes a bit on the food,' she said. . . .

'One has such ridiculous ideas of the wicked common people and the beautiful machinery of order that ropes them in. And here are these places, full of contagion!

'Of course, this is the real texture of life; this is what we refined secure people forget. We think the whole thing is straight and noble at bottom, and it isn't. We think if we just defy the friends we have and go out into the world everything will become easy and splendid. One doesn't realize that even the sort of civilization one has at Morningside Park is held together with difficulty. By policemen one mustn't shock. . . .

'This isn't a world for an innocent girl to walk about in. It's a world of dirt and skin diseases and parasites. It's a world in which the law can be a stupid pig and the police stations dirty dens. One wants helpers and protectors – and clean water.

'Am I becoming reasonable or am I being tamed?

'I'm simply discovering that life is many-sided and complex and puzzling. I thought one had only to take it by the throat.

'It hasn't *got* a throat!'

7

One day the idea of self-sacrifice came into her head, and she made, she thought, some important moral discoveries.

It came with an extreme effect of re-discovery, a remarkable novelty. 'What have I been all this time?' she asked herself, and answered: 'Just stark egotism, crude assertion of Ann Veronica, without a modest rag of religion or discipline or respect for authority to cover me!'

It seemed to her as though she had at last found the touch-stone of conduct. She perceived she had never really thought of any one but herself in all her acts and plans. Even Capes had been for her merely an excitant to passionate love, a mere idol at whose feet one could enjoy imaginative wallowings. She had set out to get a beautiful life, a free, untrammelled life, self-development, without counting the cost either for herself or others.

'I have hurt my father,' she said; 'I have hurt my aunt. I have hurt and snubbed poor Teddy. I've made no one happy. I deserve pretty much what I've got. . . .

'If only because of the way one hurts others if one kicks loose and free, one has to submit. . . .

'Broken-in people! I suppose the world is just all egotistical children and broken-in people.

'Your little flag of pride must flutter down with the rest of them, Ann Veronica. . . .

'Compromise – and kindness.'

'Compromise and kindness.'

'Who are *you* that the world should lie down at your feet?

'You've got to be a decent citizen, Ann Veronica. Take your half loaf with the others. You mustn't go clawing after a man that doesn't belong to you – that isn't even interested in you. That's one thing clear.

'You've got to take the decent reasonable way. You've got to adjust yourself to the people God has set about you. Every one else does.'

She thought more and more along that line. There was no reason why she shouldn't be Capes's friend. He did like her, anyhow; he was always pleased to be with her. There was no reason why she shouldn't be his restrained and dignified friend. After all, that was life. Nothing was given away, and no one came so rich to the stall as to command all that it had to offer. Every one has to make a deal with the world.

It would be very good to be Capes's friend.

She might be able to go on with biology, possibly even work upon the same questions that he dealt with. . . .

Perhaps her granddaughter might marry his grandson. . . .

It grew clear to her that throughout all her wild raid for independence she had done nothing for anybody, and many people had done things for her. She thought of her aunt and that purse that was dropped on the table, and of many troublesome and ill-requited kindnesses; she thought of the help of the Widgetts, of Teddy's admiration; she thought, with a new-born charity, of her father, of Manning's conscientious unselfishness, of Miss Miniver's devotion.

'And for me it has been Pride and Pride and Pride!

'I am the prodigal daughter. I will arise and go to my father, and will say unto him—

'I suppose pride and self-assertion are sin? Sinned against heaven— Yes, I have sinned against heaven and before thee. . . .

'Poor old daddy! I wonder if he'll spend much on the fatted calf? . . .

'The wrappered life – discipline! One comes to that at last. I begin to understand Jane Austen and chintz covers and decency and refinement and all the rest of it. One puts gloves on one's greedy fingers. One learns to sit up. . . .

'And somehow or other,' she added after a long interval, 'I must pay Mr Ramage back his forty pounds.'

Chapter XII

Ann Veronica Puts Things in Order

1

Ann Veronica made a strenuous attempt to carry out her good resolutions. She meditated long and carefully upon her letter to her father before she wrote it, and gravely and deliberately again before she dispatched it.

'MY DEAR FATHER,' she wrote, '*I have been thinking hard about everything since I was sent to this prison. All these experiences have taught me a great deal about life and realities. I see that compromise is more necessary to life than I ignorantly supposed it to be, and I have been trying to get Lord Morley's book on that subject,* but it does not appear to be available in the prison library, and the chaplain seems to regard him as an undesirable writer.*'

At this point she had perceived that she was drifting from her subject.

'*I must read him when I come out. But I see very clearly that as things are a daughter is necessarily dependent on her father and bound while she is in that position to live harmoniously with his ideals.*'

'Bit starchy,' said Ann Veronica, and altered the key abruptly. Her concluding paragraph was, on the whole, perhaps, hardly starchy enough.

'*Really, daddy, I am sorry for all I have done to put you out. May I come home and try to be a better daughter to you?*

'ANN VERONICA.'

2

Her aunt came to meet her outside Canongate, and, being a little confused between what was official and what was merely a rebellious slight upon our national justice, found herself involved in a triumphal procession to the Vindicator Vegetarian Restaurant, and was specifically and personally cheered by a small, shabby crowd outside that rendezvous. They decided, quite audibly:

'She's an Old Dear, anyhow. Voting wouldn't do no 'arm to 'er.' She was on the very verge of a vegetarian meal before she recovered her head again. Obeying some fine instinct she had come to the prison in a dark veil, but she had pushed this up to kiss Ann Veronica and never drawn it down again. Eggs were procured for her, and she sat out the subsequent emotions and eloquence with the dignity becoming an injured lady of good family. The quiet encounter and homecoming Ann Veronica and she had contemplated was entirely disorganized by this misadventure; there were no adequate explanations, and after they had settled things at Ann Veronica's lodgings they reached home in the early afternoon estranged and depressed, with headaches and the trumpet voice of the indomitable Kitty Brett still ringing in their ears.

'Dreadful women, my dear!' said Miss Stanley. 'And some of them quite pretty and well dressed. No need to do such things. We must never let your father know we went. Why ever did you let me get into that wagonette?'

'I thought we had to,' said Ann Veronica, who had also been a little under the compulsion of the marshals of the occasion. 'It was very tiring.'

'We will have some tea in the drawing-room as soon as ever we can – and I will take my things off. I don't think I shall ever care for this bonnet again. We'll have some buttered toast. Your poor cheeks are quite sunken and hollow. . . .'

3

When Ann Veronica found herself in her father's study that evening it seemed to her for a moment as though all the events of the past six months had been a dream. The big grey spaces of London, the shop-lit, greasy, shining streets, had become very remote; the biological laboratory with its work and emotions, the meetings and discussions, the rides in hansoms with Ramage, were like things in a book read and closed. The study seemed absolutely unaltered; there was still the same lamp with a little chip out of the shade, still the same gas fire, still the same bundle of blue and white papers, it seemed, with the same pink tape about them, at the elbow of the arm-chair, still the same father. He sat in much the same attitude, and she stood just as she had stood when he told her she could not go to the Fadden dance. Both had dropped the rather elaborate politeness of the dining-room, and in their faces an impartial observer would have discovered little lines of obstinate wilfulness in common; a certain hardness – sharp, indeed, in the father and softly rounded in the daughter – but hardness nevertheless, that made every compromise a bargain and every charity a discount.

'And so you have been thinking?' her father began, quoting her letter and looking over his slanting glasses at her. 'Well, my girl, I wish you had thought about all these things before these bothers began.'

Ann Veronica perceived that she must not forget to remain eminently reasonable.

'One has to live and learn,' she remarked with a passable imitation of her father's manner.

'So long as you learn,' said Mr Stanley.

Their conversation hung.

'I suppose, daddy, you've no objection to my going on with my work at the Imperial College?' she asked.

'If it will keep you busy,' he said with a faintly ironical smile.

'The fees are paid to the end of the session.'

He nodded twice, with his eyes on the fire, as though that was a formal statement.

'You may go on with that work,' he said. 'So long as you keep in harmony with things at home. I'm convinced that much of Russell's investigations are on wrong lines, unsound lines. Still – you must learn for yourself. You're of age – you're of age.'

'The work's almost essential for the B.Sc. exam.'

'It's scandalous, but I suppose it is.'

Their agreement so far seemed remarkable, and yet as a home-coming the thing was a little lacking in warmth. But Ann Veronica had still to get to her chief topic. They were silent for a time. 'It's a period of crude views and crude work,' said Mr Stanley. 'Still, these Mendelian fellows seem likely to give Mr Russell trouble, a good lot of trouble. Some of their specimens – wonderfully selected, wonderfully got up.'

'Daddy,' said Ann Veronica, 'these affairs – being away from home has – cost money.'

'I thought you would find that out.'

'As a matter of fact, I happen to have got a little into debt.'

'*Never*!'

Her heart sank at the change in his expression.

'Well, lodgings and things! And I paid my fees at the college.'

'Yes. But how could you get – Who gave you credit?'

'You see,' said Ann Veronica, 'my landlady kept on my room while I was in Canongate, and the fees for the college mounted up pretty considerably.' She spoke rather quickly, because she found her father's question the most awkward she had ever had to answer in her life.

'Molly and you settled about the rooms. She said you *had* some money.'

'I borrowed it,' said Ann Veronica in a casual tone, with white despair in her heart.

'But who could have lent you money?'

'I pawned my pearl necklace. I got three pounds, and there's three on my watch.'

'Six pounds. H'm. Got the tickets? Yes, but then – you said you borrowed?'

'I did, too,' said Ann Veronica.

'Who from?'

She met his eye for a second and her heart failed her. The truth was impossible, indecent. If she mentioned Ramage he might have a fit – anything might happen. She lied. 'The Widgetts,' she said.

'Tut, tut!' he said. 'Really, Vee, you seem to have advertised our relations pretty generally!'

'They – they knew, of course. Because of the dance.'

'How much do you owe them?'

She knew forty pounds was a quite impossible sum for their neighbours. She knew, too, she must not hesitate. 'Eight pounds,' she plunged, and added foolishly, 'fifteen pounds will see me clear of everything.' She muttered some unlady-like comment upon herself under her breath and engaged in secret additions.

Mr Stanley determined to improve the occasion. He seemed to deliberate. 'Well,' he said at last slowly, 'I'll pay it. I'll pay it. But I do hope, Vee, I do hope – this is the end of these adventures. I hope you have learnt your lesson now and come to see – come to realize – how things are. People, nobody, can do as they like in this world. Everywhere there are limitations.'

'I know,' said Ann Veronica (fifteen pounds!). 'I have learnt that. I mean – I mean to do what I can.' (Fifteen pounds. Fifteen from forty is twenty-five.)

He hesitated. She could think of nothing more to say.

'Well,' she achieved at last. 'Here goes for the new life!'

'Here goes for the new life!' he echoed and stood up. Father and daughter regarded each other warily, each more than a little insecure with the other. He made a movement towards her, and then recalled the circumstances of their last conversation in that study. She saw his purpose and his doubt, hesitated also, and then went to him, took his coat lapels, and kissed him on the cheek.

'Ah, Vee,' he said, 'that's better!' and kissed her back rather clumsily. 'We're going to be sensible.'

She disengaged herself from him and went out of the room with a grave, preoccupied expression. (Fifteen pounds! And she wanted forty!)

4

It was, perhaps, the natural consequence of a long and tiring and exciting day that Ann Veronica should pass a broken and distressful night, a night in which the noble and self-subduing resolutions of Canongate displayed themselves for the first time in an atmosphere of almost lurid dismay. Her father's peculiar stiffness of soul presented itself now as something altogether left out of the calculations upon which her plans were based, and, in particular, she had not anticipated the difficulty she would find in borrowing the forty pounds she needed for Ramage. That had taken her by surprise, and her tired wits had failed her. She was to have fifteen pounds, and no more. She knew that to expect more now was like anticipating a gold mine in the garden. The chance had gone. It became suddenly glaringly apparent to her that it was impossible to return fifteen pounds or any sum less than twenty pounds to Ramage – absolutely impossible. She realized that with a pang of disgust and horror.

Already she had sent him twenty pounds, and never written to explain to him why it was she had not sent it back sharply directly he returned it. She ought to have written at once and told him exactly what had happened. Now if she sent fifteen pounds the suggestion that she had spent a five-pound note in the meanwhile would be irresistible. No! That was impossible. She would have just to keep the fifteen pounds until she could make it twenty. That might happen on her birthday – in August.

She turned about, and was persecuted by visions, half memories, half dreams, of Ramage. He became ugly and monstrous, dunning her, threatening her, assailing her.

'Confound sex from first to last!' said Ann Veronica. 'Why can't we propagate by sexless spores, as the ferns do? We restrict each other, we badger each other, friendship is poisoned and buried under it! . . . I *must* pay off that forty pounds. I *must*.'

For a time there seemed no comfort for her even in Capes. She was to see Capes to-morrow, but now, in this state of misery she had achieved she felt assured he would turn his back upon her, take no notice of her at all. And if he didn't, what was the good of seeing him? 'I wish he was a woman,' she said, 'then I could make him my friend. I want him as my friend. I want to talk to him and go about with him. Just go about with him.'

She was silent for a time, with her nose on the pillow, and that brought her to: 'What's the good of pretending?

'I love him,' she said aloud to the dim forms of her room, and repeated it, and went on to imagine herself doing acts of tragically doglike devotion to the biologist, who, for the purposes of the drama, remained entirely unconscious of and indifferent to her proceedings.

At last some anodyne formed itself from these exercises, and, with eyelashes wet with such feeble tears as only three-o'clock-in-the-morning pathos can distil, she fell asleep.

5

Pursuant to some altogether private calculations she did not go up to the Imperial College until after midday, and she found the laboratory deserted, even as she desired. She went to the table under the end window at which she had been accustomed to work, and found it swept and garnished with full bottles of reagents. Everything was very neat; it had evidently been straightened up and kept for her. She put down the sketch-books and apparatus she had brought with her, pulled out her stool, and sat down. As she did so the preparation-room door opened behind her. She heard it open, but as she felt unable to look round in a careless manner she pretended not to hear it. Then Capes's footsteps approached. She turned with an effort.

'I expected you this morning,' he said. 'I saw – they knocked off your fetters yesterday.'

'I think it is very good of me to come this afternoon.'

'I began to be afraid you might not come at all.'

'Afraid!'

'Yes. I'm glad you're back for all sorts of reasons.' He spoke a little nervously. 'Among other things, you know, I didn't understand quite – I didn't understand that you were so keenly interested in this suffrage question. I have it on my conscience that I offended you –'

'Offended me, when?'

'I've been haunted by the memory of you. I was rude and stupid. We were talking about the suffrage – and I rather scoffed.'

'You weren't rude,' she said.

'I didn't know you were so keen on this suffrage business.'

'Nor I. You haven't had it on your mind all this time?'

'I have rather. I felt somehow I'd hurt you.'

'You didn't. I – I hurt myself.'

'I mean—'

'I behaved like an idiot, that's all. My nerves were in rags. I was worried. We're the hysterical animal,* Mr Capes. I got myself locked up to cool off. By a sort of instinct. As a dog eats grass. I'm right again now.'

'Because your nerves were exposed that was no excuse for my touching them. I ought to have seen—'

'It doesn't matter a rap – if you're not disposed to resent the – the way I behaved.'

'*I* resent!'

'I was only sorry, I'd been so stupid.'

'Well, I take it we're straight again,' said Capes with a note of relief, and assumed an easier position on the edge of her table. 'But if you weren't keen on the suffrage business, why on earth did you go to prison?'

Ann Veronica reflected. 'It was a phase,' she said.

He smiled. 'It's a new phase in the life history,' he remarked. 'Everybody seems to have it now. Everybody who's going to develop into a woman.'

'There's Miss Garvice.'

'She's coming on,' said Capes. 'And, you know, you're altering us all. *I'm* shaken. The campaign's a success.' He met her questioning eye, and repeated: 'Oh! it *is* a success. A man is so apt to – to take women a little too lightly. Unless they remind him now and then not to. . . . *You* did.'

'Then I didn't waste my time in prison altogether?'

'It wasn't the prison impressed me. But I liked the things you said here. I felt suddenly I understood you – as an intelligent person. If you'll forgive my saying that, and implying what goes with it. There's something – puppyish in a man's usual attitude to women. That is what I've had on my conscience. . . . I don't think we're altogether to blame if we don't take some of your lot seriously. Some of your sex, I mean. But we smirk a little, I'm afraid, habitually when we talk to you. We smirk, and we're a bit – furtive.'

He paused, with his eyes studying her gravely. 'You, anyhow, don't deserve it,' he said.

Their colloquy was ended abruptly by the apparition of Miss Klegg at the further door. When she saw Ann Veronica she stood for a moment as if entranced, and then advanced with out-stretched hands. 'Véronique!' she cried with a rising intonation, though never before had she called Ann Veronica anything but Miss Stanley, and seized her and squeezed her and kissed her with profound emotion. 'To think that you were going to do it – and never said a word! You are a little thin, but except for that you look – you look better than ever. Was it *very* horrible? I tried to get into the police court, but the crowd was ever so much too big, push as I would. . . .

'I mean to go to prison directly the session is over,' said Miss Klegg. 'Wild horses – not if they have all the mounted police in London – shan't keep me out.'

6

Capes lit things wonderfully for Ann Veronica all that afternoon, he was so friendly, so palpably interested in her, and glad to have her back with him. Tea in the laboratory was a sort of suffragette reception. Miss Garvice assumed a quality of neutrality, professed herself almost won over by Ann Veronica's example, and the Scotchman decided that if women had a distinctive sphere it was, at any rate, an enlarging sphere, and no one who believed in the doctrine of evolution could logically deny the vote to women 'ultimately', however much they might be disposed to doubt the advisability of its immediate concession. It was a refusal of expediency, he said, and not an absolute refusal. The youth with his hair like Russell cleared his throat and said rather irrelevantly that he knew a man who knew Thomas Bayard Simmons, who had rioted in the Strangers' Gallery, and then Capes, finding them all distinctly pro-Ann Veronica, if not pro-feminist, ventured to be perverse, and started a vein of speculation upon the Scotchman's idea – that there were still hopes of women evolving into something higher.

He was unusually absurd and ready, and all the time it seemed to Ann Veronica as a delightful possibility, as a thing not indeed to be entertained seriously, but to be half furtively felt, that he was being so agreeable because she had come back again. She returned home through a world that was as roseate as it had been grey overnight.

But as she got out of the train at Morningside Park station she had a shock. She saw, twenty yards down the platform, the shiny hat and broad back and inimitable swagger of Ramage. She dived at once behind the cover of the lamp room and affected serious trouble with her shoe-lace until he was out of the station, and then she followed slowly and with extreme discretion until the bifurcation of the Avenue from the field way ensured her escape. Ramage went up the Avenue, and she hurried along the path with a beating heart and a disagreeable sense of unsolved problems in her mind.

'That thing's going on,' she told herself. 'Everything goes on, confound it! One doesn't change anything one has set going by making good resolutions.'

And then ahead of her she saw the radiant and welcoming figure of Manning. He came as an agreeable diversion from an insoluble perplexity. She smiled at the sight of him, and thereat his radiation increased.

'I missed the hour of your release,' he said, 'but I was at the Vindicator Restaurant. You did not see me, I know. I was among the common herd in the place below, but I took good care to see you.'

'Of course you're converted?' she said.

'To the view that all those Splendid Women in the movement ought to have votes? Rather! Who could help it?'

He towered up over her and smiled down at her in his fatherly way.

'To the view that all women ought to have votes whether they like it or not?'

He shook his head, and his eyes and the mouth under the black moustache wrinkled with his smile. And as he walked by her side they began a wrangle that was none the less pleasant to Ann Veronica because it served to banish a disagreeable preoccupation.

It seemed to her in her restored geniality that she liked Manning extremely. The brightness Capes had diffused over the world glorified even his rival.

7

The steps by which Ann Veronica determined to engage herself to marry Manning were never very clear to her. A medley of motives warred in her, and it was certainly not one of the least of these that she knew herself to be passionately in love with Capes; at moments she had a giddy intimation that he was beginning to feel keenly interested in her. She realized more and more the quality of the brink upon which she stood – the dreadful readiness with which in certain moods she might plunge, the unmitigated wrongness and recklessness of such a self-abandonment. 'He must never know,' she would whisper to herself, 'he must never know. Or else – Else it will be impossible that I can be his friend.'

That simple statement of the case was by no means all that went on in Ann Veronica's mind. But it was the form of her ruling determination; it was the only form that she ever allowed to see daylight. What else was there lurked in shadows and deep places; if in some mood of reverie it came out into the light, it was presently overwhelmed and hustled back again into hiding. She would never look squarely at these dream forms that mocked the social order in which she lived, never admit she listened to the soft whisperings in her ear. But Manning seemed more and more clearly indicated as a refuge, as security. Certain simple purposes emerged from the disingenuous muddle of her feelings and desires. Seeing Capes from day to day made a bright eventfulness that hampered her in the course she had resolved to follow. She vanished from the laboratory for a week, a week of oddly interesting days. . . .

When she renewed her attendance at the Imperial College the third finger of her left hand was adorned with a very fine old ring with dark blue sapphires that had once belonged to a great-aunt of Manning's.

That ring manifestly occupied her thoughts a great deal. She kept pausing in her work and regarding it, and when Capes came round to her, she first put her hand in her lap and then rather awkwardly in front of him. But men are often blind to rings. He seemed to be.

In the afternoon she had considered certain doubts very carefully, and decided on a more emphatic course of action. 'Are these ordinary sapphires?' she said. He bent to her hand, and she slipped off the ring and gave it to him to examine.

'Very good,' he said. 'Rather darker than most of them. But I'm generously ignorant of gems. Is it an old ring?' he asked, returning it.

'I believe it is. It's an engagement ring. . . .' She slipped it on her finger, and added in a voice she tried to make matter-of-fact: 'It was given to me last week.'

'Oh!' he said in a colourless tone, and with his eyes on her face.

'Yes. Last week.'

She glanced at him, and it was suddenly apparent for one instant of illumination that this ring upon her finger was the crowning blunder of her life. It was apparent, and then it faded into the quality of an inevitable necessity.

'Odd!' he remarked, rather surprisingly, after a little interval.

There was a brief pause, a crowded pause, between them.

She sat very still, and his eyes rested on that ornament for a moment, and then travelled slowly to her wrist and the soft lines of her forearm.

'I suppose I ought to congratulate you,' he said. Their eyes met, and his expressed perplexity and curiosity. 'The fact is – I don't know why – this takes me by surprise. Somehow – I haven't connected the idea with you. You seemed complete – without that.'

'Did I?' she said.

'I don't know why. But this is like – like walking round a house that looks square and complete and finding an unexpected long wing running out behind.'

She looked up at him, and found he was watching her closely. For some seconds of voluminous thinking they looked at the ring between them, and neither spoke. Then Capes shifted his eyes to her microscope, and the little trays of unmounted sections beside it. 'How is that carmine working?' he asked, with a forced interest.

'Better,' said Ann Veronica, with an unreal alacrity. 'But it still misses the nucleolus.'

Chapter XIII

The Sapphire Ring

I

For a time that ring set with sapphires seemed to be, after all, the satisfactory solution of Ann Veronica's difficulties. It was like pouring a strong acid over dulled metal. A tarnish of constraint that had recently spread over her intercourse with Capes vanished again. They embarked upon an open and declared friendship. They even talked about friendship. They went to the Zoological Gardens together one Saturday to see for themselves a point of morphological interest about the toucan's bill – that friendly and entertaining bird – and they spent the rest of the afternoon walking about and elaborating in general terms this theme and the superiority of intellectual fellowship to all merely passionate relationships. Upon this topic Capes was heavy and conscientious, but that seemed to her to be just exactly what he ought to be. He was also, had she known it, more than a little insincere. 'We are only in the dawn of the Age of Friendship,' he said, 'when interests, I suppose, will take the place of passions. Either you have had to love people or hate them – which is a sort of love, too, in its way – to get anything out of them. Now, more and more, we're going to be interested in them, to be curious about them and – quite mildly – experimental with them.'

He seemed to be elaborating ideas as he talked. They watched the chimpanzees in the new apes' house, and admired the gentle humanity of their eyes – 'so much more human than human beings' – and they watched the Agile Gibbon in the next apartment doing wonderful leaps and aerial somersaults.

'I wonder which of us enjoys that most,' said Capes – 'does he, or do we?'

'He seems to get a zest—'

'He does it and forgets it. We remember it. These joyful bounds just lace into the stuff of my memories and stay there for ever. Living's just material.'

'It's very good to be alive.'

'It's better to know life than be life.'

'One may do both,' said Ann Veronica.

She was in a very uncritical state that afternoon. When he said: 'Let's go and see the wart-hog,' she thought no one ever had had so quick a flow of good ideas as he; and when he explained that sugar and not buns was the talisman of popularity among the animals, she marvelled at his practical omniscience.

Finally, at the exit into Regent's Park, they ran against Miss Klegg. It was the expression of Miss Klegg's face that put the idea into Ann Veronica's head of showing Manning at the college one day, an idea which she didn't for some reason or other carry out for a fortnight.

2

When at last she did so, the sapphire ring took on a new quality in the imagination of Capes. It ceased to be the symbol of liberty and a remote and quite abstracted person, and became suddenly and very disagreeably the token of a large and portentous body, visible and tangible.

Manning appeared just at the end of the afternoon's work, and the biologist was going through some perplexities the Scotchman had created by a metaphysical treatment of the skulls of *Hyrax* and a young African elephant. He was clearing up these difficulties by tracing a partially obliterated suture the Scotchman had overlooked when the door from the passage opened, and Manning came into his universe.

Seen down the length of the laboratory, Manning looked a very handsome and shapely gentleman indeed, and at the sight of his eager advance to his fiancée, Miss Klegg replaced one long-cherished romance about Ann Veronica by one more normal and simple. He carried a cane and a silk hat with a mourning-band in one grey-gloved hand; his frock coat and trousers were admirable; his handsome face, his black moustache, his prominent brow conveyed an eager solicitude.

'I want,' he said, with a white hand outstretched, 'to take you out to tea.'

'I've been clearing up,' said Ann Veronica brightly.

'All your dreadful scientific things?' he said, with a smile that Miss Klegg thought extraordinarily kindly.

'All my dreadful scientific things,' said Ann Veronica.

He stood back, smiling with an air of proprietorship, and looking about him at the business-like equipment of the room. The low ceiling made him seem abnormally tall. Ann Veronica wiped a scalpel, put a card over a watch-glass containing thin shreds of embryonic guinea-pig swimming in mauve stain, and dismantled her microscope.

'I wish I understood more of biology,' said Manning.

'I'm ready,' said Ann Veronica, closing her microscope box with a click, and looking for one brief instant up the laboratory. 'We have no airs and graces here, and my hat hangs from a peg in the passage.'

She led the way to the door, and Manning passed behind her and round her and opened the door for her. When Capes glanced up at them for a moment Manning seemed to be holding his arms all about her, and there was nothing but quiet acquiescence in her bearing.

After Capes had finished the Scotchman's troubles he went back into the preparation room. He sat down on the sill of the open window, folded his arms, and stared straight before him for a long time over the wilderness of tiles and chimney pots into a sky that was blue and empty. He was not addicted to monologue, and the only audible comment he permitted himself at first upon a universe that was evidently anything but satisfactory to him that afternoon, was one compact and entirely unassigned 'Damn!'

The word must have had some gratifying quality, because he repeated it. Then he stood up and repeated it again. 'The fool I have been!' he cried; and now speech was coming to him. He tried this sentence with expletives. 'Ass!' he went on, still warming. 'Muck-headed moral ass! I ought to have done anything. I ought to have done anything!

'What's a man for?

'Friendship!'

He doubled up his fist, and seemed to contemplate thrusting it through the window. He turned his back on that temptation. Then suddenly he seized a new preparation bottle that stood upon his table and contained the better part of a week's work – a displayed dissection of a snail, beautifully done – and hurled it across the room, to smash resoundingly upon the cemented floor under the bookcase; then, without either haste or pause, he swept his arm along a shelf of reagents and sent them to mingle with the debris on the floor. They fell in a diapason of smashes. 'H'm!' he said, regarding the wreckage with a calmer visage. 'Silly!' he remarked after a pause. 'One hardly knows – all the time.'

He put his hands in his pockets, his mouth puckered to a whistle, and he went to the door of the outer preparation room and stood there, looking, save for the faintest intensification of his natural ruddiness, the embodiment of blond serenity.

'Gellett,' he called, 'just come and clear up a mess, will you? I've smashed some things.'

3

There was one serious flaw in Ann Veronica's arrangements for self-rehabilitation, and that was Ramage. He hung over her – he and his loan to her and his connection with her and that terrible evening – a vague, disconcerting possibility of annoyance and exposure. She could not see any relief from this anxiety except repayment, and repayment seemed impossible. The raising of twenty-five pounds was a task altogether beyond her powers. Her birthday was four months away, and that, at its extremest point, might give her another five pounds.

The thing rankled in her mind night and day. She would wake in the night to repeat her bitter cry: 'Oh, why did I burn those notes?'

It added greatly to the annoyance of the situation that she had twice seen Ramage in the Avenue since her return to the shelter of her father's roof. He had saluted her with elaborate civility, his eyes distended with indecipherable meanings.

She felt she was bound in honour to tell the whole affair to Manning sooner or later. Indeed, it seemed inevitable that she must clear it up with his assistance, or not at all. And when Manning was not about the thing seemed simple enough. She would compose extremely lucid and honourable explanations. But when it came to broaching them, it proved to be much more difficult than she had supposed.

They went down the great staircase of the building, and, while she sought in her mind for a beginning, he broke into appreciation of her simple dress and self-congratulations upon their engagement.

'It makes me feel,' he said, 'that nothing is impossible – to have you here beside me. I said that day at Surbiton: "There's many good things in life, but there's only one best, and that's the wild-haired girl who's pulling away at that oar. I will make her my Grail, and some day, perhaps, if God wills, she shall become my wife!" '

He looked very hard before him as he said this, and his voice was full of deep feeling.

'Grail!' said Ann Veronica; and then: 'Oh, yes – of course! Anything but a holy one, I'm afraid.'

'Altogether holy, Ann Veronica. Ah! but you can't imagine what you are to me and what you mean to me! I suppose there is something mystical and wonderful about all women.'

'There is something mystical and wonderful about all human beings. I don't see that men need bank it with the women.'

'A man does,' said Manning – 'a true man, anyhow. And for me there is only one treasure house. By Jove! When I think of it I want to leap and shout!'

'It would astonish that man with the barrow.'

'It astonishes me that I don't,' said Manning, in a tone of intense self-enjoyment.

'I think,' began Ann Veronica, 'that you don't realize—'

He disregarded her entirely. He waved an arm and spoke with a peculiar resonance. 'I feel like a giant! I believe now I shall do great things. Gods! what it must be to pour out strong, splendid verse – mighty lines! mighty lines! If I do, Ann Veronica, it will be you. It will be altogether you. I will dedicate my books to you. I will lay them all at your feet.'

He beamed upon her.

'I don't think you realize,' Ann Veronica began again, 'that I am rather a defective human being.'

'I don't want to,' said Manning. 'They say there are spots on the sun. Not for me. It warms me, and lights me, and fills my world with flowers. Why should I peep at it through smoked glass to see things that don't affect me?' He smiled his delight at his companion.

'I've got bad faults.'

He shook his head slowly, smiling mysteriously.

'But perhaps I want to confess them.'

'I grant you absolution.'

'I don't want absolution. I want to make myself visible to you.'

'I wish I could make you visible to yourself. I don't believe in the faults. They're just a joyous softening of the outline – more beautiful than perfection. Like the flaws of an old marble. If you talk of your faults I shall talk of your splendours.'

'I do want to tell you things, nevertheless.'

'We'll have, thank God! ten myriad days to tell each other things. When I think of it—'

'But these are things I want to tell you now!'

'I made a little song of it. Let me say it to you. I've no name for it yet. Epithalamy might do.

> 'Like him who stood on Darien,
> 	I view uncharted sea,
> Ten thousand days, ten thousand nights
> 	Before my queen and me.

'And that only brings me up to about sixty-five!

> 'A glittering wilderness of time,
> 	That to the sunset reaches;
> No keel as yet its waves has ploughed,
> 	Or gritted on its beaches.
>
> And we will sail that splendour wide,
> 	From day to day together,
> From isle to isle of happiness,
> 	Through years of God's own weather.'

'Yes,' said his prospective fellow sailor, 'that's very pretty.' She stopped short, full of things unsaid. Pretty! Ten thousand days, ten thousand nights!

'You shall tell me your faults,' said Manning. 'If they matter to you, they matter.'

'It isn't precisely faults,' said Ann Veronica. 'It's something that bothers me.' Ten thousand! Put that way it seemed so different.

'Then assuredly!' said Manning.

She found a little difficulty in beginning. She was glad when he went on: 'I want to be your city of refuge from every sort of bother. I want to stand between you and all the force and vileness of the world. I want to make you feel that here is a place where the crowd does not clamour, nor ill winds blow.'

'That is all very well,' said Ann Veronica, unheeded.

'That is my dream of you,' said Manning, warming. 'I want my life to be beaten gold just in order to make it a fitting setting for yours. There you will be, in an inner temple. I want to enrich it with hangings and gladden it with verses. I want to fill it with fine and precious things. And by degrees, perhaps, that maiden distrust of yours that makes you shrink from my kisses, will vanish. . . . Forgive me if a certain warmth creeps into my words! The park is green and grey to-day, but I am glowing pink and gold. . . . It is difficult to express these things.'

4

They sat with tea and strawberries and cream before them at a little table in front of the pavilion in Regent's Park. Her confession was still unmade. Manning leant forward on the table, talking discursively on the probable brilliance of their married life. Ann Veronica sat back in an attitude of inattention, her eyes on a distant game of cricket, her mind perplexed and busy. She was recalling the circumstances under which she had engaged herself to Manning, and trying to understand a curious development of the quality of this relationship.

The particulars of her engagement were very clear in her memory. She had taken care he should have this momentous talk with her on a garden seat commanded by the windows of the house. They had been playing tennis, with his manifest intention looming over her.

'Let us sit down for a moment,' he had said. He made his speech a little elaborately. She plucked at the knots of her racket and heard him to the end, then spoke in a restrained undertone.

'You ask me to be engaged to you, Mr Manning,' she began.

'I want to lay all my life at your feet.'

'Mr Manning, I do not think I love you. . . . I want to be very plain with you. I have nothing, nothing that can possibly be passion for you. I am sure. Nothing at all.'

He was silent for some moments.

'Perhaps that is only sleeping,' he said. 'How can you know?'

'I think – perhaps I am rather a cold-blooded person.'

She stopped. He remained listening attentively.

'You have been very kind to me,' she said.

'I would give my life for you.'

Her heart had warmed towards him. It had seemed to her that life might be very good indeed with his kindliness and sacrifice about her. She thought of him as always courteous and helpful, as realizing, indeed, his ideal of protection and service, as chival-rously leaving her free to live her own life, rejoicing with an infinite generosity in every detail of her irresponsive being. She twanged the catgut under her fingers.

'It seems so unfair,' she said, 'to take all you offer me and give so little in return.'

'It is all the world to me. And we are not traders looking at equivalents.'

'You know, Mr Manning, I do not really want to marry.'

'No.'

'It seems so – so unworthy' – she picked among her phrases – 'of the noble love you give—'

She stopped, through the difficulty she found in expressing herself.

'But I am judge of that,' said Manning.

'Would you wait for me?'

Manning was silent for a space. 'As my lady wills.'

'Would you let me go on studying for a time?'

'If you order patience.'

'I think, Mr Manning . . . I do not know. It is so difficult. When I think of the love you give me – One ought to give you back love.'

'You like me?'

'Yes. And I am grateful to you. . . .'

Manning tapped with his racket on the turf through some moments of silence. 'You are the most perfect, the most glorious of created beings – tender, frank, intellectual, brave, beautiful. I am your servitor. I am ready to wait for you, to wait your pleasure, to give all my life to winning it. Let me only wear your livery. Give me but leave to try. You want to think for a time, to be free for a time. That is so like you, Diana – Pallas Athene! (Pallas Athene is better.) You are all the slender goddesses. I understand. Let me engage myself. That is all I ask.'

She looked at him; his face, downcast and in profile, was handsome and strong. Her gratitude swelled within her.

'You are too good for me,' she said in a low voice.

'Then you – you will?'

A long pause.

'It isn't fair. . . .'

'But will you?'

'*Yes*.'

For some seconds he had remained quite still.

'If I sit here,' he said, standing up before her abruptly, 'I shall have to shout. Let us walk about. Tum, tum, tirray tum, tum, tum, te-tum – that thing of Mendelssohn's! If making one human being absolutely happy is any satisfaction to you—'

He held out his hands, and she also stood up.

He drew her close up to him with a strong, steady pull. Then suddenly, in front of all those windows, he folded her in his arms and pressed her to him, and kissed her unresisting face.

'Don't!' cried Ann Veronica, struggling faintly, and he released her.

'Forgive me,' he said. 'But I am at singing pitch.'

She had had a moment of sheer panic at the thing she had done. 'Mr Manning,' she said, 'for a time— Will you tell no one? Will you keep this – our secret? I'm doubtful— Will you please not even tell my aunt?'

'As you will,' he said. 'But if my manner tells! I cannot help it if that shows. You only mean a secret – for a little time?'

'Just for a little time,' she said; 'yes. . . .'

But the ring, and her aunt's triumphant eye, and a note of approval in her father's manner, and a novel disposition in him to praise Manning in a just, impartial voice had soon placed very definite qualifications upon that covenanted secrecy.

5

At first the quality of her relationship to Manning seemed moving and beautiful to Ann Veronica. She admired and rather pitied him, and she was unfeignedly grateful to him. She even thought that perhaps she might come to love him, in spite of that faint indefinable flavour of absurdity that pervaded his courtly bearing. She would never love him as she loved Capes, of course, but there are grades and qualities of love. For Manning it would be a more temperate love altogether. Much more temperate; the discreet and joyless love of a virtuous, reluctant, condescending wife. She had been quite convinced that an engagement with him and at last a marriage had exactly that quality of compromise which distinguishes the ways of the wise. It would be the wrappered world almost at its best. She saw herself building up a life upon that – a life restrained, kindly, beautiful, a little pathetic and altogether dignified; a life of great disciplines and suppressions and extensive reserves. . . .

But the Ramage affair needed clearing up, of course; it was a flaw upon that project. She had to explain about and pay off that forty pounds. . . .

Then, quite insensibly, her queenliness had declined. She was never able to trace the changes her attitude had undergone, from the time when she believed herself to be the pampered Queen of Fortune, the crown of a good man's love (and secretly, but nobly, worshipping someone else), to the time when she realized she was in fact just a mannequin for her lover's imagination, and that he cared no more for the realities of her being, for the things she felt and desired, for the passions and dreams that might move her, than a child cares for the sawdust in its doll. She was the actress his whim had chosen to play a passive part. . . .

It was one of the most educational disillusionments in Ann Veronica's career.

But did many women get anything better?

This afternoon, when she was urgent to explain her hampering and tainting complication with Ramage, the realization of this alien quality in her relationship with Manning became acute. Hitherto it had been qualified by her conception of all life as a compromise, by her new effort to be unexacting of life. But she perceived that to tell Manning of her Ramage adventures as they had happened would be like tarring figures upon a water-colour. They were in a different key, they had a different timbre. How could she tell him what indeed already began to puzzle herself, why she had borrowed that money at all? The plain fact was that she had grabbed a bait. She had grabbed! She became less and less attentive to his meditative, self-complacent fragments of talk as she told herself this. Her secret thoughts made some hasty, half-hearted excursions into the possibility of telling the thing in romantic tones – Ramage as a black villain, she as a white, fantastically white, maiden. . . . She doubted if Manning would even listen to that. He would refuse to listen and absolve her unshriven.

Then it came to her with a shock, as an extraordinary oversight, that she could never tell Manning about Ramage – never.

She dismissed the idea of doing so. But that still left the forty pounds! . . .

Her mind went on generalizing. So it would always be between herself and Manning. She saw her life before her robbed of all generous illusions, the wrappered life unwrapped for ever, vistas of dull responses, crises of make-believe, years of exacting mutual disregard in a misty garden of fine sentiments.

But did any woman get anything better from a man? Perhaps every woman conceals herself from a man perforce! . . .

She thought of Capes. She could not help thinking of Capes. Surely Capes was different. Capes looked at one and not over one, spoke to one, treated one as a visible concrete fact. Capes saw her, felt for her, cared for her greatly, even if he did not love her. Anyhow, he did not sentimentalize her. And she had been doubting since that walk in the Zoological Gardens whether, indeed, he did simply care for her. Little things, almost impalpable, had happened to justify that doubt; something in his manner had belied his words. Did he not look for her in the morning when she entered – come very quickly to her? She thought of him as she had last seen him looking down the length of the laboratory to see her go. Why had he glanced up – quite in that way? . . .

The thought of Capes flooded her being like long-veiled sunlight breaking again through clouds. It came to her like a dear thing rediscovered, that she loved Capes. It came to her that to marry any one but Capes was impossible. If she could not marry him, she would not marry any one. She would end this sham with Manning. It ought never to have begun. It was cheating, pitiful cheating. And then if some day Capes wanted her – saw fit to alter his views upon friendship. . . .

Dim possibilities that she would not seem to look at even to herself gesticulated in the twilight background of her mind.

She leapt suddenly at a desperate resolution, and in one moment had made it into a new self. She flung aside every plan she had in life, every discretion. Of course, why not? She would be honest, anyhow!

She turned her eyes to Manning.

He was sitting back from the table now, with one arm over the back of his green chair and the other resting on the little table. He was smiling under his heavy moustache, and his head was a little on one side as he looked at her.

'And what was that dreadful confession you had to make?' he was saying. His quiet, kindly smile implied his serene disbelief in any confessible thing. Ann Veronica pushed aside a tea cup and the vestiges of her strawberries and cream, and put her elbows before her on the table. 'Mr Manning,' she said, 'I *have* a confession to make.'

'I wish you would use my Christian name,' he said.

She attended to that, and then dismissed it as unimportant.

Something in her voice and manner conveyed an effect of unwonted gravity to him. For the first time he seemed to wonder what it might be that she had to confess. His smile faded.

'I don't think our engagement can go on,' she plunged, and felt exactly that loss of breath that comes with a dive into icy water.

'But, how,' he said, sitting up astonished beyond measure, 'Not go on?'

'I have been thinking while you have been talking. You see – I didn't understand.'

She stared hard at her finger nails. 'It is hard to express oneself, but I do want to be honest with you. When I promised to marry you I thought I could; I thought it was a possible arrangement. I did think it could be done. I admired your chivalry. I was grateful.'

She paused.

'Go on,' he said.

She moved her elbow nearer to him and spoke in a still lower tone. 'I told you I did not love you.'

'I know,' said Manning, nodding gravely. 'It was fine and brave of you.'

'But there is something more.'

She paused again.

'I – I am sorry— I didn't explain. These things are difficult. It wasn't clear to me that I had to explain . . . . I love someone else.'

They remained looking at each other for three or four seconds. Then Manning flopped back in his chair and dropped his chin like a man shot. There was a long silence between them.

'My God!' he said at last with tremendous feeling, and then again: 'My God!'

Now that this thing was said her mind was clear and calm. She heard this standard expression of a strong soul wrung with a critical coldness that astonished herself. She realized dimly that there was no personal thing behind this cry, that countless myriads of Mannings had 'My God!'-ed with an equal gusto at situations as flatly apprehended. This mitigated her remorse enormously. He rested his brow on his hand and conveyed magnificent tragedy by his pose.

'But why,' he said in the gasping voice of one subduing an agony, and looked at her from under a pain-wrinkled brow, 'why did you not tell me this before?'

'I didn't know— I thought I might be able to control myself.'

'And you can't?'

'I don't think I ought to control myself.'

'And I have been dreaming and thinking—'

'I am frightfully sorry. . . .'

'But— This bolt from the blue! My God! Ann Veronica; you don't understand. This – this shatters a world!'

She tried to feel sorry, but her sense of his immense egotism was strong and clear.

He went on with intense urgency.

'Why did you ever let me love you? Why did you ever let me peep through the gates of paradise? Oh, my God! I don't begin to feel and realize this yet. It seems to me just talk; it seems to me like the fancy of a dream. Tell me I haven't heard. This is a joke of yours.' He made his voice very low and full, and looked closely into her face.

She twisted her fingers tightly. 'It isn't a joke,' she said. 'I feel shabby and disgraced. . . . I ought never to have thought of it. Of you, I mean. . . .'

He fell back in his chair with an expression of tremendous desolation. 'My God!' he said again. . . .

They became aware of the waitress standing over them with book and pencil ready for their bill. 'Never mind the bill,' said Manning tragically, standing up and thrusting a four-shilling piece into her hand, and turning a broad back on her astonishment. 'Let us walk across the park at least,' he said to Ann Veronica. 'Just at present my mind simply won't take hold of this at all. . . . I tell you – never mind the bill. Keep it! Keep it!'

6

They walked a long way that afternoon. They crossed the park to the westward, and then turned back and walked round the circle about the Royal Botanical Gardens and then southwardly towards Waterloo. They trudged and talked, and Manning struggled, as he said, to 'get the hang of it all'.

It was a long, meandering talk, stupid, shameful, and unavoidable. Ann Veronica was apologetic to the bottom of her soul. At the same time she was wildly exultant at the resolution she had taken, the end she had made to her blunder. She had only to get through this, to solace Manning as much as she could, to put such clumsy plasterings on his wounds as were possible, and then, anyhow, she would be free – free to put her fate to the test. She made a few protests, a few excuses for her action in accepting him, a few lame explanations, but he did not heed them or care for them. Then she realized that it was her business to let Manning talk and impose his own interpretations upon the situation so far as he was concerned. She did her best to do this. But about his unknown rival he was acutely curious.

He made her tell him the core of the difficulty.

'I cannot say who he is,' said Ann Veronica, 'but he is a married man. . . . No! I do not even know that he cares for me. It is no good going into that. Only I just want him. I just want him, and no one else will do. It is no good arguing about a thing like that.'

'But you thought you could forget him.'

'I suppose I must have thought so. I didn't understand. Now I do.'

'By God!' said Manning, making the most of the word, 'I suppose it's fate. Fate! You are so frank, so splendid!

'I'm taking this calmly now,' he said, almost as if he apologized, 'because I'm a little stunned.'

Then he asked: 'Tell me! has this man, has he *dared* to make love to you?'

Ann Veronica had a vicious moment. 'I wish he had,' she said. 'But—'

The long inconsecutive conversation by that time was getting on her nerves. 'When one wants a thing more than anything else in the world,' she said with outrageous frankness, 'one naturally wishes one had it.'

She shocked him by that. She shattered the edifice he was building up of himself as a devoted lover, waiting only his chance to win her from a hopeless and consuming passion.

'Mr Manning,' she said, 'I warned you not to idealize me. Men ought not to idealize any woman. We aren't worth it. We've done nothing to deserve it. And it hampers us. You don't know the thoughts we have; the things we can do and say. You are a sisterless man; you have never heard the ordinary talk that goes on at a girls' boarding school.'

'Oh! but you *are* splendid and open and fearless! As if I couldn't allow. What are all these little things? Nothing! Nothing! You can't sully yourself. You can't! I tell you frankly you may break off your engagement to me – I shall hold myself still engaged to you, yours just the same. As for this infatuation – it's like some obsession, some magic thing laid upon you. It's not you – not a bit. It's a thing that's happened to you. It is like some accident. I don't care. In a sense I don't care. It makes no difference. . . . All the same, I wish I had that fellow by the throat! Just the virile, unregenerate man in me wishes that. . . .

'I suppose I should let go if I had.

'You know,' he went on, 'this doesn't seem to me to end anything. I'm rather a persistent person. I'm the sort of dog, if you turn it out of the room it lies down on the mat at the door. I'm not a lovesick boy. I'm a man, and I know what I mean. It's a tremendous blow, of course – but it doesn't kill me. And the situation it makes! – the situation!'

Thus Manning, egotistical, inconsecutive, unreal. And Ann Veronica walked beside him, trying in vain to soften her heart to him by the thought of how she had ill-used him, and all the time, as her feet and mind grew weary together, rejoicing more and more that at the cost of this one interminable walk she escaped the prospect of – what was it? – 'Ten thousand days, ten thousand nights' in his company. Whatever happened she need never return to that possibility.

'For me,' Manning went on, 'this isn't final. In a sense it alters nothing. I shall still wear your favour – even if it is a stolen and forbidden favour – in my casque. . . . I shall still believe in you. Trust you.'

He repeated several times that he would trust her, though it remained obscure just exactly where the trust came in.

'Look here,' he cried out of a silence, with a sudden flash of understanding, 'did you mean to throw me over when you came out with me this afternoon?'

Ann Veronica hesitated, and with a startled mind realized the truth. 'No,' she answered reluctantly.

'Very well,' said Manning. 'Then I don't take this as final. That's all. I've bored you or something. . . . You think you love this other man! No doubt you do love him. Before you have lived—'

He became darkly prophetic. He thrust out a rhetorical hand.

'I will *make* you love me! Until he has faded – faded into a memory. . . .'

He saw her into the train at Waterloo, and stood, a tall, grave figure, with hat upraised, as the carriage moved forward slowly and hid him. Ann Veronica sat back in with a sigh of relief.

Manning might go on now idealizing her as much as he liked. She was no longer a confederate in that. He might go on as the devoted lover until he tired. She had done for ever with the Age of Chivalry, and her own base adaptations of its traditions to the compromising life. She was honest again.

But when she turned her thoughts to Morningside Park she perceived the tangled skein of life was now to be further complicated by his romantic importunity.

Chapter XIV

The Collapse of the Penitent

I

Spring had held back that year until the dawn of May, and then spring and summer came with a rush together. Two days after this conversation between Manning and Ann Veronica, Capes came into the laboratory at lunch time and found her alone there, standing by the open window, and not even pretending to be doing anything. He came in with his hands in his trouser pockets and a general air of depression in his bearing. He was engaged in detesting Manning and himself in almost equal measure. His face brightened at the sight of her, and he came towards her.

'What are you doing?' he asked.

'Nothing,' said Ann Veronica, and stared over her shoulder out of the window.

'So am I. . . . Lassitude?'

'I suppose so.'

'*I* can't work.'

'Nor I,' said Ann Veronica.

Pause.

'It's the spring,' he said. 'It's the warming up of the year, the coming of the light mornings, the way in which everything begins to run about and begin new things. Work becomes distasteful; one thinks of holidays. This year – I've got it badly. I want to get away. I've never wanted to get away so much.'

'Where do you go?'

'Oh! – Alps.'

'Climbing?'

'Yes.'

'That's rather a fine sort of holiday!'

He made no answer for three or four seconds.

'Yes,' he said, 'I want to get away. I feel at moments as though I could bolt for it. . . . Silly, isn't it? Undisciplined.'

He went to the window and fidgeted with the blind, looking out to where the tree tops of Regent's Park showed distantly over the houses. He turned round towards her and found her looking at him and standing very still.

'It's the stir of spring,' he said.

'I believe it is.'

She glanced out of the window, and the distant trees were a froth of hard spring green and almond blossom. She formed a wild resolution, and, lest she should waver from it, she set about at once to realize it. 'I've broken off my engagement,' she said in a matter-of-fact tone, and found her heart thumping in her neck. He moved slightly, and she went on, with a slight catching of her breath: 'It's a bother and disturbance, but you see—' She had to go through with it now, because she could think of nothing but her preconceived words. Her voice was weak and flat. 'I've fallen in love.'

He never helped her by a sound.

'I – I didn't love the man I was engaged to,' she said.

She met his eyes for a moment, and could not interpret their expression. They struck her as cold and indifferent.

Her heart failed her and her resolution became water. She remained standing stiffly, unable even to move. She could not look at him through an interval that seemed to her a vast gulf of time. But she felt his lax figure become rigid.

At last his voice came to release her tension.

'I thought you weren't keeping up to the mark. You— It's jolly of you to confide in me. Still—' Then, with incredible and obviously deliberate stupidity, and a voice as flat as her own, he asked: 'Who is the man?'

Her spirit raged within her at the dumbness, the paralysis that had fallen upon her. Grace, confidence, the power of movement even, seemed gone from her. A fever of shame ran through her being. Horrible doubts assailed her. She sat down awkwardly and helplessly on one of the little stools by her table and covered her face with her hands.

'Can't you *see* how things are?' she said.

2

Before Capes could answer her in any way the door at the end of the laboratory opened noisily and Miss Klegg appeared. She went to her own table and sat down. At the sound of the door Ann

Veronica uncovered a tearless face, and with one swift movement assumed a conversational attitude. Things hung for a moment in an awkward silence.

'You see,' said Ann Veronica, staring before her at the window sash, 'that's the form my question takes at the present time.'

Capes had not quite the same power of recovery. He stood with his hands in his pockets looking at Miss Klegg's back. His face was white. 'It's – it's a difficult question.' He appeared to be paralysed by abstruse acoustic calculations. Then, very awkwardly, he took a stool and placed it at the end of Ann Veronica's table, and sat down. He glanced at Miss Klegg again, and spoke quickly and furtively, with eager eyes on Ann Veronica's face.

'I had a faint idea once that things were as you say they are, but the affair of the ring – of the unexpected ring – puzzled me. Wish *she*' – he indicated Miss Klegg's back with a nod – 'was at the bottom of the sea. . . . I would like to talk to you about this – soon. If you don't think it would be a social outrage, perhaps I might walk with you to your railway station.'

'I will wait,' said Ann Veronica, still not looking at him, 'and we will go into Regent's Park. No – you shall come with me to Waterloo.'

'Right!' he said, and hesitated, and then got up and went into the preparation room.

3

For a time they walked in silence through the back streets that lead southward from the college. Capes bore a face of infinite perplexity.

'The thing I feel most disposed to say, Miss Stanley,' he began at last, 'is that this is very sudden.'

'It's been coming on since first I came into the laboratory.'

'What do you want?' he asked bluntly.

'You!' said Ann Veronica.

The sense of publicity, of people coming and going about them, kept them both unemotional. And neither had any of that theatricality which demands gestures and facial expression.

'I suppose you know I like you tremendously?' he pursued.

'You told me that in the Zoological Gardens.'

She found her muscles a-tremble. But there was nothing in her bearing that a passer-by would have noted, to tell of the excitement that possessed her.

'I' – he seemed to have a difficulty with the word – 'I love you. I've told you that practically already. But I can give it its name now. You needn't be in any doubt about it. I tell you that because it puts us on a footing. . . .'

They went on for a time without another word.

'But don't you know about me?' he said at last.

'Something. Not much.'

'I'm a married man. And my wife won't live with me for reasons that I think most women would consider sound. . . . Or I should have made love to you long ago.'

There came a silence again.

'I don't care,' said Ann Veronica.

'But if you knew anything of that. . . .'

'I did. It doesn't matter.'

'Why did you tell me? I thought – I thought we were going to be friends.'

He was suddenly resentful. He seemed to charge her with the ruin of their situation. 'Why on earth did you *tell* me?' he cried.

'I couldn't help it. It was an impulse. I *had* to.'

'But it changes things. I thought you understood.'

'I had to,' she repeated. 'I was sick of the make-believe. I don't care! I'm glad I did. I'm glad I did.'

'Look here!' said Capes, 'what on earth do you want? What do you think we can do? Don't you know what men are, and what life is? – to come to me and talk to me like this!'

'I know – something, anyhow. But I don't care; I haven't a spark of shame. I don't see any good in life if it hasn't got you in it. I wanted you to know. And now you know. And the fences are down for good. You can't look me in the eyes and say you don't care for me.'

'I've told you,' he said.

'Very well,' said Ann Veronica, with an air of concluding the discussion.

They walked side by side for a time.

'In that laboratory one gets to disregard these passions,' began Capes. 'Men are curious animals, with a trick of falling in love readily with girls about your age. One has to train oneself not to. I've accustomed myself to think of you – as if you were like every other girl who works at the schools – as something quite outside these possibilities. If only out of loyalty to co-education one has to do that. Apart from everything else, this meeting of ours is a breach of a good rule.'

'Rules are for every day,' said Ann Veronica. 'This is not every day. This is something above all rules.'

'For you.'

'Not for you?'

'No. No; I'm going to stick to the rules. . . . It's odd, but nothing but *cliché* seems to meet this case. You've placed me in a very exceptional position, Miss Stanley.' The note of his own voice exasperated him. 'Oh, damn!' he said.

She made no answer, and for a time he debated some problems with himself.

'No!' he said aloud at last.

'The plain common sense of the case,' he said, 'is that we can't possibly be lovers in the ordinary sense. That, I think, is manifest. You know, I've done no work at all this afternoon. I've been smoking cigarettes in the preparation room and thinking this out. We can't be lovers in the ordinary sense, but we can be great and intimate friends.'

'We are,' said Ann Veronica.

'You've interested me enormously. . . .'

He paused with a sense of ineptitude. 'I want to be your friend,' he said. 'I said that at the Zoo, and I mean it. Let us be friends – as near and close as friends can be.'

Ann Veronica gave him a pallid profile.

'What is the good of pretending?' she said.

'We don't pretend.'

'We do. Love is one thing and friendship quite another. Because I'm younger than you. . . . I've got imagination. . . . I know what I am talking about. Mr Capes, do you think . . . do you think I don't know the meaning of love?'

4

Capes made no answer for a time.

'My mind is full of confused stuff,' he said at length. 'I've been thinking – all the afternoon. Oh, and weeks and months of thought and feeling there are bottled up too. . . . I feel a mixture of beast and uncle. I feel like a fraudulent trustee. Every rule is against me— Why did I let you begin this? I might have told—'

'I don't see that you could help—'

'I might have helped—'

'You couldn't.'

'I ought to have – all the same.

'I wonder,' he said, and went off at a tangent. 'You know about my scandalous past?'

'Very little. It doesn't seem to matter. Does it?'

'I think it does. Profoundly.'

'How?'

'It prevents our marrying. It forbids – all sorts of things.'

'It can't prevent our loving.'

'I'm afraid it can't. But, by Jove! it's going to make our loving a fiercely abstract thing.'

'You are separated from your wife?'

'Yes, but do you know how?'

'Not exactly.'

'Why on earth—? A man ought to be labelled. You see, I'm separated from my wife. But she doesn't and won't divorce me. You don't understand the fix I am in. And you don't know what led to our separation. And, in fact, all round the problem you don't know and I don't see how I could possibly have told you before. I wanted to, that day in the Zoo. But I trusted to that ring of yours.'

'Poor old ring!' said Ann Veronica.

'I ought never to have gone to the Zoo, I suppose. I asked you to go. But a man is a mixed creature. . . . I wanted the time with you. I wanted it badly.'

'Tell me about yourself,' said Ann Veronica.

'To begin with, I was – I was in the divorce court. I was – I was a co-respondent. You understand that term?'

Ann Veronica smiled faintly. 'A modern girl does understand these terms. She reads novels – and history – and all sorts of things. Did you really doubt if I knew?'

'No. But I don't suppose you can understand.'

'I don't see why I shouldn't.'

'To know things by name is one thing; to know them by seeing them and feeling them and being them quite another. That is where life takes advantage of youth. You don't understand.'

'Perhaps I don't.'

'You don't. That's the difficulty. If I told you the facts, I expect, since you are in love with me, you'd explain the whole business as being very fine and honourable for me – the Higher Morality, or something of that sort . . . It wasn't.'

'I don't deal very much,' said Ann Veronica, 'in the Higher Morality, or the Higher Truth, or any of those things.'

'Perhaps you don't. But a human being who is young and clean, as you are, is apt to ennoble – or explain away.'

'I've had a biological training. I'm a hard young woman.'

'Nice clean hardness, anyhow. I think you are hard. There's something – something *adult* about you. I'm talking to you now as though you had all the wisdom and charity in the world. I'm going to tell you things plainly. Plainly. It's best. And then you can go home and think things over before we talk again. I want you to be clear what you're really and truly up to, anyhow.'

'I don't mind knowing,' said Ann Veronica.

'It's precious unromantic.'

'Well, tell me.'

'I married pretty young,' said Capes. 'I've got – I have to tell you this to make myself clear – a streak of ardent animal in my composition. I married – I married a woman whom I still think one of the most beautiful persons in the world. She is a year or so older than I am, and she is, well, of a very serene and proud and dignified temperament. If you met her you would, I am certain, think her as fine as I do. She has never done a really ignoble thing that I know of – never. I met her when we were both very young, as young as you are. I loved her and made love to her, and I don't think she quite loved me back in the same way.'

He paused for a time. Ann Veronica said nothing.

'These are the sort of things that aren't supposed to happen. They leave them out of novels – these incompatibilities. Young people ignore them until they find themselves up against them. My wife doesn't understand, doesn't understand now. She despises me, I suppose. . . . We married, and for a time we were happy. She was fine and tender, I worshipped her and subdued myself.'

He left off abruptly. 'Do you understand what I am talking about? It's no good if you don't.'

'I think so,' said Ann Veronica, and coloured. 'In fact, yes, I do.'

'Do you think of these things – these matters – as belonging to our Higher Nature or our Lower?'

'I don't deal in Higher Things, I tell you,' said Ann Veronica, 'or lower, for the matter of that. I don't classify.' She hesitated. 'Flesh and flowers are all alike to me.'

'That's the comfort of you. Well, after a time there came a fever in my blood. Don't think it was anything better than fever – or a bit beautiful. It wasn't. Quite soon, after we were married – it was just within a year – I formed a friendship with the wife of a friend, a woman eight years older than myself. . . . It wasn't anything splendid, you know. It was just a shabby, stupid, furtive business that began between us. Like stealing. We dressed it in a little music. . . . I want you to understand clearly that I was indebted to the man in many small ways. I was mean to him. . . . It was the gratification of an immense necessity. We were two people with a craving. We felt like thieves. We *were* thieves. . . . We *liked* each other well enough. Well, my friend found us out, and would give no quarter. He divorced her. How do you like the story?'

'Go on,' said Ann Veronica, a little hoarsely; 'tell me all of it.'

'My wife was astounded – wounded beyond measure. She thought me – filthy. All her pride raged at me. One particularly humiliating thing came out – humiliating for me. There was a second co-respondent. I hadn't heard of him before the trial. I don't know why that should be so acutely humiliating. There's no logic in these things. It was.'

'Poor you!' said Ann Veronica.

'My wife refused absolutely to have anything more to do with me. She could hardly speak to me; she insisted relentlessly upon a separation. She had money of her own – much more than I have – and there was no need to squabble about that. She has given herself up to social work.'

'Well—'

'That's all. Practically all. And yet— Wait a little, you'd better have every bit of it. One doesn't go about with these passions allayed simply because they have made wreckage and a scandal. There one is! The same stuff still! One has a craving in one's blood, a craving roused, cut off from its redeeming and guiding emotional side. A man has more freedom to do evil than a woman. Irregularly, in a quite inglorious and unromantic way, you know, I am a vicious man. That's – that's my private life. Until the last few months. It isn't what I have been but what I am. I haven't taken much account of it until now. My honour has been in my scientific work and public discussion and the things I write. Lots of us are like that. But, you see, I'm smirched. For the sort of love-making you think about. I've muddled all this business. I've had my time, and lost my chances. I'm damaged goods. And you're as clean as fire. You come with those clear eyes of yours, as valiant as an angel. . . .'

He stopped abruptly.

'Well?' she said.

'That's all.'

'It's so strange to think of you – troubled by such things. I didn't think— I don't know what I thought. Suddenly all this makes you human. Makes you real.'

'But don't you see how I must stand to you? Don't you see how it bars us from being lovers— You can't – at first. You must think it over. It's all outside the world of your experience.'

'I don't think it makes a rap of difference, except for one thing. I love you more. I've wanted you – always. I didn't dream, not even in my wildest dreaming, that – you might have any need of me.'

He made a little noise in his throat as if something had cried out within him, and for a time they were both too full for speech.

They were going up the slope into Waterloo station.

'You go home and think of all this,' he said, 'and talk about it to-morrow. Don't, don't say anything now, not anything. As for loving you, I do. I do – with all my heart. It's no good hiding it any more. I could never have talked to you like this, forgetting everything that parts us, forgetting even your age, if I did not love you utterly. If I were a clean, free man— We'll have to talk of all these things. Thank goodness there's plenty of opportunity! And we two can talk. Anyhow, now you've begun it, there's nothing to keep us in all this from being the best friends in the world. And talking of every conceivable thing. Is there?'

'Nothing,' said Ann Veronica, with a radiant face.

'Before this there was a sort of restraint – a make-believe. It's gone.'

'It's gone!'

'Friendship and love being separate things. And that confounded engagement!'

'Gone!'

They came upon a platform, and stood before her compartment.

He took her hand and looked into her eyes and spoke, divided against himself, in a voice that was forced and insincere.

'I shall be very glad to have you for a friend,' he said, 'loving friend. I had never dreamt of such a friend as you.'

She smiled, sure of herself beyond any pretending, into his troubled eyes. Hadn't they settled that already?

'I want you as a friend,' he persisted, almost as if he disputed something.

5

The next morning she waited in the laboratory at the lunch hour in the reasonable certainty that he would come to her.

'Well, you have thought it over?' he said, sitting down beside her.

'I've been thinking of you all night,' she answered.

'Well?'

'I don't care a rap for all these things.'

He said nothing for a space.

'I don't see there's any getting away from the fact that you and I love each other,' he said slowly. 'So far you've got me and I you. . . . You've got me. I'm like a creature just wakened up. My eyes are open to you. I keep on thinking of you. I keep on thinking of little details and aspects of your voice, your eyes, the way you walk, the way your hair goes back from the side of your forehead. I believe I have always been in love with you. Always. Before ever I knew you.'

She sat motionless, with her hand tightening over the edge of the table, and he, too, said no more. She began to tremble violently.

She stood up abruptly and went to the window.

'We have,' he said, 'to be the utmost friends.'

She stood up and held her arms towards him. 'I want you to kiss me,' she said.

He gripped the window sill behind him.

'If I do,' he said. . . . 'No! I want to do without that. I want to do without that for a time. I want to give you time to think. I am a man – of a sort of experience. You are a girl with very little. Just sit down on that stool again and let's talk of this in cold blood. People of your sort— I don't want the instincts to – to rush our situation. Are you sure what it is you want of me?'

'I want you. I want you to be my lover. I want to give myself to you. I want to be whatever I can to you.' She paused for a moment. 'Is that plain?' she asked.

'If I didn't love you better than myself,' said Capes, 'I wouldn't fence like this with you.

'I am convinced you haven't thought this out,' he went on. 'You do not know what such a relation means. We are in love. Our heads swim with the thought of being together. But what can we do? Here am I, fixed to respectability and this laboratory; you're living at home. It means . . . just furtive meetings.'

'I don't care how we meet,' she said.

'It will spoil your life.'

'It will make it. I want you. I am clear I want you. You are different from all the world for me. You can think all round me. You are the one person I can understand and feel – feel right with. I don't idealize you. Don't imagine that. It isn't because you're good, but because I may be rotten bad; and there's something – something living and understanding in you. Something that is born anew each time we meet, and pines when we are separated. You see, I'm selfish. I'm rather scornful. I think too much about myself. You're the only person I've really given good, straight, unselfish thought to. I'm making a mess of my life – unless you come in and take it. I am. In you – if you can love me – there is salvation. Salvation. I know what I am doing better than you do. Think – think of that engagement!'

Their talk had come to eloquent silences that contradicted all he had to say.

She stood up before him, smiling faintly.

'I think we've exhausted this discussion,' she said.

'I think we have,' he answered gravely, and took her in his arms, and smoothed her hair from her forehead, and very tenderly kissed her lips.

6

They spent the next Sunday in Richmond Park, and mingled the happy sensation of being together uninterruptedly through the long sunshine of a summer's day with the ample discussion of their position. 'This has all the clean freshness of spring and youth,' said Capes; 'it is love with the down on; it is like the glitter of dew in the sunlight to be lovers such as we are, with no more than one warm kiss between us. I love everything to-day, and all of you, but I love this, this – this innocence upon us most of all.

'You can't imagine,' he said, 'what a beastly thing a furtive love affair can be.'

'This isn't furtive,' said Ann Veronica.

'Not a bit of it. And we won't make it so. . . . We mustn't make it so.'

They loitered under trees, they sat on mossy banks, they gossiped on friendly benches, they came back to lunch at the 'Star and Garter', and talked their afternoon away in the garden that looks out upon the crescent of the river. They had a universe to talk about – two universes.

'What are we going to do?' said Capes, with his eyes on the broad distances beyond the ribbon of the river.

'I will do whatever you want,' said Ann Veronica.

'My first love was all blundering,' said Capes.

He thought for a moment, and went on: 'Love is something that has to be taken care of. One has to be so careful. . . . It's a beautiful plant, but a tender one. . . . I didn't know. I've a dread of love dropping its petals, becoming mean and ugly. How can I tell you all I feel? I love you beyond measure. And I'm afraid. . . . I'm anxious, joyfully anxious, like a man when he has found a treasure.'

'*You* know,' said Ann Veronica. 'I just came to you and put myself in your hands.'

'That's why, in a way, I'm prudish. I've – dreads. I don't want to tear at you with hot, rough hands.'

'As you will, dear lover. But for me it doesn't matter. Nothing is wrong that you do. Nothing. I am quite clear about this. I know exactly what I am doing. I give myself to you.'

'God send you may never repent it!' cried Capes.

She put her hand in his to be squeezed.

'You see,' he said, 'it is doubtful if we can ever marry. Very doubtful. I have been thinking— I will go to my wife again. I will do my utmost. But for a long time, anyhow, we lovers have to be as if we were no more than friends.'

He paused. She answered slowly. 'That is as you will,' she said.

'Why should it matter?' he said.

And then, as she answered nothing: 'Seeing that we are lovers.'

7

It was rather less than a week after that walk that Capes came and sat down beside Ann Veronica for their customary talk in the lunch hour. He took a handful of almonds and raisins that she held out to him – for both these young people had given up the practice of going out for luncheon – and kept her hand for a moment to kiss her finger-tips. He did not speak for a moment.

'Well?' she said.

'I say!' he said, without any movement. 'Let's go.'

'Go!' She did not understand him at first, and then her heart began to beat very rapidly.

'Stop this – this humbugging,' he explained. 'It's like the Statue and the Bust.* I can't stand it. Let's go. Go off and live together – until we can marry. Dare you?'

'Do you mean *now*?'

'At the end of the session. It's the only clean way for us. Are you prepared to do it?'

Her hands clenched. 'Yes,' she said very faintly. And then: 'Of course! Always. It is what I have wanted, what I have meant all along.'

She stared before her, trying to keep back a rush of tears.

Capes kept obstinately stiff, and spoke between his teeth.

'There's endless reasons, no doubt, why we shouldn't,' he said. 'Endless. It's wrong in the eyes of most people. For many of them it will smirch us for ever. . . . You *do* understand?'

'Who cares for most people?' she said, not looking at him.

'I do. It means social isolation – struggle.'

'If you dare – I dare,' said Ann Veronica. 'I was never so clear in all my life as I have been in this business.' She lifted steadfast eyes to him. 'Dare!' she said. The tears were welling over now, but her voice was steady. 'You're not a man for me – not one of a sex, I mean. You're just a particular being with nothing else in the world to class with you. You are just necessary to life for me. I've never met any one like you. To have you is all-important. Nothing else weighs against it. Morals only begin when that is settled. I shan't care a rap if we can never marry. I'm not a bit afraid of anything – scandal, difficulty, struggle. . . . I rather want them. I do want them.'

'You'll get them,' he said. 'This means a plunge.'

'Are you afraid?'

'Only for you! Most of my income will vanish. Even unbelieving biological demonstrators must respect decorum; and besides, you see – you were a student. We shall have – hardly any money.'

'I don't care.'

'Hardship and danger.'

'With you!'

'And as for your people?'

'They don't count. That is the dreadful truth. This – all this swamps them. They don't count, and I don't care.'

Capes suddenly abandoned his attitude of meditative restraint. 'By Jove!' he broke out, 'one tries to take a serious, sober view. I don't quite know why. But this is a great lark, Ann Veronica! This turns life into a glorious adventure!'

'Ah!' she cried in triumph.

'I shall have to give up biology, anyhow. I've always had a sneaking desire for the writing trade. That is what I must do. I can.'

'Of course you can.'

'And biology was beginning to bore me a bit. One research is very like another. . . . Latterly I've been doing things. . . . Creative work appeals to me wonderfully. Things seem to come rather easily. . . . But that, and that sort of thing, is just a day-dream. For a time I must do journalism and work hard. . . . What isn't a day-dream is this – that you and I are going to put an end to flummery – and go!'

'Go!' said Ann Veronica, clenching her hands.

'For better or worse.'

'For richer or poorer.'

She could not go on, for she was laughing and crying at the same time. 'We were bound to do this when you kissed me,' she sobbed through her tears. 'We have been all this time— Only your queer code of honour— Honour! Once you begin with love you have to see it through.'

Chapter XV

The Last Days at Home

I

They decided to go to Switzerland at the session's end. 'We'll clean up everything tidy,' said Capes. . . .

For her pride's sake, and to save herself from long day-dreams and an unappeasable longing for her lover, Ann Veronica worked hard at her biology during those closing weeks. She was, as Capes had said, a hard young woman. She was keenly resolved to do well in the school examination, and not to be drowned in the seas of emotion that threatened to submerge her intellectual being.

Nevertheless, she could not prevent a rising excitement as the dawn of the new life drew near to her – a thrilling of the nerves, a secret and delicious exaltation above the common circumstances of existence. Sometimes her straying mind would become astonishingly active – embroidering bright and decorative things that she could say to Capes; sometimes it passed into a state of passive acquiescence, into a radiant, formless, golden joy. She was aware of people – her aunt, her father, her fellow students, friends, and neighbours – moving about outside this glowing secret, very much as an actor is aware of the dim audience beyond the barrier of the footlights. They might applaud, or object, or interfere, but the drama was her very own. She was going through with that, anyhow.

The feeling of last days grew stronger with her as their number diminished. She went about the familiar home with a clearer and clearer sense of inevitable conclusions. She became exceptionally considerate and affectionate with her father and aunt, and more and more concerned about the coming catastrophe that she was about to precipitate upon them. Her aunt had a once exasperating habit of interrupting her work with demands for small household services, but now Ann Veronica rendered them with a queer readiness of anticipatory propitiation. She was greatly exercised by the problem of confiding in the Widgetts; they were dears, and she talked away two evenings with Constance without broaching the topic; she made some vague intimations in letters to Miss Miniver that Miss Miniver failed to mark. But she did not bother her head very much about her relations with these sympathizers.

And at length her penultimate day in Morningside Park dawned for her. She got up early, and walked about the garden in the dewy June sunshine and revived her childhood. She was saying good-bye to childhood, and home, and her making; she was going out into the great, multitudinous world; this time there would be no returning. She was at the end of girlhood and on the eve of a woman's crowning experience. She visited the corner that had been her own little garden – her forget-me-nots and candytuft had long since been elbowed into insignificance by weeds; she visited the raspberry canes that had sheltered that first love affair with the little boy in velvet, and the greenhouse where she had been wont to read her secret letters. Here was the place behind the shed where she had used to hide from Roddy's persecutions, and here the border of herbaceous perennials under whose stems was fairyland. The back of the house had been the Alps for climbing, and the shrubs in front of it a Terai. The knots and broken pale that made the garden fence scalable, and gave access to the fields behind, were still to be traced. And here against a wall were the plum-trees. In spite of God and wasps and her father she had stolen plums; and once because of discovered misdeeds, and once because she had realized that her mother was dead, she had lain on her face in the unmown grass, beneath the elm-trees that came beyond the vegetables, and poured out her soul in weeping.

Remote little Ann Veronica! She would never know the heart of that child again! That child had loved fairy princes with velvet suits and golden locks, and she was in love with a real man named Capes, with little gleams of gold on his cheek and a pleasant voice and firm and shapely hands. She was going to him soon and certainly, going to his strong, embracing arms. She was going through a new world with him side by side. She had been so busy with life that, for a vast gulf of time, as it seemed, she had given no thought to those ancient, imagined things of her childhood. Now, abruptly, they were real again, though very distant, and she had come to say farewell to them across one sundering year.

She was unusually helpful at breakfast, and unselfish about the eggs; and then she went off to catch the train before her father's. She did this to please him. He hated travelling second class with her – indeed, he never did – but he also disliked travelling in the same train when his daughter was in an inferior class, because of the look of the thing. So he liked to go by a different train. And in the Avenue she had an encounter with Ramage.

It was an odd little encounter, that left vague and dubitable impressions in her mind. She was aware of him – a silk-hatted, shiny-black figure on the opposite side of the avenue; and then, abruptly and startlingly, he crossed the road and saluted and spoke to her.

'I *must* speak to you,' he said. 'I can't keep away from you.'

She made some inane response. She was struck by a change in his appearance. His eyes looked a little bloodshot to her; his face had lost something of its ruddy freshness.

He began a jerky, broken conversation that lasted until they reached the station, and left her puzzled at its drift and meaning. She quickened her pace, and so did he, talking at her slightly averted ear. She made lumpish and inadequate interruptions rather than replies. At times he seemed to be claiming pity from her; at times he was threatening her with her cheque and exposure; at times he was boasting of his inflexible will, and how, in the end, he always got what he wanted. He said that his life was boring and stupid without her. Something or other – she did not catch what – he was damned if he could stand. He was evidently nervous, and very anxious to be impressive; his projecting eyes sought to dominate. The crowning aspect of the incident, for her mind, was the discovery that he and her indiscretion with him no longer mattered very much. Its importance had vanished with her abandonment of compromise. Even her debt to him was a triviality now.

And of course! She had a brilliant idea. It surprised her she hadn't thought of it before! She tried to explain that she was going to pay him forty pounds without fail next week. She said as much to him. She repeated this breathlessly.

'I was glad you did not send it back again,' he said.

He touched a long-standing sore, and Ann Veronica found herself vainly trying to explain – the inexplicable. 'It's because I mean to send it back altogether,' she said.

He ignored her protests in order to pursue some impressive line of his own.

'Here we are, living in the same suburb,' he began. 'We have to be – modern.'

Her heart leapt within her as she caught that phrase. That knot also would be cut. Modern indeed! She was going to be as primordial as chipped flint.

2

In the late afternoon, as Ann Veronica was gathering flowers for the dinner table, her father came strolling across the lawn towards her with an affectation of great deliberation.

'I want to speak to you about a little thing, Vee,' said Mr Stanley.

Ann Veronica's tense nerves started, and she stood still with her eyes upon him, wondering what it might be that impended.

'You were talking to that fellow Ramage to-day – in the Avenue. Walking to the station with him.'

So that was it!

'He came and talked to me.'

'Ye-e-es.' Mr Stanley considered. 'Well, I don't want you to talk to him,' he said very firmly.

Ann Veronica paused before she answered. 'Don't you think I ought to?' she asked very submissively.

'No.' Mr Stanley coughed and faced towards the house. 'He is not— I don't like him. I think it inadvisable— I don't want an intimacy to spring up between you and a man of that type.'

Ann Veronica reflected. 'I *have* – had one or two talks with him, daddy.'

'Don't let there be any more. I— In fact, I dislike him extremely.'

'Suppose he comes and talks to me?'

'A girl can always keep a man at a distance if she cares to do it. She— She can snub him.'

Ann Veronica picked a cornflower.

'I wouldn't make this objection,' Mr Stanley went on, 'but there are things— there are stories about Ramage. He's – He lives in a world of possibilities outside your imagination. His treatment of his wife is most unsatisfactory. Most unsatisfactory. A bad man, in fact. A dissipated, loose-living man.'

'I'll try not to see him again,' said Ann Veronica. 'I didn't know you objected to him, daddy.'

'Strongly,' said Mr Stanley, 'very strongly.'

The conversation hung. Ann Veronica wondered what her father would do if she were to tell him the full story of her relations with Ramage.

'A man like that taints a girl by looking at her, by his mere conversation.' He adjusted his glasses on his nose. There was another little thing he had to say. 'One has to be so careful of one's friends and acquaintances,' he remarked by way of transition. 'They mould one insensibly.' His voice assumed an easy, detached tone. 'I suppose, Vee, you don't see much of those Widgetts now?'

'I go in and talk to Constance sometimes.'

'Do you?'

'We were great friends at school.'

'No doubt. . . . Still— I don't know whether I quite like— Something ramshackle about those people, Vee. While I am talking about your friends, I feel— I think you ought to know how I look at it.' His voice conveyed studied moderation. 'I don't mind, of course, your seeing her sometimes, still there are differences – differences in social atmospheres. One gets drawn into things. Before you know where you are you find yourself in a complication. I don't want to influence you unduly— But— They're artistic people, Vee. That's the fact about them. We're different.'

'I suppose we are,' said Vee, rearranging the flowers in her hand.

'Friendships that are all very well between schoolgirls don't always go on into later life. It's – it's a social difference.'

'I like Constance very much.'

'No doubt. Still, one has to be reasonable. As you admitted to me – one has to square oneself with the world. You don't know. With people of that sort all sorts of things may happen. We don't want things to happen.'

Ann Veronica made no answer.

A vague desire to justify himself ruffled her father. 'I may seem unduly – anxious. I can't forget about your sister. It's that has always made me— *She*, you know, was drawn into a set – didn't discriminate. Private theatricals.'

Ann Veronica remained anxious to hear more of her sister's story from her father's point of view, but he did not go on. Even so much allusion as this to that family shadow, she felt, was an immense recognition of her ripening years. She glanced at him. He stood, a little anxious and fussy, bothered by the responsibility of her, entirely careless of what her life was or was likely to be, ignoring her thoughts and feelings, ignorant of every fact of importance in her life, explaining everything he could not understand in her as nonsense and perversity, concerned only with a terror of bothers and undesirable situations. 'We don't want things to happen!' Never had he shown his daughter so clearly that the womenkind he was persuaded he had to protect and control could please him in one way, and in one way only, and that was by doing nothing except the punctual domestic duties and being nothing except restful appearances. He had quite enough to see to and worry about in the City without their doing things. He had no use for Ann Veronica; he had never had a use for her since she had been too old to sit upon his knee. Nothing but the constraint of social usage now linked him to her. And the less 'anything' happened the better. The less she lived, in fact, the better. These realizations rushed into Ann Veronica's mind and hardened her heart against him. She spoke slowly. 'I may not see the Widgetts for some little time, father,' she said. 'I don't think I shall.'

'Some little tiff?'

'No; but I don't think I shall see them.'

Suppose she were to add: 'I am going away!'

'I'm glad to hear you say it,' said Mr Stanley, and was so evidently pleased that Ann Veronica's heart smote her.

'I am very glad to hear you say it,' he repeated, and refrained from further inquiry. 'I think we are growing sensible,' he said. 'I think you are getting to understand me better.'

He hesitated, and walked away from her towards the house. Her eyes followed him. The curve of his shoulders, the very angle of his feet, expressed relief at her apparent obedience. 'Thank goodness!' said that retreating aspect, '*that*'s said and over. Vee's all right. There's nothing happened at all!' She didn't mean, he concluded, to give him any more trouble ever, and he was free to begin a fresh chromatic novel – he had just finished the *Blue Lagoon*,* which he thought very beautiful and tender and absolutely irrelevant to Morningside Park – or work in peace at his microtome without bothering about her in the least.

The immense disillusionment that awaited him! The devastating disillusionment! She had a vague desire to run after him, to state her case to him, to wring some understanding from him of what life was to her. She felt a cheat and a sneak to his unsuspecting retreating back.

'But what can one do?' asked Ann Veronica.

3

She dressed carefully for dinner in a black dress that her father liked, and that made her look serious and responsible. Dinner was quite uneventful. Her father read a draft prospectus warily, and her aunt dropped fragments of her projects for managing while the cook had a holiday. After dinner Ann Veronica went into the drawing-room with Miss Stanley, and her father went up to his den for his pipe and pensive petrography. Later in the evening she heard him whistling, poor man!

She felt very restless and excited. She refused coffee, though she knew that anyhow she was doomed to a sleepless night. She took up one of her father's novels and put it down again, fretted up to her own room for some work, sat on her bed and meditated upon the room that she was now really abandoning for ever, and returned at length with a stocking to darn. Her aunt was making herself cuffs out of little slips of insertion under the newly lit lamp.

Ann Veronica sat down in the other arm-chair and darned badly for a minute or so. Then she looked at her aunt, and traced with a curious eye the careful arrangement of her hair, her sharp nose, the little drooping lines of mouth and chin and cheek.

Her thought spoke aloud. 'Were you ever in love, aunt?' she asked.

Her aunt glanced up, startled, and then sat very still, with hands that had ceased to work. 'What makes you ask such a question, Vee?' she said.

'I wondered.'

Her aunt answered in a low voice: 'I was engaged to Him, dear, for seven years, and then he died.'

Ann Veronica made a sympathetic little murmur.

'He was in holy orders, and we were to have been married when he got a living. He was a Wiltshire Edmondshaw, a very old family.'

She sat very still.

Ann Veronica hesitated with a question that had leapt up in her mind, and that she felt was cruel. 'Are you sorry you waited, aunt?' she said.

Her aunt was a long time before she answered. 'His stipend forbade it,' she said, and seemed to fall into a train of thought. 'It would have been rash and unwise,' she said at the end of a meditation. 'What he had was altogether insufficient.'

Ann Veronica looked at the mildly pensive grey eyes and the comfortable, rather refined face with a penetrating curiosity. Presently her aunt sighed deeply and looked at the clock. 'Time for my patience,' she said. She got up, put the neat cuffs she had made into her work-basket, and went to the bureau for the little cards in the morocco case. Ann Veronica jumped up to get her the card table. 'I haven't seen the new patience, dear,' she said. 'May I sit beside you?'

'It's a very difficult one,' said her aunt. 'Perhaps you will help me shuffle?'

Ann Veronica did, and also assisted nimbly with the arrangements of the rows of eight with which the struggle began. Then she sat watching the play, sometimes offering a helpful suggestion, sometimes letting her attention wander to the smoothly shining arms she had folded across her knees just below the edge of the table. She was feeling extraordinarily well that night, so that the sense of her body was a deep delight, a realization of a gentle warmth and strength and elastic firmness. Then she glanced at the cards again, over which her aunt's many-ringed hand played, and then at the rather weak, rather plump face that surveyed its operations.

It came to Ann Veronica that life was wonderful beyond measure. It seemed incredible that she and her aunt were, indeed, creatures of the same blood, only by a birth or so different beings, and part of that same broad interlacing stream of human life that has invented the fauns and nymphs, Astarte, Aphrodite, Freya, and all the twining beauty of the gods. The love songs of all the ages were singing in her blood, the scent of night stock from the garden filled the air, and the moths that beat upon the closed frames of the window next the lamp set her mind dreaming of kisses in the dusk. Yet her aunt, with a ringed hand flitting to her lips and a puzzled, worried look in her eyes, deaf to all this riot of warmth and flitting desire, was playing patience – playing patience, as if Dionysus and her curate had died together. A faint buzz above the ceiling witnessed that petrography, too, was active. Grey and tranquil world! Amazing passionless world! A world in which days without meaning, days in which 'we don't want things to happen' followed days without meaning – until the last thing happened, the ultimate, unavoidable, coarse 'disagreeable'. It was her last evening in that wrappered life against which she had rebelled. Warm reality was now so near her she could hear it beating in her ears. Away in London even now Capes was packing and preparing; Capes, the magic man whose touch turned one to trembling fire. What was he doing? What was he thinking? It was less than a day now, less than twenty hours. Seventeen hours, sixteen hours. She glanced at the soft-ticking clock with the exposed brass pendulum upon the white marble mantel, and made a rapid calculation. To be exact, it was just sixteen hours and twenty minutes. The slow stars circled on to the moment of their meeting. The softly glittering summer stars! She saw them shining over mountains of snow, over valleys of haze and warm darkness. . . . There would be no moon.

'I believe after all it's coming out!' said Miss Stanley. 'The aces made it easy.'

Ann Veronica started from her reverie, sat up in her chair, became attentive. 'Look, dear,' she said, presently, 'you can put the ten on the jack.'

Chapter XVI

In the Mountains

I

Next day Ann Veronica and Capes felt like new-born things. It seemed to them they could never have been really alive before, but only dimly anticipating existence. They sat face to face beneath an experienced-looking rucksack and a brand-new portmanteau and a leather handbag, in the afternoon boat train that goes from Charing Cross to Folkestone for Boulogne. They tried to read illustrated papers in an unconcerned manner and with forced attention, lest they should catch the leaping exultation in each other's eyes. And they admired Kent sedulously from the windows.

They crossed the Channel in sunshine and a breeze that just ruffled the sea to glittering scales of silver. Some of the people who watched them standing side by side thought they must be newly wedded because of their happy faces, and others that they were an old-established couple because of their easy confidence in each other.

At Boulogne they took train to Basle; next morning they breakfasted together in the buffet of that station, and thence they caught the Interlaken express, and so went by way of Spies to Frutigen. There was no railway beyond Frutigen in those days; they sent their baggage by post to Kandersteg, and walked along the mule path to the left of the stream to that queer hollow among the precipices, Blauer See, where the petrifying branches of trees lie in the blue deeps of an icy lake, and pine-trees clamber among gigantic boulders. A little inn flying a Swiss flag nestles under a great rock, and there they put aside their knapsacks and lunched and rested in the midday shadow of the gorge and the scent of resin. And later they paddled in a boat above the mysterious deeps of the See, and peered down into the green-blues and the blue-greens together. By that time it seemed to them they had lived together twenty years.

Except for one memorable school excursion to Paris, Ann Veronica had never yet been outside England. So that it seemed to her the whole world had changed – the very light of it had changed. Instead of English villas and cottages there were châlets and Italian-built houses shining white; there were lakes of emerald and sapphire and clustering castles, and such sweeps of hill and mountain, such shining uplands of snow, as she had never seen before. Everything was fresh and bright, from the kindly manners of the Frutigen cobbler, who hammered mountain nails into her boots, to the unfamiliar wild flowers that spangled the wayside. And Capes had changed into the easiest and jolliest companion in the world. The mere fact that he was there in the train alongside her, helping her, sitting opposite to her in the dining-car, presently sleeping on a seat within a yard of her, made her heart sing until she was afraid their fellow passengers would hear it. It was too good to be true. She would not sleep for fear of losing a moment of that sense of his proximity. To walk beside him, dressed akin to him, rucksacked and companionable, was bliss in itself; each step she took was like stepping once more across the threshold of heaven.

One trouble, however, shot its slanting bolts athwart the shining warmth of that opening day and marred its perfection, and that was the thought of her father.

She had treated him badly; she had hurt him and her aunt; she had done wrong by their standards, and she would never persuade them that she had done right. She thought of her father in the garden, and of her aunt with her patience, as she had seen them – how many ages was it ago? Just one day intervened. She felt as if she had struck them unawares. The thought of them distressed her without subtracting at all from the oceans of happiness in which she swam. But she wished she could put the thing she had done in some way to them so that it would not hurt them so much as the truth would certainly do. The thought of their faces, and particularly of her aunt's, as it would meet the fact – disconcerted, unfriendly, condemning, pained – occurred to her again and again.

'Oh! I wish,' she said, 'that people thought alike about these things.'

Capes watched the limpid water dripping from his oar. 'I wish they did,' he said, 'but they don't.'

'I feel— All this is the rightest of all conceivable things. I want to tell every one. I want to boast myself.'

'I know.'

'I told them a lie. I told them lies. I wrote three letters yesterday and tore them up. It was so hopeless to put it to them. At last – I told a story.'

'You didn't tell them our position?'

'I implied we had married.'

'They'll find out. They'll know.'

'Not yet.'

'Sooner or later.'

'Possibly – bit by bit. . . . But it was hopelessly hard to put. I said I knew he disliked and distrusted you and your work – that you shared all Russell's opinions: he hates Russell beyond measure – and that we couldn't possibly face a conventional marriage. What else could one say? I left him to suppose – a registry perhaps. . . .'

Capes let his oar smack on the water.

'Do you mind very much?'

He shook his head.

'But it makes me feel inhuman,' he added.

'And me. . . .'

'It's the perpetual trouble,' he said, 'of parent and child. They can't help seeing things in the way they do. Nor can we. *We* don't think they're right, but they don't think we are. A deadlock. In a very definite sense we are in the wrong – hopelessly in the wrong. But— It's just this: who was to be hurt?'

'I wish no one had to be hurt,' said Ann Veronica. 'When one is happy— I don't like to think of them. Last time I left home I felt as hard as nails. But this is all different. It is different.'

'There's a sort of instinct of rebellion,' said Capes. 'It isn't anything to do with our times particularly. People think it is, but they are wrong. It's to do with adolescence. Long before religion and Society heard of Doubt, girls were all for midnight coaches and Gretna Green. It's a sort of home-leaving instinct.'

He followed up a line of thought.

'There's another instinct, too,' he went on, 'in a state of suppression, unless I'm very much mistaken; a child-expelling instinct. . . . I wonder. . . . There's no family-uniting instinct, anyhow; it's habit and sentiment and material convenience hold families together after adolescence. There's always friction, conflict, unwilling concessions. Always! I don't believe there is any strong natural affection at all between parents and growing-up children. There wasn't, I know, between myself and my father. I didn't allow myself to see things as they were in those days; now I do. I bored him. I hated him. I suppose that shocks one's ideas. . . . It's true. . . . There are sentimental and traditional deferences and reverences, I know, between father and son; but that's just exactly what prevents the development of an easy friendship. Father-worshipping sons are abnormal – and they're no good. No good at all. One's got to be a better man than one's father, or what is the good of successive generations? Life is rebellion, or nothing.'

He rowed a stroke and watched the swirl of water from his oar broaden and die away. At last he took up his thoughts again: 'I wonder if, some day, one won't need to rebel against customs and laws? If this discord will have gone? Some day, perhaps – who knows? – the old won't coddle and hamper the young, and the young won't need to fly in the faces of the old. They'll face facts as facts, and understand. Oh, to face facts! Gods! what a world it might be if people faced facts! Understanding! Understanding! There is no other salvation. Some day, older people, perhaps, will trouble to understand younger people, and there won't be these fierce disruptions; there won't be barriers one must defy or perish. . . . That's really our choice now, defy – or futility. . . . The world, perhaps, will be educated out of its idea of fixed standards. . . . I wonder, Ann Veronica, if, when our time comes, we shall be any wiser?'

Ann Veronica watched a water-beetle fussing across the green depths. 'One can't tell. I'm a female thing at bottom. I like high tone for a flourish and stars and ideas; but I want my things.'

2

Capes thought.

'It's odd – I have no doubt in my mind that what we are doing is wrong,' he said. 'And yet I do it without compunction.'

'I never felt so absolutely right,' said Ann Veronica.

'You *are* a female thing at bottom,' he admitted. 'I'm not nearly so sure as you. As for me, I look twice at it. . . . Life is two things, that's how I see it; two things mixed and muddled up together. Life is morality – life is adventure. Squire and master. Adventure rules and morality – looks up the trains in the Bradshaw. Morality tells you what is right, and adventure moves you. If morality means anything it means keeping bounds, respecting implications, respecting implicit bounds. If individuality means anything it means breaking bounds – adventure. Will you be moral and your species, or immoral and yourself? We've decided to be immoral. We needn't try and give ourselves airs. We've deserted the posts in which we found ourselves, cut our duties, exposed ourselves to risks that may destroy any sort of social usefulness in us. . . . I don't know. One keeps rules in order to be oneself. One studies nature in order not to be blindly ruled by her. There's no sense in morality, I suppose, unless you are fundamentally immoral.'

She watched his face as he traced his way through these speculative thickets.

'Look at our affair,' he went on, looking up at her. 'No power on earth will persuade me we're not two rather disreputable persons. You desert your home; I throw up useful teaching, risk every hope in your career. Here we are absconding, pretending to be what we are not; shady, to say the least of it. It's not a bit of good pretending there's any Higher Truth or wonderful principle in this business. There isn't. We never started out in any high-browed manner to scandalize and Shelleyfy.* When first you left your home you had no idea that I was the hidden impulse. I wasn't. You came out like an ant for your nuptial flight. It was just a chance that we in particular hit against each other – nothing predestined about it. We just hit against each other, and here we are flying off at a tangent, a little surprised at what we are doing, all our principles abandoned, and tremendously and quite unreasonably proud of ourselves. Out of all this we have struck a sort of harmony. . . . And it's gorgeous!'

'Glorious!' said Ann Veronica.

'Would *you* like us – if someone told you the bare outline of our story? – and what we are doing?'

'I shouldn't mind,' said Ann Veronica.

'But if someone else asked your advice? If someone else said: "Here is my teacher, a jaded married man on the verge of middle age, and he and I have a violent passion for one another. We propose to disregard all our ties, all our obligations, all the established prohibitions of society, and begin life together afresh. What would you tell her?" '

'If she asked advice, I should say that having a doubt was enough to condemn it.'

'But waive that point.'

'It would be different all the same. It wouldn't be you.'

'It wouldn't be you either. I suppose that's the gist of the whole thing.' He stared at a little eddy. 'The rule's all right, so long as there isn't a case. Rules are for established things, like the pieces and positions of a game. Men and women are not established things; they're experiments, all of them. Every human being is a new thing, exists to do new things. Find the thing you want to do most intensely, make sure that's it, and do it with all your might. If you live, well and good; if you die, well and good. Your purpose is done. . . . Well, this is *our* thing.'

He woke the glassy water to swirling activity again, and made the deep blue shapes below writhe and shiver.

'This is *my* thing,' said Ann Veronica softly, with thoughtful eyes upon him.

Then she looked up the sweep of pine-trees to the towering sunlit cliffs and the high heaven above and then back to his face. She drew in a deep breath of the sweet mountain air. Her eyes were soft and grave, and there was the faintest of smiles upon her resolute lips.

3

Later they loitered along a winding path above the inn, and made love to one another. Their journey had made them indolent, the afternoon was warm, and it seemed impossible to breathe a sweeter air. The flowers and turf, a wild strawberry, a rare butterfly, and suchlike little intimate things had become more interesting than mountains. Their flitting hands were always touching. Deep silences came between them. . . .

'I had thought to go on to Kandersteg,' said Capes, 'but this is a pleasant place. There is not a soul in the inn but ourselves. Let us stay the night here. Then we can loiter and gossip to our hearts' content.'

'Agreed,' said Ann Veronica.

'After all, it's our honeymoon.'

'All we shall get,' said Ann Veronica.

'This place is very beautiful.'

'Any place would be beautiful,' said Ann Veronica in a low voice. For a time they walked in silence.

'I wonder,' she began presently, 'why I love you – and love you so much? . . . I know now what it is to be an abandoned female. I *am* an abandoned female. I'm not ashamed – of the things I'm doing. I want to put myself into your hands. You know I wish I could roll my little body up small and squeeze it into your hand and grip your fingers upon it. Tight. I want you to hold me and have me *so.* . . . . Everything. Everything. It's a pure joy of giving – giving to *you.* I have never spoken of these things to any human being. Just dreamt – and ran away even from my dreams. It is as if my lips had been sealed about them. And now I break the seals – for you. Only I wish – I wish to-day I was a thousand times, ten thousand times more beautiful.'

Capes lifted her hand and kissed it.

'You are a thousand times more beautiful,' he said, 'than anything else could be. . . . You are you. You are all the beauty in the world. Beauty doesn't mean, never has meant, anything – anything at all but you. It heralded you, promised you. . . .'

4

They lay side by side in a shallow nest of turf and mosses among boulders and stunted bushes on a high rock, and watched the day sky deepen to evening between the vast precipices overhead and looked over the tree tops down the widening gorge. A distant suggestion of châlets and a glimpse of the road set them talking for a time of the world they had left behind.

Capes spoke casually of their plans for work. 'It's a flabby, loose-willed world we have to face. It won't even know whether to be scandalized at us or forgiving. It will hold aloof, a little undecided whether to pelt or not—'

'That depends on whether we carry ourselves as though we expected pelting,' said Ann Veronica.

'We won't.'

'No fear!'

'Then, as we succeed, it will begin to sidle back to us. It will do its best to overlook things—'

'If we let it, poor dear.'

'That's if we succeed. If we fail,' said Capes, 'then—'

'We aren't going to fail,' said Ann Veronica.

Life seemed a very brave and glorious enterprise to Ann Veronica that day. She was quivering with the sense of Capes at her side and glowing with heroic love; it seemed to her that if they put their hands jointly against the Alps and pushed they would be able to push them aside. She lay and nibbled at a sprig of dwarf rhododendron.

'*Fail*!' she said.

5

Presently it occurred to Ann Veronica to ask about the journey he had planned. He had his sections of the Siegfried map folded in his pocket, and he squatted up with his legs crossed like an Indian idol while she lay prone beside him and followed every movement of his indicatory finger.

'Here,' he said, 'is this Blauer See, and here we rest until to-morrow. I think we rest here until to-morrow?'

There was a brief silence.

'It is a very pleasant place,' said Ann Veronica, biting a rhododendron stalk through, and with that faint shadow of a smile returning to her lips. . . .

'And then?' said Ann Veronica.

'Then we go on to this place, the Oeschinensee. It's a lake among precipices, and there is a little inn where we can stay, and sit and eat our dinner at a pleasant table that looks upon the lake. For some days we shall be very idle there among the trees and rocks. There are boats on the lake and shady depths and wildernesses of pine wood. After a day or so, perhaps, we will go on one or two little excursions and see how good your head is – a mild scramble or so; and then up to a hut on a pass just here, and out upon the Blumlisalp glacier that spreads out so and so.'

She roused herself from some dream at the word. 'Glaciers?' she said.

'Under the Wilde Frau – which was named after you.'

He bent and kissed her hair and paused, and then forced his attention back to the map. 'One day,' he resumed, 'we will start off early and come down into Kandersteg and up these zigzags and here and here, and so past this Daubensee to a tiny inn – it won't be busy yet though, we may get it all to ourselves – on the brim of the steepest zigzag you can imagine, thousands of feet of zigzag; and you will sit and eat lunch with me and look out across the Rhône valley and over blue distances beyond blue distances to the Matterhorn and Monte Rosa and a long regiment of sunny, snowy mountains. And when we see them we shall at once want

to go to them – that's the way with beautiful things – and down
we shall go, like flies down a wall, to Leukerbad, and so to Leuk
station, here, and then by train up the Rhône valley and this little
side valley to Stalden; and there, in the cool of the afternoon, we
shall start off up a gorge, torrents and cliffs below us and above
us, to sleep in a half-way inn, and go on next day to Saas Fée, Saas
of the Magic, Saas of the Pagan People. And there, about Saas,
are ice and snows again, and sometimes we will loiter among the
rocks and trees about Saas or peep into Samuel Butler's chapels,
and sometimes we will climb up out of the way of the other people
on to the glaciers and snow. And, for one expedition at least, we
will go up this desolate valley here to Mattmark, and so on to
Monte Moro. There indeed you see Monte Rosa. Almost the best
of all.'

'Is it very beautiful?'

'When I saw it there it was very beautiful. It was wonderful. It
was the crowned queen of mountains in her robes of shining
white. It towered up high above the level of the pass, thousands
of feet, still, shining and white, and below, thousands of feet
below, was a floor of little woolly clouds. And then presently these
clouds began to wear thin and expose steep, deep slopes, going
down and down, with grass and pine-trees, down and down, and
at last, through a great rent in the clouds, bare roofs, shining like
very minute pin-heads, and a road like a fibre of white silk –
Macugnana, in Italy. That will be a fine day – it will have to be,
when first you set eyes on Italy. . . . That's as far as we go.'

'Can't we go down into Italy?'

'No,' he said; 'it won't run to that now. We must wave our hands
at the blue hills far away there and go back to London and work.'

'But Italy—'

'Italy's for a good girl,' he said, and laid his hand for a moment
on her shoulder. 'She must look forward to Italy.'

'I say,' she reflected, 'you *are* rather the master, you know.'

The idea struck him as novel. 'Of course, I'm manager for this
expedition,' he said, after an interval of self-examination.

She slid her cheek down the tweed sleeve of his coat. 'Nice
sleeve,' she said, and came to his hand and kissed it.

'I say,' he cried. 'Look here! Aren't you going a little too far?
This – this is degradation – making a fuss with sleeves. You
mustn't do things like that.'

'Why not?'

'Free woman – and equal.'

'I do it – of my own free will,' said Ann Veronica, kissing his hand again. 'It's nothing to what I *will* do.'

'Oh, well!' he said a little doubtfully, 'it's just a phase,' and bent down and rested his hand on her shoulder for a moment, with his heart beating and his nerves a-quiver. Then as she lay very still, with her hands clenched and her black hair tumbled about her face, he came still closer and softly kissed the nape of her neck. . . .

6

Most of the things that he had planned they did. But they climbed more than he had intended because Ann Veronica proved rather a good climber, steady-headed and plucky, rather daring, but quite willing to be cautious at his command.

One of the things that most surprised him in her was her capacity for blind obedience. She loved to be told to do things.

He knew the circle of mountains about Saas Fée fairly well; he had been there twice before, and it was fine to get away from the straggling pedestrians into the high, lonely places, and sit and munch sandwiches and talk together and do things together that were just a little difficult and dangerous. And they could talk, they found; and never once, it seemed, did their meaning and intention hitch. They were enormously pleased with one another; they found each other beyond measure better than they had expected, if only because of the want of substance in mere expectation. Their conversation degenerated again and again into a strain of self-congratulation that would have irked an eavesdropper.

'You're – I don't know,' said Ann Veronica. 'You're splendid.'

'It isn't that you're splendid or I,' said Capes. 'But we satisfy one another. Heaven alone knows why. So completely! The oddest fitness! What is it made of? Texture of skin and texture of mind? Complexion and voice. I don't think I've got illusions, nor you. . . . If I had never met anything of you at all but a scrap of your skin binding a book, Ann Veronica, I know I would have kept that somewhere near to me. . . . All your faults are just jolly modelling to make you real and solid.'

'The faults are the best part of it,' said Ann Veronica; 'why, even our little vicious strains run the same way. Even our coarseness.'

'Coarse?' said Capes. 'We're not coarse.'

'But if we were?' said Ann Veronica.

'I can talk to you and you to me without a scrap of effort,' said Capes; 'that's the essence of it. It's made up of things as small as the diameter of hairs and big as life and death. . . . One always dreamt of this and never believed it. It's the rarest luck, the wildest, most impossible accident. Most people, every one I know else, seem to have mated with foreigners and to talk uneasily in unfamiliar tongues, to be afraid of the knowledge the other one has, of the other one's perpetual misjudgment and misunderstandings.

'Why don't they wait?' he added.

Ann Veronica had one of her flashes of insight.

'One doesn't wait,' said Ann Veronica.

She expanded that. 'I shouldn't have waited,' she said. 'I might have muddled for a time. But it's as you say. I've had the rarest luck and fallen on my feet.'

'We've both fallen on our feet! We're the rarest of mortals! The real thing! There's not a compromise nor a sham nor a concession between us. We aren't afraid; we don't bother. We don't consider each other; we needn't. That wrappered life, as you call it – we've burnt the confounded rags! Danced out of it! We're stark!'

'Stark!' echoed Ann Veronica.

7

As they came back from that day's climb – it was up the Mittaghorn – they had to cross a shining space of wet, steep rocks between two grass slopes that needed a little care. There were a few loose, broken fragments of rock to reckon with upon the ledges, and one place where hands did as much work as toes. They used the rope – not that a rope was at all necessary, but because Ann Veronica's exalted state of mind made the fact of the rope agreeably symbolical; and, anyhow, it did ensure a joint death in the event of some remotely possible mischance. Capes went first, finding footholds and, where the drops in the strata-edges came like long, awkward steps, placing Ann Veronica's feet. About half-way across this interval, when everything seemed going well, Capes had a shock.

'Heavens!' exclaimed Ann Veronica, with extraordinary passion. 'My God!' and ceased to move.

Capes became rigid and adhesive. Nothing ensued. 'All right?' he asked.

'I'll have to pay it.'

'Eh?'

'I've forgotten something. Oh, cuss it!'

'Eh?'

'He said I would.'

'What?'

'That's the devil of it!'

'Devil of what? . . . You *do* use vile language!'

'Forget about it like this.'

'Forget *what*?'

'And I said I wouldn't. I said I'd do anything. I said I'd make shirts.'

'Shirts?'

'Shirts at one and something a dozen. Oh, goodness! Bilking! Ann Veronica, you're a bilker!'

Pause.

'Will you tell me what all this is about?' said Capes.

'It's about forty pounds.'

Capes waited patiently.

'G. I'm sorry. . . . But you've got to lend me forty pounds.'

'It's some sort of delirium,' said Capes. 'The rarefied air? I thought you had a better head.'

'No! I'll explain lower. It's all right. Let's go on climbing now. It's a thing I've unaccountably overlooked. All right really. It can wait a bit longer. I borrowed forty pounds from Mr Ramage. Thank goodness you'll understand. That's why I chucked Manning. . . . All right, I'm coming. But all this business has driven it clean out of my head. . . . That's why he was so annoyed, you know.'

'Who was annoyed?'

'Mr Ramage – about the forty pounds.' She took a step. 'My dear,' she added, by way of afterthought, 'you *do* obliterate things!'

8

They found themselves next day talking love to one another high up on some rocks above a steep bank of snow that overhung a precipice on the eastern side of the Fée glacier. By this time Capes's hair had bleached nearly white, and his skin had become a skin of red copper shot with gold. They were now both in a state of unprecedented physical fitness. And such skirts as Ann Veronica had had when she entered the valley of Saas were safely packed away in the hotel, and she wore a leather belt and loose knicker-bockers and puttees – a costume that suited the fine, long lines of her limbs far better than any feminine walking dress could do. Her complexion had resisted the snow glare wonderfully; her skin had only deepened its natural warmth a little under the Alpine sun. She had pushed aside her azure veil, taken off her snow glasses, and sat smiling under her hand at the shining glories – the lit cornices, the blue shadows, the softly rounded, enormous snow masses, the deep places full of quivering luminosity – of the Taschhorn and Dom. The sky was cloudless, effulgent blue.

Capes sat watching and admiring her, and then he fell praising the day and fortune and their love for each other.

'Here we are,' he said, 'shining through each other like light through a stained-glass window. With this air in our blood, this sunlight soaking us. . . . Life is so good. Can it ever be so good again?'

Ann Veronica put out a firm hand and squeezed his arm. 'It's very good,' she said. 'It's glorious good!'

'Suppose now – look at this long snow slope and then that blue deep beyond – do you see that round pool of colour in the ice – a thousand feet or more below? Yes? Well, think – we've got to go but ten steps and lie down and put our arms about each other. See? Down we should rush in a foam – in a cloud of snow – to flight and a dream. All the rest of our lives would be together then, Ann Veronica. Every moment. And no ill chances.'

'If you tempt me too much,' she said, after a silence, 'I shall do it. I need only just jump up and throw myself upon you. I'm a desperate young woman. And then as we went down you'd try to explain. And that would spoil it. . . . You know you don't mean it.'

'No, I don't. But I liked to say it.'

'Rather! But I wonder why you don't mean it?'

'Because, I suppose, the other thing is better. What other reason could there be? It's more complex, but it's better. *This*, this glissade, would be damned scoundrelism. You know that, and I know that, though we might be put to it to find a reason why. It would be swindling. Drawing the pay of life and then not living. And besides – We're going to live, Ann Veronica! Oh, the things we'll do, the life we'll lead! There'll be trouble in it at times – you and I aren't going to run without friction. But we've got the brains to get over that, and tongues in our heads to talk to one another. We shan't hang up on any misunderstanding. Not us. And we're going to fight that old world down there. That old world that had shoved up that silly old hotel, and all the rest of it. . . . If we don't live it will think we are afraid of it. . . . Die, indeed! We're going to do work; we're going to unfold about each other; we're going to have children.'

'Girls!' cried Ann Veronica.

'Boys!' said Capes.

'Both!' said Ann Veronica. 'Lots of 'em!'

Capes chuckled. 'You delicate female!'

'Who cares,' said Ann Veronica, 'seeing it's you? Warm, soft little wonders! Of course I want them.'

9

'All sorts of things we're going to do,' said Capes; 'all sorts of times we're going to have. Sooner or later we'll certainly do something to clean those prisons you told me about – limewash the underside of life. You and I. We can love on a snow cornice, we can love over a pail of white-wash. Love anywhere. Anywhere! Moonlight and music – pleasing, you know, but quite unnecessary. We met dissecting dogfish. . . . Do you remember your first day with me? . . . Do you indeed remember? The smell of decay and cheap methylated spirit! . . . My dear! we've had so many moments! I used to go over the times we'd had together, the things we'd said – like a rosary of beads. But now it's beads by the cask – like the hold of a West African trader. It feels like too much gold dust clutched in one's hand. One doesn't want to lose a grain. And one must – some of it must slip through one's fingers.'

'I don't care if it does,' said Ann Veronica. 'I don't care a rap for remembering. I care for you. This moment couldn't be better until the next moment comes. That's how it takes me. Why should *we* hoard? We aren't going out presently, like Japanese lanterns in a gale. It's the poor dears who do, who know they will, know they will, know they can't keep it up, who need to clutch at wayside flowers. And put 'em in little books for remembrance.

Flattened flowers aren't for the likes of us. Moments, indeed! We like each other fresh and fresh. It isn't illusions – for us. We two just love each other – the real, identical other – all the time.'

'The real, identical other,' said Capes, and took and bit the tip of her little finger.

'There's no delusions, so far as I know,' said Ann Veronica.

'I don't believe there is one. If there is, it's a mere wrapping – there's better underneath. It's only as if I'd begun to know you the day before yesterday or thereabouts. You keep on coming truer, after you have seemed to come altogether true. You . . . brick!'

10

'To think,' he cried, 'you are ten years younger than I! . . . There are times when you make me feel a little thing at your feet – a young, silly, protected thing. Do you know, Ann Veronica, it is all a lie about your birth certificate; a forgery – and fooling at that. You are one of the Immortals. Immortal! You were in the beginning, and all the men in the world who have known what love is have worshipped at your feet. You have converted me to – Lester Ward!* You are my dear friend, you are a slip of a girl, but there are moments when my head has been on your breast, when your heart has been beating close to my ears, when I have known you for the goddess, when I have wished myself your slave, when I have wished that you could kill me for the joy of being killed by you. You are the High Priestess of Life. . . .'

'Your priestess,' whispered Ann Veronica softly. 'A silly little priestess who knew nothing of life at all until she came to you.'

11

They sat for a time without speaking a word, in an enormous shining globe of mutual satisfaction.

'Well,' said Capes at length, 'we've to go down, Ann Veronica. Life waits for us.'

He stood up and waited for her to move.

'Gods!' cried Ann Veronica, and kept him standing. 'And to think that it's not a full year ago since I was a black-hearted rebel schoolgirl, distressed, puzzled, perplexed, not understanding that this great force of love was bursting its way through me! All those nameless discontents – they were no more than love's birth-pangs. I felt – I felt living in a masked world. I felt as though I had bandaged eyes. I felt – wrapped in thick cobwebs. They blinded me. They got in my mouth. And now— Dear! Dear! The day-spring from on high hath visited me. I love. I am loved. I want to shout! I want to sing! I am glad! I am glad to be alive because you are alive! I am glad to be a woman because you are a man! I am glad! I am glad! I am glad! I thank God for life and you. I thank God for His sunlight on your face. I thank God for the beauty you love and the faults you love. I thank God for the very skin that is peeling from your nose, for all things great and small that make us what we are. This is grace I am saying! Oh, my dear! all the joy and weeping of life are mixed in me now and all the gratitude. Never a new-born dragon-fly that spread its wings in the morning has felt as glad as I!'

Chapter XVII

In Perspective

I

About four years and a quarter later, to be exact it was four years and four months, Mr and Mrs Capes stood side by side upon an old Persian carpet that did duty as a hearthrug in the dining-room of their flat and surveyed a shining dinner table set for four people, lit by skilfully shaded electric lights, brightened by frequent gleams of silver, and carefully and simply adorned with sweet-pea blossom. Capes had altered scarcely at all during the interval, except for a new quality of smartness in the cut of his clothes, but Ann Veronica was nearly half an inch taller; her face was at once stronger and softer, her neck firmer and rounder, and her carriage definitely more womanly than it had been in the days of her rebellion. She was a woman now to the tips of her fingers; she had said good-bye to her girlhood in the old garden four years and a quarter ago. She was dressed in a simple evening gown of soft creamy silk, with a yoke of dark old embroidery that enhanced the gentle gravity of her style, and her black hair flowed off her open forehead to pass under the control of a simple ribbon of silver. A silver necklace enhanced the dusky beauty of her neck. Both husband and wife affected an unnatural ease of manner for the benefit of the efficient parlour-maid, who was putting the finishing touches to the sideboard arrangements.

'It looks all right,' said Capes.

'I think everything's right,' said Ann Veronica, with the roaming eye of a capable but not devoted house mistress.

'I wonder if they will seem altered,' she remarked for the third time.

'There I can't help,' said Capes.

He walked through a wide open archway, curtained, with deep blue curtains, into the apartment that served as a reception room. Ann Veronica, after a last survey of the dinner appointments, followed him, rustling, came to his side by the high brass fender, and touched two or three ornaments on the mantel above the cheerful fire-place.

'It's still a marvel to me that we are to be forgiven,' she said, turning.

'My charm of manner, I suppose. But, indeed, he's very human.'

'Did you tell him of the registry office?'

'No-o – certainly not so emphatically as I did about the play.'

'It was an inspiration – your speaking to him?'

'I felt impudent. I believe I am getting impudent. I had not been near the Royal Society since – since you disgraced me. What's that?'

They both stood listening. It was not the arrival of the guests, but merely the maid moving about in the hall.

'Wonderful man!' said Ann Veronica, reassured, and stroking his cheek with her finger.

Capes made a quick movement as if to bite that aggressive digit, but it withdrew to Ann Veronica's side.

'I was really interested in his stuff. I *was* talking to him before I saw his name on the card beside the row of microscopes. Then, naturally, I went on talking. He – he has rather a poor opinion of his contemporaries. Of course, he had no idea who I was.'

'But how did you tell him? You've never told me. Wasn't it – a little bit of a scene?'

'Oh! let me see. I said I hadn't been at the Royal Society soirée for four years, and got him to tell me about some of the fresh Mendelian work. He loves the Mendelians because he hates all the big names of the eighties and nineties. Then I think I remarked that science was disgracefully under-endowed, and confessed I'd had to take to more profitable courses. "The fact of it is," I said, "I'm the new playwright, Thomas More. Perhaps you've heard—?" Well, you know, he had.'

'Fame!'

'Isn't it? "I've not seen your play, Mr More," he said, "but I'm told it's the most amusing thing in London at the present time. A friend of mine, Ogilvy" – I suppose that's Ogilvy & Ogilvy, who do so many divorces, Vee? – "was speaking very highly of it – very highly!" ' He smiled into her eyes.

'You are developing far too retentive a memory for praises,' said Ann Veronica.

'I'm still new to them. But after that it was easy. I told him instantly and shamelessly that the play was going to be worth ten thousand pounds. He agreed it was disgraceful. Then I assumed a rather portentous manner to prepare him.'

'How? Show me.'

'I can't be portentous, dear, when you're about. It's my other side of the moon.* But I was portentous, I can assure you. "My name's *not* More, Mr Stanley," I said. "That's my pen name." '

'Yes?'

'I think – yes, I went on in a pleasing blend of the casual and *sotto voce*: "The fact of it is, sir, I happen to be your son-in-law, Capes. I do wish you could come and dine with us some evening. It would make my wife very happy." '

'What did he say?'

'What does any one say to an invitation to dinner point-blank? One tries to collect one's wits. "She is constantly thinking of you," I said.'

'And he accepted meekly?'

'Practically. What else could he do? You can't kick up a scene on the spur of the moment in the face of such conflicting values as he had before him. With me behaving as if everything was infinitely matter-of-fact, what could he do? And just then heaven sent old Manningtree – I didn't tell you before of the fortunate intervention of Manningtree, did I? He was looking quite infernally distinguished, with a wide crimson ribbon across him – what *is* a wide crimson ribbon? Some sort of knight, I suppose. He is a knight. "Well, young man," he said, "we haven't seen you lately," and something about "Bateson & Co." – he's frightfully anti-Mendelian – having it all their own way. So I introduced him to my father-in-law like a shot. I think that *was* decision. Yes, it was Manningtree really secured your father. He –'

'Here they are!' said Ann Veronica as the bell sounded.

2

They received the guests in their pretty little hall with genuine effusion. Miss Stanley threw aside a black cloak to reveal a discreet and dignified arrangement of brown silk, and then embraced Ann Veronica with warmth. 'So very clear and cold,' she said. 'I feared we might have a fog.' The housemaid's presence acted as a useful restraint. Ann Veronica passed from her aunt to her father, and put her arms about him and kissed his cheek. 'Dear old daddy!' she said, and was amazed to find herself shedding tears. She veiled her emotion by taking off his overcoat. 'And this is Mr Capes?' she heard her aunt saying.

All four people moved a little nervously into the drawing-room, maintaining a sort of fluttered amiability of sound and movement. Mr Stanley professed a great solicitude to warm his hands. 'Quite unusually cold for the time of year,' he said. 'Everything very nice, I am sure,' Miss Stanley murmured to Capes as he steered her to a place upon the little sofa before the fire. Also she made little pussy-like sounds of a reassuring nature.

'And let's have a look at you, Vee!' said Mr Stanley, standing up with a sudden geniality and rubbing his hands together.

Ann Veronica, who knew her dress became her, dropped a curtsy to her father's regard.

Happily they had no one else to wait for, and it heartened her mightily to think that she had ordered the promptest possible service of the dinner. Capes stood beside Miss Stanley, who was beaming unnaturally, and Mr Stanley, in his effort to seem at ease, took entire possession of the hearth-rug.

'You found the flat easily?' said Capes in the pause. 'The numbers are a little difficult to see in the archway. They ought to put a lamp.'

Her father declared there had been no difficulty.

'Dinner is served, m'm,' said the efficient parlour-maid in the archway, and the worst was over.

'Come, daddy,' said Ann Veronica, following her husband and Miss Stanley; and in the fullness of her heart she gave a friendly squeeze to the parental arm.

'Excellent fellow!' he answered a little irrelevantly. 'I didn't understand, Vee.'

'Quite charming apartments,' Miss Stanley admired; 'charming! Everything is so pretty and convenient.'

The dinner was admirable as a dinner; nothing went wrong, from the golden and excellent clear soup to the delightful iced *marrons* and cream; and Miss Stanley's praises died away to an appreciative acquiescence. A brisk talk sprang up between Capes and Mr Stanley, to which the two ladies subordinated themselves intelligently. The burning topic of the Mendelian controversy was approached on one or two occasions, but avoided dexterously; and they talked chiefly of letters and art and the censorship of the English stage. Mr Stanley was inclined to think the censorship should be extended to the supply of what he styled latter-day fiction; good wholesome stories were being ousted, he said, by 'vicious, corrupting stuff' that 'left a bad taste in the mouth'. He declared that no book could be satisfactory that left a bad taste in the mouth, however much it seized and interested the reader at the time. He did not like, he said, with a significant look, to be reminded of either his books or his dinners after he had done with them. Capes agreed with the utmost cordiality.

'Life is upsetting enough, without the novels taking a share,' said Mr Stanley.

For a time Ann Veronica's attention was diverted by her aunt's interest in the salted almonds.

'Quite particularly nice,' said her aunt. 'Exceptionally so.'

When Ann Veronica could attend again she found the men were discussing the ethics of the depreciation of house property through the increasing tumult of traffic in the West End, and agreeing with each other to a devastating extent. It came into her head with real emotional force that this must be some particularly fantastic sort of dream. It seemed to her that her father was in some inexplicable way meaner-looking than she had supposed, and yet also, as unaccountably, appealing. His tie had demanded a struggle; he ought to have taken a clean one after his first failure. Why was she noting things like this? Capes seemed self-possessed and elaborately genial and commonplace, but she knew him to be nervous by a little occasional clumsiness, by the faintest shadow of vulgarity in the urgency of his hospitality. She wished he could smoke and dull his nerves a little. A gust of irrational impatience blew through her being. Well, they'd got to the pheasants, and in a little while he would smoke. What was it she had expected? Surely her moods were getting a little out of hand.

She wished her father and aunt would not enjoy their dinner with such quiet determination. Her father and her husband, who had both been a little pale at their first encounter, were growing now just faintly flushed. It was a pity people had to eat food.

'I suppose,' said her father, 'I have read at least half the novels that have been at all successful during the last twenty years. Three a week is my allowance, and, if I get short ones, four. I change them in the morning at Cannon Street, and take my book as I come down.'

It occurred to her that she had never seen her father dining out before, never watched him critically as an equal. To Capes he was almost deferential, and she had never seen him deferential in the old time, never. The dinner was stranger than she had ever anticipated. It was as if she had grown right past her father into something older and of infinitely wider outlook, as if he had always been unsuspectedly a flattened figure, and now she had discovered him from the other side.

It was a great relief to arrive at last at that pause when she could say to her aunt: 'Now, dear?' and rise and hold back the curtain through the archway. Capes and her father stood up, and her father made a belated movement towards the curtain. She realized that he was the sort of man one does not think much about at dinners. And Capes was thinking that his wife was a supremely beautiful woman. He reached a silver cigar and cigarette box from the sideboard and put it before his father-in-law, and for a time the preliminaries of smoking occupied them both. Then Capes flitted to the hearth-rug and poked the fire, stood up, and turned about. 'Ann Veronica is looking very well, don't you think?' he said a little awkwardly.

'Very,' said Mr Stanley. 'Very,' and cracked a walnut appreciatively.

'Life – things— I don't think her prospects now— Hopeful outlook.'

'You were in difficult position,' Mr Stanley pronounced, and seemed to hesitate whether he had not gone too far. He looked at his port wine as though that tawny ruby contained the solution of the matter. 'All's well that ends well,' he said; 'and the less one says about things the better.'

'Of course,' said Capes, and threw a newly lit cigar into the fire through sheer nervousness. 'Have some more port wine, sir?'

'It's a very sound wine,' said Mr Stanley, consenting with dignity.

'Ann Veronica has never looked quite so well, I think,' said Capes, clinging, because of a preconceived plan, to the suppressed topic.

3

At last the evening was over, and Capes and his wife had gone down to see Mr Stanley and his sister into a taxi-cab, and had waved an amiable farewell from the pavement steps.

'Great dears!' said Capes, as the vehicle passed out of sight.

'Yes, aren't they?' said Ann Veronica, after a thoughtful pause. And then: 'They seemed changed.'

'Come in out of the cold,' said Capes, and took her arm.

'They seem smaller, you know, even physically smaller,' she said.

'You've grown out of them. . . . Your aunt liked the pheasant.'

'She liked everything. Did you hear us through the archway, talking cookery?'

They went up by the lift in silence.

'It's odd,' said Ann Veronica, re-entering the flat.

'What's odd?'

'Oh, everything!'

She shivered, and went to the fire and poked it. Capes sat down in the arm-chair beside her.

'Life's so queer,' she said, kneeling and looking into the flames. 'I wonder – I wonder if we shall ever get like that.'

She turned a firelit face to her husband. 'Did you tell him?'

Capes smiled faintly. 'Yes.'

'How?'

'Well – a little clumsily.'

'But how?'

'I poured him out some port wine, and I said – let me see – oh: "You are going to be a grandfather!" '

'Yes. Was he pleased?'

'Calmly! He said – you won't mind my telling you?'

'Not a bit.'

'He said: "Poor Alice has got no end!" '

'Alice's are different,' said Ann Veronica after an interval. 'Quite different. She didn't choose her man. . . . Well, I told aunt. . . . Husband of mine, I think we have rather overrated the emotional capacity of those – those dears.'

'What did your aunt say?'

'She didn't even kiss me. She said' – Ann Veronica shivered again – ' "I hope it won't make you uncomfortable, my dear" – like that – "and whatever you do, do be careful of your hair!" I think – I judge from her manner – that she thought it was just a little indelicate of us – considering everything; but she tried to be practical and sympathetic and live down to our standards.'

Capes looked at his wife's unsmiling face.

'Your father,' he said, 'remarked that all's well that ends well, and that he was disposed to let bygones be bygones. He then spoke with a certain fatherly kindliness of the past. . . .'

'And my heart has ached for him!'

'Oh, no doubt it cut him at the time. It must have cut him.'

'We might even have – given it up for them!'

'I wonder if we could.'

'I suppose all *is* well that ends well. Somehow to-night – I don't know.'

'I suppose so. I'm glad the old sore is assuaged. Very glad. But if we had gone under—!'

They regarded one another silently, and Ann Veronica had one of her penetrating flashes.

'We are not the sort that goes under,' said Ann Veronica, holding her hands so that the red reflections vanished from her eyes. 'We settled long ago – we're hard stuff. We're hard stuff!'

Then she went on: 'To think that is my father! Oh, my dear! He stood over me like a cliff; the thought of him nearly turned me aside from everything we have done. He was the social order; he was law and wisdom. And they come here, and they look at our furniture to see if it is good; and they are not glad, it does not stir them, that at last, at last we can dare to have children.'

She dropped back into a crouching attitude and began to weep. 'Oh, my dear!' she cried, and suddenly flung herself kneeling into her husband's arms.

'Do you remember the mountains? Do you remember how we loved one another? How intensely we loved one another! Do you remember the light on things and the glory of things? I'm greedy, I'm greedy! I want children like the mountains and life like the sky. Oh! and love – love! We've had so splendid a time, and fought our fight and won. And it's like the petals falling from a flower. Oh, I've loved love, dear! I've loved love and you, and the glory of you; and the great time is over, and I have to go carefully and bear children, and – take care of my hair – and when I am done with that I shall be an old woman. The petals have fallen – the red petals we loved so. We're hedged about with discretions – and all this furniture – and successes! We are successful at last! Successful! But the mountains, dear! We won't forget the mountains, dear, ever. That shining slope of snow, and how we talked of death! We might have died! Even when we are old, when we are rich as we may be, we won't forget the time when we cared nothing for anything but the joy of one another, when we risked everything for one another, when all the wrappings and coverings seemed to have fallen from life and left it light and fire. Stark and stark! Do you remember it all? . . . Say you will never forget! That these common things and secondary things shan't overwhelm us. These petals! I've been wanting to cry all the evening, cry here on your shoulder, for my petals. Petals! . . . Silly woman! . . . I've never had these crying fits before. . . .'

'Blood of my heart!' whispered Capes, holding her close to him. 'I know. I understand.'

NOTES

p.7 **The Imperial College at Westminster:** The title of the institution to which Huxley was originally appointed was the Government School of Mines and Science, situated in Jermyn Street. Later in *Ann Veronica*, however, Wells says the Central Imperial College 'towers up from among the back streets in the angle between Euston Road and Great Portland Street'. Presumably this institution would have been one of the laboratories scattered around London which transferred eventually to South Kensington to form the Imperial College of Science and Technology in 1907.

p.7 **Russell:** clearly based on T. H. Huxley (1825–95), friend and ally of Charles Darwin, and staunch defender of his theory of evolution; he was professor of natural history at the Normal School of Science, which H. G. Wells attended from 1884 to 1887. Wells's first year at the School was Huxley's last as professor, and in his autobiography, Wells claims: 'That year I spent in Huxley's class was beyond all question the most educational year of my life.' Mr Stanley's objection to Russell's 'unbridled classes' probably relates to Huxley's religious views as much as to his scientific theories (Huxley coined the word 'agnostic' to describe his own doubts).

p.19 **Lydia Languish:** the heroine of Richard Brinsley Sheridan's *The Rivals* (1775). Despite her attempts to thwart the wishes of her elders and guardians, Lydia ends up by complying with every one of them.

p.19 **Women Who Dids:** Grant Allen's influential novel, *The Woman Who Did* (1895) is about a woman, with advanced ideas, who refuses to marry her lover on principle because she considers marriage a degradation for women. When she becomes pregnant, she and her lover go to Italy, where he dies suddenly; she returns to London with the baby and finds herself a social outcast. When the daughter grows up, marries a country gentleman, and denounces her mother for her depravity, the latter commits suicide. The novel was widely read – there were nineteen editions within its first nine months – and produced a number of imitations. When Wells reviewed *The Woman Who Did* for the *Saturday Review* in 9 March 1895 he objected to the book on the grounds that it failed to understand what emancipation meant.

p.31 **euphuistic**: This word, which refers to 'high flown or affected language', occurs twice in *Ann Veronica* (see note to p.149). In this context it is just about acceptable – Lady Palworthy is a social leader who clearly lives in some style – but since we are told she and her friend spend their time bringing people together 'And they never talked of anything at all, never discussed, never even encouraged gossip', 'euphemistic' would seem the more appropriate word.

p.55 **The New Woman**: a phrase fashionable in the 1880s and 1890s which described a woman who was independent, possessed advanced ideas and was often a feminist; writing in 1902 about his own plays of this period, Shaw comments, 'we, of course, called everything advanced "the New" at that time.' (*Plays Unpleasant*, p.11). By 1909 it had become a dated term – in a review of *Jude the Obscure* for the *Saturday Review* in 1896, H. G. Wells commented: 'It is now the better part of a year ago since the collapse of the "New Woman" fiction began.' It is significant, therefore, that it is the aging *roué*, Ramage, whose youth dates back to the 1880s, who uses the phrase.

p.71 **Vivie Warren**: the young heroine of Shaw's play, *Mrs Warren's Profession*, written in 1894. The play ends with Vivie determined to make her own way in the world, and to reject the allowance given by her mother, Mrs Warren, whose capital (as her daughter has discovered in the course of the play) derives from a chain of brothels. The fact that Ann Veronica saw the play helps date the events of the book. *Mrs Warren's Profession* had been refused a licence by the Lord Chamberlain, so the play did not appear on stage for eight years, then the Stage Society (which was a club and therefore not subject to the Lord Chamberlain's jurisdiction) put on two performances at the New Lyric Club in 1902, the first a matinée, and this is the one Ann Veronica and Hetty Widgett attended.

p.90   **Woman-who-diddery**: see note to p.19.

p.90   **Ouida**: the pen-name of Marie Louise de la Ramée (1839–1908) who wrote forty-five romantic novels in the 1860s to 1880s, all with exotic settings and featuring dashing guardsmen bearing a striking resemblance to Mr Manning, with faces 'handsome, thoro'bred, languid and nonchalant' and eyes 'with a certain gentle mournful love-me look'. (Eileen Bigland, *Ouida: The Passionate Victorian*, London, Jarrolds, 1950, P.47.)

p.90   **Haldane**: Richard Burdon Haldane (1856–1928), a prominent liberal politician and a philosopher whom Wells came to know during the early years of the century. Both he and the newly established London School of Economics played a prominent part in the 'Edwardian cult of Efficiency' movement.

p.90   **The Keltic School**: the Irish Keltic (or Celtic) school movement associated with Yeats and the Irish Revival of the 1880s and 1890s was characterized by its mysticism and its romantic approach to Irish folklore. Taken together, these references sum up Mr Manning's combination of romantic self-absorption and business efficiency.

p.94   **Vivie Warren was what is called an 'ideal'**: Vivie Warren had received an excellent education at Newnham College, Cambridge where she distinguished herself in the mathematical tripos and tied with the third wrangler. By the end of the play she is sharing chambers in the City, preparing for a career on the stock exchange.

p.98   **the Fabians**: Wells joined the socialist Fabian Society in 1903. In 1906 he became embroiled in a quarrel with his fellow executive members, particularly G. Bernard Shaw and Beatrice and Sidney Webb, over the way the Society should be organized, and there were also disputes about his advocacy of freer sexual behaviour. In 1908, Wells resigned from the Society and revenged himself by ridiculing its members in *Ann Veronica*.

p.102   **Wilkins the author**: Wilkins is the name by which Wells portrays himself in his novels.

p.103   *Looking Backwards* **and** *News from Nowhere*: Edward Bellamy's *Looking Backwards* (1887) and William Morris's *News from Nowhere* (1891) are both socialist Utopian fantasies in which the narrators are projected into the future.

p.117 **Bebel:** Ferdinand August Bebel (1840–1913) was a German socialist who rose to be a leader of the German Social Democratic movement and its chief spokesman in the Reichstag. He wrote widely on socialism and on the status of women.

p.124 **Atkinson:** J. J. Atkinson's book *Primal Law* (1903) is essentially patriarchal. It explains the earliest forms of social life in terms of small herds, each under the leadership of a dominant male, the 'Old Man', who drove off the younger males who challenged his position and his possession of the females of the group.

p.124 **Lester Ward:** F. Lester Ward (1841–1913) was an American sociologist who believed that the primary responsibility of sociology was to teach methods of achieving a better society. His 1906 book, *Applied Sociology*, puts forward his ideas for a 'telic' or planned society, and he developed a gynæococentric theory of the primacy of the female which was taken up by supporters of women's emancipation.

p.149 **Euphuism:** The word 'euphuism' in this context is clearly inappropriate because Ramage's use of 'loan' *was* a euphemism for his real intent, as he himself is acknowledging. It would seem that at this stage of his career, Wells was not aware of the difference between these two words (see note to p.31).

p.155 **Belfort Bax:** Ernest Belfort Bax (1854–1926) was an English writer and reformer; a co-founder with William Morris of the Socialist League.

p.166 **a raid upon the House of Commons:** The militant activities of the Women's Suffrage and Political Union (WSPU) were at their height when Wells was writing *Ann Veronica*, and the details of the Women's Bond of Freedom raid described in this chapter are modelled very closely on those of an actual raid on the House of Commons by the WSPU on 11 February 1908.

p.184 **Lord Morley's book on the subject:** John, 1st Viscount Morley (1838–1923), an eminent man of letters, was Editor of the *Fortnightly Review* for twenty years, and biographer of Gladstone. His works include *On Compromise* (1874).

p.190 **We're the hysterical animal:** In this statement Wells is drawing on medical theories which categorized certain forms of neurosis – which were regarded as peculiar to women – as hysteria. The First World War and the male experience of shellshock challenged these assumptions. (See Elaine Showalter, *The Female Malady: Women, Madness and English Culture, 1830–1980*, London, Virago, 1988.)

p.223 **the Statue and the Bust**: Robert Browning's poem, 'The Statue and the Bust,' tells the story of a Duke in Renaissance Florence who falls in love with a bride on her wedding day, and she with him. Each vows to run away and join the other, but they never do, and since the lady is confined to her room, they see one another only when the Duke rides past her window. When they perceive that youth and beauty are fading, the duke has a bronze statue of himself on horseback placed in the square, the lady a bust of herself sitting in the window.

p.230 **the Blue Lagoon**: H. De Vere Stacpoole's *The Blue Lagoon* was a best-selling romance, which first appeared in 1908. The story describes the adventures of two eight-year-old cousins, a boy and a girl, who are marooned on a South Sea island, their only companion a drunken Irish seaman, who dies after they have been on the island for two years. It is ironic that Mr Stanley should consider the book 'very beautiful and tender and nothing at all to do with Morningside Park' since the bulk of the novel concerns the way in which the two young people discover and explore their sexuality.

p.238 **Shelleyfy**: The life and work of the Romantic poet, Percy Bysshe Shelley (1792–1822) later became synonymous with youthful idealism and principled rebellion against injustice and conventional morality.

p.248 **Lester Ward**: See note to p.102.

p.252 **my other side of the moon**: probably a reference to Robert Browning's love poem, 'One Word More' addressed to his wife, Elizabeth Barrett Browning, in which the poet rejoices that, like the moon, 'the meanest of God's creatures/Boasts two soul sides, one to face the world with,/One to show a woman when he loves her.'

H. G. WELLS AND HIS CRITICS

The critical response to *Ann Veronica* predates the publication of the novel. When, in the autumn of 1908, H. G. Wells sent the completed manuscript to Frederick Macmillan, he was surprised to have it rejected. This was a serious step for the publisher to take because Wells had signed a contract with him in 1903 which gave him sole publishing rights. In a letter dated 19 October, Macmillan wrote:

> I regret that we cannot publish *Ann Veronica* as it seems to me a very well written book and there is a great deal in it that is attractive, but the plot develops on lines that would be exceedingly distasteful to the public which buys books published by our firm. The early part of the book with the picture of middle-class suburban life is very entertaining, indeed up to and including the episode of the suffragette girl there is nothing to object to. When, however, Ann Veronica begins her pursuit of the Professor at the International College, offers herself to him as his mistress and almost forces herself into his arms, the story ceases to be amusing and is certainly not edifying.[1]

Although Wells found another publisher right away, Frederick Macmillan's reaction was a mild foretaste of what Wells was later to term the 'hysterical animosity' which greeted the novel.[2]

One of the earliest responses, however, came in a private letter from an eminent literary figure, the distinguished writer and critic Edmund Gosse, who wrote to Wells to give his impressions of the book on 13 October 1909 only a week after its publication (*Ann Veronica* was published on 3 October). The letter is interesting because although it is in the main commendatory, it does raise questions about aspects of the novel which have been a subject of controversy ever since – Wells's treatment of parent-child relations, his depiction of the family and the novel's ending:

> My dear Wells
>
> I have just finished *Ann Veronica*, which deserves to stand among the finest of your writings. You never were more vivid, more direct or more luminous. The book is really a wonderful commentary on the

febrility of a certain section of women today. It would be a mistake, of course – you are the last to make the mistake – to take these revolutionaries as the body of female society.

There are a thousand points which your admirable story lights up, on which talk would be interesting. You present to us the Family as practically a bankrupt concern. This, if true, is a peculiarly English condition. I find the Family going strong in France, in Germany, in Italy even. ... It must not be held that the novelist recommends what he describes, but there are some impersonal remarks, which I read with close attention, wherein you seem to rejoice in the insolvency of the patriarchal system. I don't quite know why? I seem to see much more happiness (and after all happiness, you admit, is the aim of existence) in the serried domestic life of the French than in our centrifugal modern English plan. I should like to hear from you – with your great experience, your remarkable observation – what has led you to think affection between parents and children such an objectionable thing. On your pp.324, 325 [Capes's explication of the'child-expelling instinct'] you get quite away from what seems to me to be helpful or sane. But I daresay I am wrong.

One thing, and one thing alone in *Ann Veronica* I must protest against. The last chapter (XVIII) seems to me to be entirely wrong. Is not all this a concession to the romantic fallacy? Up to p.341, I had been carried on by the sense of reality, the pathetic commonness of everything, the absence of the heroic exception; and then suddenly, in order to get the necessary English close in luxury, we are told (without any preface) that Mr Capes is a highly successful dramatist, making £10,000 by a play. That is to say, from having been up to that moment a pawn in the game of life, thrillingly interesting because of his fragility and poverty, he suddenly is presented to us as Haroun-al-Raschid, as one of the six or seven persons out of six or seven millions who makes a preposterous accidental fortune. I cannot tell you how this end, in which you beg everything and shirk all the sinister problems of such a life as that of Capes and Ann Veronica, disappoints me.

Yours most sincerely

Edmund Gosse[3]

The first newspaper and periodical reviews were mild in comparison with what was to come later. The reviewer in the *Daily News* had some criticisms of the social theory underlying the book, but concedes:

Nevertheless it is an excellent novel. The characters gradually grow into vital personalities. The heroine from whom the book takes its name begins as an impetuous, capricious girl with a sense of humour, and ideals which she does not understand. She becomes a woman, experienced, self-reliant, reflective, capable of discipline yet with a capacity of concentrated passion which she is willing to regard as the true channel of her destiny.[4]

The reviewer in the *Globe* Literary Supplement did object to Ann Veronica's overt sexuality. He sees Wells as suggesting 'that in a normal, healthy young woman, education and mental development go for nought when the animal and instinctive side of her nature asserted itself.'[5] The John O'London review of 22 October has more reservations, and takes the opportunity for some rhetorical moralizing about the role of women in society. *Ann Veronica* is seen as 'a dangerous novel' because it may influence young women to behave as the heroine does:

> Self-fulfilment at any price is Ann Veronica's motto. It is a rule of life, or an absence of rule, full of a wild attraction. Mr Wells as the disposer of Ann Veronica's fate can bring her through, but in real life the girl who thus threw the reins on the neck of Destiny would be courting irretrievable disaster.... The legal husband, wife and child are still the units of society. The best woman is still the good woman, who maintains her culture by imparting it to her children, who interpolates her mother wit in a world of pioneering and argument and who, as far as may be, makes her own home a microcosm of Utopia. It may be all very difficult and may require some self-limitation in exchange for some self-fulfilment. Such a woman will suffer, as all men and women suffer, but she will be lovely and lovable in her life, and in her coffin more beautiful than she whose beauty launched a thousand ships and burned the topless towers of Ilium.[6]

It was in November that the storm broke. The proprietor of the *Spectator*, St Loe Strachey, was the only London editor who was an active supporter of the influential National Social Purity Crusade. In May 1908, the Crusade had launched a campaign called 'The Forward Movement' with the aim of raising 'the standard of social and personal purity' both in London and 'in all great cities and towns'[7] and the unsigned review, entitled 'A Poisonous Book', which appeared in the *Spectator* on 20 November was clearly a contribution to this campaign. The reviewer begins by stating that the journal has no intention of being puritanical, that it would not denounce a book as likely to poison the minds of its readers 'merely because it was coarse in language, or dealt plainly, or even brutally, with the facts of human life', but:

Between such books and a book like *Ann Veronica* there is a gulf deep and wide. *Ann Veronica* has not a coarse word in it, nor are the 'suggestive' passages open to any very severe criticism. The loathing and indignation which the book inspires in us are due to the effect it is likely to have in undermining that sense of continence and self-control in the individual which is essential to a sound and healthy State. The book is based on the negation of woman's purity and of man's good faith in the relations of sex. It teaches, in effect, that there is no such thing as woman's honour, or if there is, it is only to be a bulwark against a weak temptation. When the temptation is strong enough, not only is the tempted person justified in yielding, but such yielding becomes not merely inevitable but something to be welcomed and glorified. If an animal yearning or lust is only sufficiently absorbing, it is to be obeyed. Self-sacrifice is a dream and self-restraint a delusion. Such things have no place in the muddy world of Mr Wells's imaginings. His is a community of scuffling stoats and ferrets, unenlightened by a ray of duty or abnegation.

The review goes on to describe Capes as 'an erotic science lecturer' who has 'broken his own marriage vows in circumstances of bestial depravity' and ends by suggesting that although real life Ann Veronicas should be forgiven, there should be no attempt to excuse such behaviour with 'the slime of ... faint-scented sophistries':

> Boswell tells us of a conversation in which he defended with sophistical excuses a woman who had betrayed her husband. Dr Johnson cut him short with his immortal – 'My dear Sir, never accustom your mind to mingle virtue and vice. The woman's a—, and there's an end on't.'[8]

Writing a quarter of a century later in his autobiography, Wells comments wryly:

> A reviewer in his columns rallied the last resources of our noble language, made no bones about it, pulled himself together as men must do when the fundamentals of life are at stake, and said in so many words that Ann Veronica was a whore. It was I think an illegitimate extension of the term.[9]

At the time, he made a more vigorous response, and in a letter printed in the *Spectator* on 4 December, Wells took the battle into the enemy camp by appealing – as the National Crusade for Social Purity had – to anxieties about the decline in the birth rate and its effects on the nation but arguing from the opposite position: 'I know your keen and vigorous patriotism, and it seems to me that you overlook the fact that in practice the arrangement you manifestly approve is not giving the modern State enough children, or fine enough children for its needs.' The review itself sparked off a correspondence in the *Spectator* which continued for many months; the novel was banned by libraries and preached against by clergymen – the Reverend Herbert Bull of Westgate-on-Sea received contributions of £720. 18s when he announced a plan for setting a Watch Committee which would bring an immediate prosecution against any book likely to 'contaminate' its readers[10] – and the more the controversy raged, the better the sales.[11]

Ann Veronica has never been written about at such length since. For a number of reasons, H. G. Wells's literary reputation declined during the 1920s. This was partly a consequence of significant changes in literary fashion. The modernist novel was in the ascendant, younger writers like Virginia Woolf and James Joyce were creating a new novel form and Wells refused to have anything to do with modernist techniques. It was a consequence, too, of the emphasis he himself gave to his non-fiction, to his writings on history, politics and social comment. The books published about him during this period tend to concentrate on these aspects of his work and if the novels are mentioned at all, it is usually in relation to the author's social theories.[12]

During the 1930s and 1940s, the decline in Wells's reputation as a literary figure continued. In his 1930 biography of H. G. Wells, Geoffrey West suggests that *Ann Veronica* marks the beginning of a new phase in Wells's writing, and this is the view taken in two 1950s studies. Norman Nicholson's examination of Wells's fiction and Vincent Brome's critical biography both start from the assumption that the early scientific romances and the novels *Love and Mr Lewisham*, *Kipps*, *The History of Mr Polly* and *Tono-Bungay* constitute Wells's best work as an imaginative writer, that after these books his fiction deteriorates because he becomes more interested in conveying a message than in writing a story. Nicholson does, however, consider that *Ann Veronica* has merit:

> Certainly the subject, which is roughly that of women's rights, is never allowed to run away with the narrative. The picture of Ann Veronica, stifled by an affectionate father and aunt whose views on young girls are thoroughly Victorian, is convincingly drawn, and Ann herself is a lively and attractive character, not so brilliant but more human than Shaw's Vivie Warren on whom she is obviously modelled.

But he has major reservations:

> The other characters, however, are surface caricatures, Miss Miniver (the suffragette) and the odious Ramage.... Nevertheless, *Ann Veronica* is a most enjoyable and readable book apart from the last part of it. Ann Veronica goes to a science school in London and there she falls in love with a teacher, a man called Capes, who is separated from his wife. After some struggle, with most of the reluctance on Capes' side, they decide to run away together, even though it means giving up Capes' career ... They go to Switzerland and here Wells shows his inability to write a convincing love-scene between educated people. Capes seems to have read nothing outside his text-books but tuppenny magazines.[13]

Brome's central thesis in *H. G. Wells: A Biography* is that throughout Wells's career, Wells the artist was engaged in a struggle with Wells the scientist, with the latter becoming more dominant as time went on. *Ann Veronica* he associates with the latter phase, but Brome seems to respond to the novel almost in spite of himself:

> There might be an emotional queasiness about certain passages towards the end of the book, the exit remark of Capes – 'Blood of my heart, I know, I understand' – might curl something inside one, and Ann herself lacks the finer line of any deeply interesting character; she might prove that Wells could never 'successfully draw the portrait of a really cultivated woman', and show him as 'no profound connoisseur of the human heart'; but there was a pace about the book, the writing had enormous movement, and for the ordinary reader Ann lived and that was enough.[14]

In 1961, Bernard Bergonzi's book, *The Early H. G. Wells*, did a great deal to revive scholarly and popular interest in Wells as an imaginative writer, but only in relation to the scientific romances. It had a correspondingly deleterious effect on his later fiction, because it takes it for granted that much of Wells's later work is not worth reading. 'I am assuming as axiomatic,' writes Bergonzi, 'that the bulk of Wells's published output has lost whatever *literary* interest it might have had, and is not likely to regain it in the foreseeable future, whatever value it may possess for the social historian or the historian of ideas.'[15] It is, of course, arguable whether 'literary' interests can be separated out in such arbitrary fashion, but there is no doubt that Bergonzi's line on the later fiction is reflected in a number of comments on *Ann Veronica* in the 1960s and 1970s.

In their influential critical biography of Wells, *The Time Traveller*, published in 1973, Norman and Jeanne MacKenzie are scathing in their judgement of *Ann Veronica*'s literary qualities. The book's appeal, they suggest, has always been dependent on extrinsic factors:

> *Ann Veronica* was a tract masquerading as a piece of romantic fiction. Had the plot not been blatantly immoral by the standards of the day it would have been dismissed as banal, humourless and sentimental. Being 'in love' turns out to be some kind of intellectualized attraction between two 'partners' challenging the world together.

And they stress, too, the autobiographical aspects:

> It is the escapist's daydream fulfilled. The married man runs away with the beautiful and intelligent girl to live happily ever after, and even her parents are ultimately reconciled to the elopement. 'Life is rebellion or nothing', said Capes. 'That's really our choice now, defy – or futility.' These words which Wells wrote for Capes described his own feelings. The book, indeed, was another instalment of autobiography in which H. G. rewrote the past to make it fit his current concerns.[16]

Similarly, like Vincent Brome, Lovat Dickson, writing in 1971, is less enthusiastic about the novel as a whole than he is about its heroine:

> *Ann Veronica* is not one of Wells's most highly regarded books, although Ann Veronica as a character is one of the most attractive of Wells's heroines, and the book has an assured place in the emancipation of the modern novel from the inhibitions of Victorianism.[17]

He, too, discusses the book mainly in relation to the Amber Reeves affair.

The most detailed and perceptive study of *Ann Veronica* to appear in the 1970s is Patrick Parrinder's *H. G. Wells*, although he, too, groups it with 'the discussion novels' and not with the comedies. He gives close attention to the text of *Ann Veronica* and claims that it lacks qualities possessed by the earlier novels:

> The first few chapters introduce the world of an intelligent middle-class girl rebelling against the stuffiness of a London suburb. It is a solid, recognizable world ... and yet it is shallower, flatter and less intimately seen than the world of Kipps and Polly.... When Ann is handed a note from her father forbidding her to go to a dance, we are told that 'she had at first a wild, fantastic idea that it contained a tip'.

In contrast to *Tono-Bungay* and *Mr Polly*, however, there is no thread of grotesque language and striking metaphor connecting such moments together. *Ann Veronica*'s healthy spontaneity is a more conventional quality, like hockey sticks in the drawing-room; it lacks the note of obsession.

In common with most other critics, Parrinder finds the ending of the novel unsatisfactory: 'The book ends in an atmosphere of embarrassing mutual uplift – Wells's world outlook simplified for immediate consumption.' But, he concludes: 'In its less didactic moments... *Ann Veronica* remains enjoyably fresh and observant.'[18]

In the last twenty years there has been some resurgence of interest in Wells's fiction and in his status as a literary figure. This was triggered initially by the publication of the Wells-James correspondence[19] in 1959, which threw a new light on Wells's approach to fiction. In his 1985 study of Wells, John Batchelor argues persuasively that Wells's side of the debate about the nature and function of the novel has never been given the attention it deserves – '[Wells] was in possession of a defensible alternative to James's view of the novelist's art but failed to defend it responsibly.'[20]

Recent developments in literary theory, too, have led to new appraisals of how we should judge and respond to texts. In the introduction to his 1982 study, *The Natural History of H. G. Wells*, John Reed asks, 'Was Wells a fine novelist?' and then replies, 'The question may be beside the point.'[21] Reed's book is not interested in making value judgements but in tracing through Wells's vast output various interrelated motifs which reveal an underlying pattern and consistency in his writing. *Ann Veronica* is discussed, for instance, in relation to the motif of liberation:

> Ann Veronica feels that she 'walks out of a cell into a free and spacious world' when she leaves her restrictive suburban home for an independent life in London. Later she discovers that she is still living in a pit because her sex prevents her from achieving true freedom. Finally she escapes with Capes to a truly free and courageous life that begins auspiciously in the high, open country of the Alps.[22]

Although *Ann Veronica* focuses on women's experience, very few women have written about the novel. Nancy Steffen-Fluhr's essay, 'Paper Tiger: Women and H. G. Wells'[23] looks at Wells's life rather than his work but it is applicable to *Ann Veronica* nonetheless because it examines *H. G. Wells in Love* from a feminist and psychoanalytic perspective, and this has relevance to all depictions of women in his fiction. In an article in *H. G. Wells Under Revision*, Cliona Murphy examines Wells's attitude to women's education in his novels and concludes that despite his protestations to the contrary, he is not in favour of educated women:

> Educated women would have control over their own destiny. In the end Wells's females always have to return to the fact that they are women, reminded either by their emotions or their health – these in his view control them. One cannot help concluding that the concept of a woman educated to the extent that, in intellectual terms, she is finally independent of man was not one which Wells, despite his desires to be avant-garde, could not entertain.[24]

The most extensive study of *Ann Veronica* by a feminist critic is to be found in Patricia Stubb's *Women and Fiction*. In a chapter entitled 'Mr Wells's Sexual Utopia', Stubbs examines Wells's depiction of women in four of his novels and concludes that looked at from the perspective of the late twentieth century, his attempt to portray women as sexual beings – as in *Ann Veronica* – has not had entirely positive results:

> In the nineteenth century the only acceptable image of women was as pure beings who were both repulsed and mystified by sexuality. By the middle of the twentieth century this had been largely reversed, so that the popular fictional image of women became sexualized to the point where they had little reality beyond a psycho-sexual one. Wells must bear some of the responsibility for this development.[25]

Notes

[1] Lovat Dickson, *H. G. Wells: His Turbulent Life and Times* (London, Macmillan, 1971) p.166.

[2] In his preface to *Ann Veronica* in vol.8 of the Atlantic Edition of his work, published in 1925, Wells comments that 'In England the book was not so much criticized as attacked with hysterical animosity by people who did not like the heroine or disapproved of her thoughts and ways.' Wells pairs the *Ann Veronica* with his 1914 novel *Boon*, 'another book that also had its stormy consequences'.

[3] Wells Archive, University of Urbana-Champaign, Illinois.

[4] R. A. Scott-James, review in the *Daily News*, 4 October 1909.

[5] The *Globe* Literary Supplement 6 October 1909; Ingvald Raknem, *H. G. Wells and his Critics* (Norway, Allen & Unwin, 1962).

[6] John O'London, *T. P.'s Weekly*, 22 October 1909 quoted by *H. G. Wells: The Critical Heritage*, ed. Patrick Parrinder (London, Routledge & Kegan Paul, 1972) pp.160–64.

[7] Samuel Hynes, *The Edwardian Turn of Mind* (Princeton, Princeton UP, 1971) p.281.

[8] Unsigned Review, 'A Poisonous Book', *Spectator*, 20 November 1909.

[9] H. G. Wells, *Experiment in Autobiography* (London, Jonathan Cape, 1934) p.471.

[10] Lovat Dickson, p.176.

[11] Wells records that the controversy over *Ann Veronica* brought him 'a new type of reader', his earlier books were bought 'by eager seekers after obscenity – to their extreme disillusionment. They decided after a baffled perusal that I was dreadfully overrated and superficial, and my brief reputation in the cloacal recesses of the bookish world evaporated speedily enough.' *Experiment in Autobiography*, p.472.

[12] See Sidney Dark, *The Outline of H. G. Wells: The Superman on the Street* (London, Leonard Parsons, 1922); Ivor Brown, *H. G. Wells* (London, Nisbet, 1923); Patrick Braybrooke, *Some Aspects of H. G. Wells* (London, C. W. Daniel, 1928).

[13] Norman Nicholson, *H. G. Wells* (London, Arthur Barker Ltd, 1950) pp.69–70.

[14] Vincent Brome, *H. G. Wells: A Biography* (London, Longman, 1951) pp.111–12.

[15] Bernard Bergonzi, *The Early H. G. Wells: A Study of the Scientific Romances* (Manchester, Manchester UP, 1961) p.165.

[16] Norman & Jeanne Mackenzie, pp.248–9.

[17] Lovat Dickson, p.158.

[18] Patrick Parrinder, *H. G. Wells* (Edinburgh, Oliver & Boyd, 1970) pp.91–2.

[19] Edel & Ray, eds. *Henry James and H. G. Wells: A Record of their Friendship, their Debate on the Art of Fiction, and their Quarrel* (London, Rupert Hart-Davis, 1959).

[20] John Batchelor, *H. G. Wells* (Cambridge, Cambridge UP, 1985) p.159.

[21] John Reed, *The Natural History of H. G. Wells* (Athens Ohio, Ohio UP, 1982) p.2.

[22] John Reed, p.19.

[23] Nancy Steffen-Fluhr, 'Paper Tiger: Women and H. G. Wells', *Science Fiction Studies*, vol.37, 1985.

[24] Cliona Murphy, 'H. G. Wells: Educationist, Utopian, Feminist', *H. G. Wells Under Revision*, eds. Patrick Parrinder & Christopher Rolfe (London, Associated UP, 1990) p.225.

[25] Patricia Stubbs, *Women and Fiction: Feminism and the Novel 1880–1920.* (London, Methuen, 1979) pp.193–4.

SUGGESTIONS FOR FURTHER READING

Autobiography

Wells, H. G., *Experiment in Autobiography* (2 vols) (Jonathan Cape, 1934)

The first volume of Wells's autobiography gives a lively and readable account of his early life. In the second volume there is an interesting retrospective account, too, of the controversy which followed the publication of *Ann Veronica*.

Wells, H. G., *H. G. Wells in Love*, ed. G. P. Wells (Faber, 1984)

Autobiography, like all forms of writing, involves processes of selection and rearrangement; the selective processes which appear to have influenced Wells in this extended account of his love life are fascinating, particularly when the book is read in conjunction with the Brandon text mentioned below.

Biography

MacKenzie, Norman and Jeanne, *The Time Traveller: The Life of H. G. Wells* (Weidenfield & Nicholson, 1973)

This is a clear and well-researched account of Wells's life and work which provides an interesting biographical context for his novels.

General Background

Brandon, Ruth, *The New Women and the Old Men: Love, Sex and the Woman Question* (Flamingo, 1991)

This book looks at Wells's relations with a number of women in relation to other unorthodox love affairs of the Edwardian period and concludes that although all of the people considered – men *and* women – saw themselves as free spirits, challenging social convention and the accepted view of sexual behaviour, only the men were truly free, few of the women emerged unscathed.

Hynes, Samuel, *The Edwardian Turn of Mind* (Princeton UP, 1971)

An excellent, readable introduction to the political, historical and social ideas which shaped the period in which *Ann Veronica* was written.

Literary Criticism

There are no full-length studies of *Ann Veronica*, and most books on

H. G. Wells's fiction tend either to concentrate on his earlier work, or to survey his output as a whole. The three texts listed below, however, do look in some detail at the novel itself.

Batchelor, John, *H. G. Wells* (Cambridge UP, 1985)
This writer does see *Ann Veronica* as 'an entirely serious feminist novel' and discusses it in these terms.

Parrinder, Patrick, *H. G. Wells* (Edinburgh, Oliver & Boyd, 1970)
This is one of the few critical accounts to examine the text of the novel as well as – and in relation to – its ideas.

Stubbs, Patricia, *Women and Fiction: Feminism and the Novel 1880–1920* (Methuen, 1979)
An interesting account of the ways in which male writers this period depict women, which includes a lengthy chapter on Wells's novels, including *Ann Veronica*.

TEXT SUMMARY

Chapter I: Twenty-one-year-old Ann Veronica Stanley gets off the train from London at the south London suburb, Morningside Park. She lives at home with her widowed father and her aunt and is resolved to have things out with her father because he has forbidden her to attend a fancy-dress ball with her art student friends, the Widgetts.

Chapter II: Ann Veronica visits the Widgetts and meets Miss Miniver, a supporter of the women's suffrage movement, who assures her that women will only get what they want through the vote. She then goes with her aunt to call on Lady Palsworthy, a leading figure in local society, and attempts, unsuccessfully, to avoid an encounter with Lady Palsworthy's nephew, Mr Manning, an eligible bachelor who has already shown an interest in knowing her better.

Chapter III: two days later, the day of the fancy-dress ball, Ann Veronica receives a letter from Mr Manning proposing marriage. She goes for a walk to think it over and decides not only that she does not want to marry, but also that – in contravention of her father's wishes – she will find a way of attending Imperial College and she *will* go to the ball. During her walk, Ann Veronica meets Mr Ramage, who engages her in a conversation about the changes the modern world has brought to man/woman relationships. Meanwhile, her aunt has discovered the corsair's costume hanging in Ann Veronica's wardrobe and tells Mr Stanley about it.

Chapter IV: Ann Veronica comes downstairs, dressed for the ball, and confronts her father.

Chapter V: Ann Veronica is resolved to leave home. She takes the train to Waterloo, finds a hotel near the Embankment, and then wanders around central London, half-aware of but puzzled by the air of sexual menace she senses, a feeling which comes to a head when she discovers she is being followed. That evening she sends a telegram to her father announcing that she is safe, and the next day is spent searching for a suitable apartment.

Chapter VI: Ann Veronica receives various visitors. First her aunt, then her father arrive and attempt to persuade, then order, her home. She also receives a letter from her married sister, and a visit from her brother, and eventually Mr Manning comes, urging her to reconsider his proposal, and enthusing about her courage.

Chapter VII: Ann Veronica discovers how unqualified she is for any suitable occupation, and all attempts to find a post prove unsuccessful. Miss Miniver visits, full of admiration for Ann Veronica's spirit, and she organizes visits to the Fabian Society and suffragette meetings. By December, Ann Veronica is so short of money she decides to visit Ramage at his office in the City to ask his advice. He suggests that she further her scientific education and offers to lend her money, at five per cent interest. At first she is rather shocked by the idea, but before Christmas she visits him again and accepts a loan of forty pounds.

Chapter VIII: In January, Ann Veronica begins her biological studies at Imperial College. From the beginning she is attracted by Russell's demonstrator, Capes, and after a while realizes that she is falling in love with him.

Chapter IX: Ann Veronica discovers the real motives behind Mr Ramage's generosity. She has been seeing him almost weekly since December, and in February is pleased to receive a telegram inviting her to have dinner with him. They attend a performance of *Tristan and Isolde*, and Ann Veronica is both surprised and dismayed when he puts his hand on her waist and declares his love for her, but when he apologizes she agrees to see him for dinner the following night so they can 'talk things out'. In the private room of the restaurant the next evening Ramage makes a sexual assault on Ann Veronica, and is astonished by the effectiveness with which she defends herself. But although she escapes physically unscathed, she is overcome by self-disgust at her naivety in accepting a loan from a philanderer. The next morning she draws out twenty pounds of the twenty-two pounds left in her post office savings account, and sends it to Ramage. At the laboratory, because she is upset, she quarrels with Capes about women's rights, and then discovers from a fellow student that he is married. When she gets home and finds that Ramage has sent back the money, she throws both envelope and banknotes on the fire in a moment of passion.

Chapter X: Ann Veronica is determined to engage herself in

the struggle for women's liberation. She goes to the Woman's Bond of Freedom and meets one of its leaders, Kitty Brett, and in early March offers to take part in a raid on the House of Commons, which results in her arrest and a month's imprisonment.

Chapter XI: Ann Veronica realizes that she is far more interested in Capes than in political rights, and she also feels contrite about her treatment of her father and aunt.

Chapter XII: Ann Veronica writes a letter of apology to her father, and when she is released from prison her aunt is there to meet her. On her return to Imperial College, she finds herself treated as a hero, and her joy at seeing Capes again overflows on to her feelings for Mr Manning. Partly in order to disguise her love for Capes, Ann Veronica agrees to become engaged to Manning.

Chapter XIII: The circumstances that led up to the engagement are described, together with Ann Veronica's gradual realization that Manning will never love her as she is but only as his imagination conceives her. She breaks the engagement and acknowledges to herself that she could never marry anyone but Capes.

Chapter XIV: Ann Veronica takes the initiative and declares her love for Capes. He tells her about his past and urges caution, but Ann Veronica brushes aside all impediments. A week or so later, Capes suggests that they should go off and live together.

Chapter XV: Ann Veronica is at home, preparing for her elopement.

Chapter XVI: Capes and Ann Veronica depart for their illicit honeymoon in the Alps. In the middle of a difficult climb Ann Veronica suddenly remembers the anxiety which had dominated her thoughts for so long – the debt to Ramage.

Chapter XVII: Four years on, the couple are now married. Capes has made a new and successful career as a playwright; Ann Veronica is pregnant and content. Mr Stanley and Ann Veronica's aunt come to dinner, and the family is reconciled.

CLASSIC FICTION
IN EVERYMAN

A SELECTION

Frankenstein
MARY SHELLEY
A masterpiece of Gothic terror in its
original 1818 version **£3.99**

Dracula
BRAM STOKER
One of the best known horror stories
in the world **£3.99**

The Diary of A Nobody
GEORGE AND WEEDON
GROSSMITH
A hilarious account of suburban life
in Edwardian London **£4.99**

Some Experiences
and Further Experiences
of an Irish R. M.
SOMERVILLE AND ROSS
Gems of comic exuberance and
improvisation **£4.50**

Three Men in a Boat
JEROME K. JEROME
English humour at its best **£2.99**

Twenty Thousand Leagues
under the Sea
JULES VERNE
Scientific fact combines with
fantasy in this prophetic tale of
underwater adventure **£4.99**

The Best of Father Brown
G. K. CHESTERTON
An irresistible selection of crime
stories – unique to Everyman **£3.99**

The Collected Raffles
E. W. HORNUNG
Dashing exploits from the most glam-
orous figure in crime fiction **£4.99**

£2.99

£5.99

£5.99

AVAILABILITY

All books are available from your local bookshop or direct from
**Littlehampton Book Services Cash Sales, 14 Eldon Way, LinesideEstate,
Littlehampton, West Sussex BN17 7HE.** PRICES ARE SUBJECT TO CHANGE.

To order any of the books, please enclose a cheque (in £ sterling) made payable to
Littlehampton Book Services, or phone your order through with credit card details (Access,
Visa or Mastercard) on 0903 721596 (24 hour answering service) stating card number and
expiry date. Please add £1.25 for package and postage to the total value of your order.

CLASSIC NOVELS
IN EVERYMAN

A SELECTION

The Way of All Flesh
SAMUEL BUTLER
A savagely funny odyssey from joyless duty to unbridled liberalism **£4.99**

Born in Exile
GEORGE GISSING
A rationalist's progress towards love and compromise in class-ridden Victorian England **£4.99**

David Copperfield
CHARLES DICKENS
One of Dickens' best-loved novels, brimming with humour **£3.99**

The Last Chronicle of Barset
ANTHONY TROLLOPE
Trollope's magnificent conclusion to his Barsetshire novels **£4.99**

He Knew He Was Right
ANTHONY TROLLOPE
Sexual jealousy, money and women's rights within marriage – a novel ahead of its time **£6.99**

Tess of the D'Urbervilles
THOMAS HARDY
The powerful, poetic classic of wronged innocence **£3.99**

Wuthering Heights and Poems
EMILY BRONTE
A powerful work of genius – one of the great masterpieces of literature **£3.50**

Tom Jones
HENRY FIELDING
The wayward adventures of one of literatures most likable heroes **£5.99**

The Master of Ballantrae and Weir of Hermiston
R. L. STEVENSON
Together in one volume, two great novels of high adventure and family conflict **£4.99**

£3.99

£2.99

£3.99

AVAILABILITY

All books are available from your local bookshop or direct from
**Littlehampton Book Services Cash Sales, 14 Eldon Way, LinesideEstate,
Littlehampton, West Sussex BN17 7HE.** PRICES ARE SUBJECT TO CHANGE.

To order any of the books, please enclose a cheque (in £ sterling) made payable to Littlehampton Book Services, or phone your order through with credit card details (Access, Visa or Mastercard) on 0903 721596 (24 hour answering service) stating card number and expiry date. Please add £1.25 for package and postage to the total value of your order.

ESSAYS, CRITICISM AND HISTORY IN EVERYMAN

A SELECTION

The Embassy to Constantinople and Other Writings
LIUDPRAND OF CREMONA
An insider's view of political machinations in medieval Europe
£5.99

The Rights of Man
THOMAS PAINE
One of the great masterpieces of English radicalism **£4.99**

Speeches and Letters
ABRAHAM LINCOLN
A key document of the American Civil War **£4.99**

Essays
FRANCIS BACON
An excellent introduction to Bacon's incisive wit and moral outlook **£3.99**

Puritanism and Liberty: Being the Army Debates (1647-49) from the Clarke Manuscripts
A fascinating revelation of Puritan minds in action **£7.99**

History of His Own Time
BISHOP GILBERT BURNET
A highly readable contemporary account of the Glorious Revolution of 1688 **£7.99**

Biographia Literaria
SAMUEL TAYLOR COLERIDGE
A masterpiece of criticism, marrying the study of literature with philosophy **£4.99**

Essays on Literature and Art
WALTER PATER
Insights on culture and literature from a major voice of the 1890s **£3.99**

Chesterton on Dickens: Criticisms and Appreciations
A landmark in Dickens criticism, rarely surpassed **£4.99**

Essays and Poems
R. L. STEVENSON
Stevenson's hidden treasures in a new selection **£4.99**

£3.99

THE NATURAL HISTORY OF SELBORNE
GILBERT WHITE

THE COMPLEAT ANGLER
IZAAK WALTON

£4.99

AVAILABILITY

All books are available from your local bookshop or direct from
Littlehampton Book Services Cash Sales, 14 Eldon Way, LinesideEstate, Littlehampton, West Sussex BN17 7HE. PRICES ARE SUBJECT TO CHANGE.

To order any of the books, please enclose a cheque (in £ sterling) made payable to Littlehampton Book Services, or phone your order through with credit card details (Access, Visa or Mastercard) on 0903 721596 (24 hour answering service) stating card number and expiry date. Please add £1.25 for package and postage to the total value of your order.

AMERICAN LITERATURE
IN EVERYMAN

A SELECTION

Selected Poems
HENRY LONGFELLOW
A new selection spanning the whole
of Longfellow's literary career **£7.99**

Typee
HERMAN MELVILLE
Melville's stirring debut, drawing
directly on his own adventures in the
South Sea **£4.99**

Billy Budd
and Other Stories
HERMAN MELVILLE
The compelling parable of
innocence destroyed by a fallen
world **£4.99**

The Scarlet Letter
NATHANIEL HAWTHORNE
The compelling tale of an
independent woman's struggle
against a crushing moral code **£3.99**

The Last of The Mohicans
JAMES FENIMORE COOPER
The classic tale of old America, full
of romantic adventure **£5.99**

The Red Badge of Courage
STEPHEN CRANE
A vivid portrayal of a young
soldier's experience of the
American Civil War **£2.99**

Essays and Poems
RALPH WALDO EMERSON
An indispensable edition celebrating
one of the most influential
American writers **£5.99**

The Federalist
HAMILTON, MADISON, AND JAY
Classics of political science, these
essays helped to found the
American Constitution **£6.99**

Leaves of Grass and
Selected Prose
WALT WHITMAN
The best of Whitman in one volume
£6.99

£5.99

£4.99

£4.99